TURBO CHICKS
Talking Young Feminisms

TURBO CHICKS

TALKING YOUNG FEMINISMS

EDITED BY

Allyson Mitchell
Lisa Bryn Rundle
& Lara Karaian

SUMACH
PRESS

WOMEN'S ISSUES PUBLISHING PROGRAM

SERIES EDITOR BETH MCAULEY

To the Raging Grannies and Turbo Chicks everywhere.

Keep your motors running!

CANADIAN CATALOGUING IN PUBLICATION DATA
Main entry under title:
Turbo chicks: talking young feminisms

Includes bibliographical references.
ISBN 978-1-894549-06-6

1. Feminist theory. 2. Feminism. I. Mitchell, Allyson.
II. Rundle, Lisa Bryn. III. Karaian, Lara.

HQ1190.T87 2001   305.42   C2001-930150-2

Edited by Beth McAuley
Cover & Design by Liz Martin
Cover image by Missy Kulik

Printed in Canada

Published by
SUMACH PRESS

1415 Bathurst Street, Suite 202
Toronto ON Canada M5R 3H8
info@sumachpress.com

www.sumachpress.com

Contents

Part III Schooling Feminisms: Big Brained Girls Crack the Codes with Chainsaws

Acknowledgements

Turbo Chicks was kick-started by the "Graduate Women's Studies: Visions and Realities" conference held in 1995 at York University. In 1996, it went from "0 to 60" at the one-day "Revolution Girl Style" conference sponsored by the Summer Institute of the York University Centre for Feminist Research. Some of the essays in this collection were inspired by presentations there; the overall collection, however, has been inspired by young feminists wanting to add their creativity and intelligence to the third wave.

This collection is the end result of a great deal of work on the part of many people. We would like to thank all our contributors for their patience during this long process and all our artists and zinesters for generously letting us use their work. We would like to thank Sumach Press for believing in this project and seeing it to fruition. Our sincere gratitude to Sumach's editor Beth McAuley for her tireless work and endless patience amid our long-winded discussions, for helping to bridge generational gaps and for encouraging us to launch into this project, even when she knew how much work it would really take.

We would also like to thank, in random order, Candis Steenbergen for facing down piles of paper in her room to help compile the suggested readings; Alex Vamos for her isolating work on the momentous glossary, and Alaina Hardie for help with some of the terms; Krista Scott-Dixon for compiling our feminist Web site resources; Catherine Dean for photos where we really look like ourselves; Missy Kulik for flexibility and super-charged genius in creating our turbo chick for the cover; Jane Farrow for the title idea and jump starts along the way; Katherine McKittrick and Cate Barnes for early roadside assistance; Chris Mitchell, Lisa Hayes, Joe Callaghan, Lisa Cupoli and Chandra Bulucon for postering and envelope stuffing and everyone else who helped spread the word; Tom and Daphne Mitchell for encouragement and benefactorial support; and Nancy Mandell, Linda Briskin, Linda Peake, Sharon Rosenberg, Joan Grant Cummings, Didi Khayatt and Susanne Luhmann for ideas, advice and the generous gift of a sense of possibility.

Lara would like to thank Chris Kinkaid for his unlimited love and support and for clearing out of the house (or hiding in the bedroom) for way too many meetings. She would also like to thank her family and especially her dad (1932-2000) for all their love and support through this and all her other endeavours.

Lisa would like to thank her friends, family and colleagues who put up with endless excitements, discussions, cancelled plans and casual references to "the book."

Allyson wants to thank Lex Vaughn for sweet sweet love and pep talks. She dedicates this book to her niece Madelyne Beckles because she is such a smart cookie.

INTRODUCTION

A Conversation with
Allyson, Lisa and Lara

"And everytime you move, you make a woman's movement."

— ani difranco, "Hour Follows Hour,"
Not a Pretty Girl

Start Talking

Photos by Catherine Dean

How do we adequately introduce a book this diverse, a book we know people will come to with so many assumptions (because we always come to new encounters with assumptions, because we ourselves came with assumptions), we ask ourselves. How can we shrink what was a huge, long and sometimes confused process into a catchy intro? Should we, even if we could? Questions. We are always asking ourselves questions. Sometimes in doubt, because we've never done this before; sometimes because we believe that questioning is the way to informed decisions. You have to question everything in a world that often hands you the short end of the stick. You have to question yourself and others. So we did, and we hope that in the process of doing so (not in the finding of absolute answers) that we would produce a book fantastic in its diversity, fair in its process and that would embody what we feel about young women, not-so-young women, young feminism and the need for sharing across women's movements. At the risk of sounding absolute, we think we did.

Well, almost did. As feminists we know it's always more complicated than that. In the following pages, then, you will see us struggling with the issues, not smoothing them out neatly. They are the issues feminists are struggling with everywhere: issues of how to put our convictions into practice, of how to adequately talk about issues of race, class, education, religion, language, sexuality and ability, of representation and the privileging of voice. Below, then, is one part of our numerous conversations about these issues and more, what this book is and what it all means to us. You'll see what we're happy with, what we learned, and what we wish we could do better. We hope you'll have your own conversations about it.

We thought about doing a more traditional introduction — you know, where all the pieces are tied together, themes are traced, the collection is contextualized and, while we do some of these things in our conversation (we're graduate students, after all), we felt that format was too artificial to suit this collection. And being among the first Canadian young feminist collections, we're forging new ground. A regular introduction just didn't seem to cut it for our irregular book.

Besides (the truth comes out) we found no truths! And our themes, loose as they were, at times hampered our writers, we don't want them to hamper our readers. If there's one thing we learned, or were reminded of, it's that no one fits easily into categories. (Here's where that questioning comes in again.) And questioning requires an ongoing conversation. To us, this book is a conversation. Below, we took turns asking questions, answering them, making jokes, interrupting each other in excitement and trailing off in confusion. All in all, pretty representative of what young women do with feminism. You can see conversations going on within and among the pieces too, but we're not going to tell you where; you're going to have to listen in yourself. Our process, which was, as you can gather, one big conversation with a lot of work in between, will continue as our conversation continues. We know we will keep growing and changing our minds and, hopefully, still speaking them as the girls and women do in this book — speaking fast and furiously, energetically, reflectively, academically, passionately, angrily and poetically about that inspirer of innumerable discussions, debates, fights, support and, of course, questions: FEMINISM. To that we say, Thanks feminism, for telling us, for once, to keep our mouths open.

Our Definition of Feminism

Feminism is a critical awareness of how the world works and a conscious resistance to who gets what.

Feminism is made up of infinite variety; its strength based on its diversity. This collection demonstrates just some of the wonderfully wide spectrum of feminisms and varying relationships to feminism experienced by women today. Each contributor's own distinct perspective will stand out as you flip through the book. Go ahead, give it a flip. We'll wait. You see how with each take on the topic/politic/way of life that connects this collection — feminism — it grows and changes, whether it is taken up, used, moulded or discarded by the women it was made for, young and old alike.

DATES: November 20, 1999, and January 26, 2001
PLACES: Lisa's place and Lara's place

Why This Book?

LARA: Ally, you were the instigator, you should start.

ALLYSON: OK. I was at an academic conference on feminism and all these older academic women (older to me at the time, although I've aged significantly since the process started) were talking about the young women in their classes and how apathetic they were and how they were apolitical and how, when they were that age, they were hanging out together in their living rooms over bottles of wine and talking about women's issues. I looked at my friend who was sitting beside me and we were like, that's what we do, only not with the wine. And I had also read *Listen Up: Voices from the Next Feminist Generation* (it was something like six years ago) and I was just so blown away and so inspired by the writings in that book. Some of them, like Nomy Lamm's "It's a Big Fat Revolution," brought me to tears. It transformed my feminism in a big way to hear these young women's voices. I put together a call for submissions for a young feminist anthology and plastered it wherever I went, in Toronto and around the country when I travelled. Lisa submitted an essay and when I realized the project was too big for me, I asked her and Lara (you were both doing work on young feminists at York University at this point) to join me. It was really crucial to me to create a space for more young women to talk about their lives. Interestingly enough, I've started my PhD in Women's Studies now and I'm following the track of these women who moved me to do something to counter their opinions, and I've found that a lot of young women in my classes *are* really apathetic. There are a few of them who need a lifeline to feminism and a few who've already found it, but a lot of them are just at the very beginning stages of their consciousness-raising. I want to present feminism in a way that speaks to all these women. So, why did you guys get involved?

14

LARA: For me it was very personal; I always wanted to find out more about young women and feminism. It really took off in a graduate course in methodology when I did a research project that focused on what young women saw as influences and barriers to their feminism. I always wondered about that for myself. I presented the paper at the 1996 Canadian Women's Studies Association conference (at the "Learneds") and our editor Beth McAuley was there. She spoke with me afterward about your project, Ally, because she loved the paper and wanted me to submit it. (Check out Lara's essay in Part I.) So when you asked me to be part of the collection I thought, Well here's a chance to broaden what I'd learned about myself and five other young women. Not just in terms of becoming a feminist, but in terms of how young women understand feminist theory and activism. I thought this was a perfect opportunity to learn more about the way young women are relating to feminism and what they are doing with it, because they *are* doing things with it, even if they're not recognized for it.

LISA: I think I have personal and political reasons, mostly personal. I thought it would be really fun. I find it energizing to talk to young women, and sometimes frustrating. We've all had the experience now where we've been teachers and it makes me see how important it is to get the word out about what feminism actually is. I remember sitting there on the first day of a tutorial I was leading in an introductory Women's Studies course and having people say, I don't hate men and I'm not a lesbian so I don't know if I should be here. It's hard to know where to begin. There are so many assumptions and people have so much misinformation. I find it really exciting to hear from young women who are thinking deeply about feminism and who've had more experience with it, as well as from older women who take young feminists seriously.

Generation Gap?

ALLYSON: The idea of young women not being feminists is a self-fulfilling prophecy. So if their voices aren't out there and other young women don't have access to that community then they just feel like this crazy person, this angry person, all alone. (Check out Ally's piece about girl graffiti in Part III and see that you're not alone!)

LARA: And if older women don't have access to that community, it fosters the belief that younger women have nothing to add to the women's movement, that we're all wet behind the ears. I'm twenty-seven and I get that a lot! (Of course, lots of older feminists know how much we contribute; see Joan Grant Cumming's essay in Part IV.)

LISA: Actually, I've written an article about this relationship between young women and the women's movement (you can find it in *Herizons,* Fall 1998). Writing it led me to feel that there was some miscommunication happening between generations of feminists. And when people look around and see lots of apathetic women, I think, Ya, that's true. And if you looked around in the late '60s and the '70s, when feminism was so much in the public eye, I bet you'd find lots of women who weren't involved with it too. It's always a small part of the population that's politicized or that calls themselves feminist.

ALLYSON: If we think young women who are feminist are isolated now, think how isolated they must have felt then!

LARA: This book really lays out how there are many women's movements, not just one. Young women today are entering multiple movements, not just one monolithic white middle-class movement — not that there was only one in the past. There are so many manifestations of feminism now that some women of previous generations might not even associate new voices with the feminism that they themselves practise. (See Susanne Luhmann in Part I and Candis Steenbergen in Part III on generational feminism.)

ALLYSON: And that generation gap can cause a kind of illiteracy of feminism where we may not understand each other due to such different cultures of feminisms.

LISA: Back to how the second-wave feminist movement wasn't

monolithic but it appeared to be. I think that had to do with whose voices got into the media, who got public attention. It was Gloria Steinem all over the place. And Gloria's great, but we know that black women were organizing, union women were organizing, they may or may not have used the same language, but regardless, they didn't get the same kind of media attention. They didn't get to go down in history in the same way. That's part of what we're conscious of in *Turbo Chicks,* we don't want to only give space to one view or make it appear as though there is just one voice of feminism. (Check it out, our contributors barely agree with each other about anything; well, maybe they do, but you'll sure see lots of room for debate.)

Who Are These Women?

LISA: We're talking about young feminists, older women, generational differences — what do we mean by these terms? What is young and old? Is it a number or a concept? What are the assumptions? (See Jessica Lara Ticktin in Part I for one woman's exploration of age and feminism.) In our proposal to the publisher we said, "Not surprisingly, we've found that respectful, appropriate and accurate language is difficult to find that describes women's identities and relationships to feminist and generational experiences. The best we can do is draw attention to these concerns. Age is a culturally and personally relative identity that is experienced differently by different individuals. 'Young' and 'old' are ambiguous terms that we use tentatively because of the often negative connotations associated with them. We simply want to point to the generational differences between feminist women while avoiding the characterization of young women as inexperienced and older women as experts, or young women as necessarily innovative and older women as has-beens."

LARA: We don't want to get too specific about what our definitions are about young and old because the more specific you get, the more you start to exclude.

LISA: As soon as you try to pin people down, you leave people out.

ALLYSON: We didn't leave anybody out because of biological age, and we aren't necessarily flagging the age of the contributors. We left it up to them to identify their age. One person's young is another person's old. And it's not just about maturity or biological age. It's about class, economics, personality. So "young" for us is almost more a spirit or an aesthetic or ... I'm grappling for words ...

LARA: One of our writers, Sharon Rosenberg, identifies as a young feminist because of how she thinks about teaching and learning. (Sharon's piece is in Part III.) But what about other aspects of identity? What about boys? Are they excluded by the mere fact we're talking about young feminists, which usually means girls? Where do feminist male voices get heard if not in a feminist anthology? What about transgendered and transsexual people?

LISA: We started this discussion because of that photo I saw and liked that was taken by a boy (see Sean MacEachern's photo essay of his sister in Part II). And we have another contributor for whom male and female don't work as gender categories at all (Cat Pyne's exploration of this very topic is also in Part II).

ALLYSON: In terms of boys, there is the issue of men taking up some of our space. There are important historical reasons for women-only spaces — like women-run presses, dyke marches, women's music festivals. They've been crucial places of power for women. And they should be places of power for transgender and transsexual people as well, and for those who don't identify with any gender category.

LARA: I think if we're asking ourselves whose voices get heard, we have to ask ourselves what forums are available for other voices to get heard. My partner (who is a boy) is more feminist than many women I know. And feminism is not just about women.

LISA: That's true. The politics of inclusion and identity are tricky things. Like we've already talked about, it's hard to have a young feminist collection without tacitly supporting the idea that "young" and "feminist" mean the same thing to everyone. But we're all so different within that and that's the way we like it. To me, if young women have anything in common as a group, it's whatever commonalities come from having grown up at a certain time, in a certain place. What does it mean to have grown up in Canada after the women's movement's influence of the 1970s? I was born in 1974, which means that I've grown up in a society already infused with feminism. Judy Rebick talks about how when she was applying for her first job, the classifieds would read "Help Wanted, Men" and "Help Wanted, Women." She was turned down for work because of being a woman. A lot of these structural equality rights had been won by the time we came along and we grew up with different expectations and different struggles, and with a different relationship to feminism. So to me that means that as young feminists, in Canada, now, we have something in common, but what I love about the selections in this book is that we don't have much more in common than that. The room for all these different opinions is what part of the spirit of young feminism means to me.

LARA: And we can see how location, whether across Canada or in different communities in the same province, comes out in some contributions and not in others. Just because you're a young black woman doesn't mean you're writing about your experiences of being black; if you're disabled, you're not necessarily writing about being disabled; and just because you live in Saskatoon, doesn't mean that's what you're going to write about. Identities are complex things, and we weren't interested in telling contributors what we wanted them to produce for this collection.

ALLYSON: I think the point too is that despite the outreach we've done to different communities across Canada, the collection is still pretty urban and tied to universities. Some people just didn't respond as eagerly as others. But we did achieve a great deal of diversity in terms of sexuality and race.

LISA: I think it's important to say, we had goals in terms of representation across culture, age, location in Canada, education, activist/academic ...

LARA: ... race, class, ability, everything.

LISA: But we couldn't always reach our goals. And there was a sense of struggle too between aiming for representation and avoiding tokenism. The space between those is what you're talking about I think, Lara. Of course, we also just wanted engaging, interesting writing. (Some of the pieces about identity, race and sexuality include Sarmishta Subramanian's, Kristen Warder's in Part II and Cassandra Lord's in Part III.)

LARA: It upsets me when I do a lot of reading and find one-line disclaimers from authors that say, "We haven't taken race into consideration because of such and such, but we realize it's still important to the discussion." It's so important that they don't even talk about it? I think it's important that we don't do this — make a disclaimer that says this book is just a snapshot and that things are going to be different next time. We have to recognize that we are taking these voices from a certain time and framing them, structuring them and then leaving them for the future.

ALLYSON: I wish we'd reached people in the Territories and I'm disappointed that we didn't receive submissions from Native women. Achieving fair representation is always hard, but I do think we are making positive changes toward the decolonization of feminism. That's part of what young women are trying to contribute to feminism. (See T.J. Bryan in Part II and Carmela Murdocca in Part III on related topics.)

LISA: We hope we are moving forward and helping to break down the structural barriers we see. We have to think about what it is about the book, the process, who we are, our style, our call for submissions or feminism itself that makes some people feel more comfortable, more entitled or more interested than others, and about who wants to express themselves in this forum. These are things that are in some ways outside of us, yet still things that affected the shape of this book.

LARA: When you're trying to pull together a collection like this one, you've got to think about a huge number of things, like access to communities, whether the people you want to hear from have access to resources and time and if there is trust between you — especially trust because often a community's history with the women's movement hasn't been all positive. And you've got to think about confidence. Especially with young women; sometimes you have to convince them what they have to say is worthwhile.

Learn Much?

ALLYSON: One of the most exciting things I learned in approaching people to write for the book is that people may not be used to having their ideas recognized as important. It's like handing the microphone to somebody who has never even considered that they have a voice in that way and just watching them take it and run with it. It's so exciting when young women get that kind of spark. Of course, there are also lots of women in this collection (like Mariko Tamaki in Part I) who are quite young in age but they are professional writers; they have a stockpile of writing in a drawer that they can just grab because they've been doing it forever. And even if it's not their career, a lot of these women write incessantly, continuously — if not in a journal, they e-mail or create zines or perform their poetry. It's not like they're just babes out in the woods that we scooped up; they've been writing since they had a pen in their hand.

LISA: There's this great range from those who write for a living to the women who haven't written before or have never been published before. (Check out first-time writers Alessia Di Virgilio and Ana Ratcliffe in Part I and Miriam Johnson in Part III). For me, I think I was reminded how difficult it can be to put your feminist convictions into practice when it's you who's suddenly making decisions and controlling things, and also, of course, how vital and energizing young women and their writing can be. Lara, how about you?

LARA: I thought of the question more structurally, in terms of how we had to negotiate the institution of putting together a book and ensuring that our common philosophy was carried out. I've learned a lot about how we negotiate what we think will be marketable versus what we think is most important. This book is about getting the voices of turbo chicks out there, but we still have to think of our criteria for doing that — what we pick and what we don't and how not to silence. These are the questions we had to struggle with and hopefully we learned from the challenge of taking them on.

Is This Activism?
Convictions Into Practice

ALLYSON: Feminism has not necessarily always had strictly positive effects on the lives of young women. Sometimes studying oppression can freeze a person to some degree. We need to ask: What does it mean to raise a person's consciousness and not tell them what to do with that? First year Women's Studies students are often frustrated and depressed and angry. Not necessarily just at what they're learning but at their professors because they're generally not teaching them action.

LARA: I think the book is good in that respect because action is really such a part of this. We asked what the difference is between theory and activism, and some of the pieces in the book shed light on that question. (See Carly Stasko and Lisa Mesbur in Part IV.) Writing can be activism in many ways.

LISA: But activists might say it's not. It's not like freezing your butt off outside the parliament buildings at a protest or getting tear-gassed by riot police. It can be gruelling in its own way, though.

ALLYSON: Being an activist isn't necessarily just picketing or demonstrating. But that's often what my first year Women's Studies students equate feminism with — carrying a sign.

LISA: In my own life it hasn't been the marches I've been to that felt the most political. It was things like telling my family I had a girlfriend. That took more courage for me, and I think that type of action changes more about the way people think than walking topless down Yonge Street in the Dyke March does, which also takes courage. A lot of young women change the world just by being who they are in the world and challenging the way others think and see them in it.

LARA: And even the act of educating yourself on issues is a form of activism to me. I think we're broadening the sense of what action is. Writing is action. Even just declaring yourself a feminist is a political act.

ALLYSON: Your activism incorporates your whole life, your public and private actions.

LISA: Going out with friends and not accepting assumptions about people feels like activism. It takes guts to challenge friends on things when it's so uncomfortable to do it and you know you'll get dubbed "too political," when you know there will be personal ramifications, like wrecking a night that you wanted to be fun, and all those types of things ...

ALLYSON: ... ruining a family dinner!

LISA: Exactly!

Girl Power?

ALLYSON: We can't talk about young feminism without talking about the emergence in the media of Girl Power and the co-optation and commercialization of Girl Power. Now we've got *Girl Cosmopolitan;* we've got *Dawson's Creek.* We used to have Spice Girls (remember them?) and now we have their spin-offs. So how does this book fit into all this? Does it have anything to do with Girl Power? Is it a Riot Grrrly kind of power or what?

LISA: I hope it has to do with real Girl Power. I hope that the girls and women who contributed to *Turbo Chicks* felt in some way empowered and that those who read it do too. I kind of see the turbo chick as the antidote to fakey Girl Power. (Jennifer O'Connor profiles a true turbo chick in Part IV.)

23

LARA: But Girl Power, in the way it's out there, is the consciousness-raising of the '90s and beyond. It's like the awareness campaigns of the '60s and '70s but repackaged and aimed at a different market, though I wonder if the capitalist language is appropriate here. I think that's the main problem with Girl Power now, the notion that it can be bought and sold. (See Leah Rumack's discussion of Girl Power in Part II.)

ALLYSON: I don't think you should shy away from "market" when you're talking about Girl Power. You're right it's consciousness-raising updated but it's also a marketing ploy (see Jennifer Harris on this and more in Part III). It's hard-core politics that gets watered down into tight T-shirts and pink bubblegum feminism, and that's sexy and cute. It's Girl Power for a certain young, cutsie, fashionable, specific body type; it's a specific look and specific politic. There isn't very much Girl Power for fat, ugly, hairy dykes. You're not going to see them on a lollipop. But I still buy into it; I still have some tight Girl Power T-shirts. Because even though it is about selling things, I can still see the positive in it because there are people who never would have said something like "Girl Power!" who are saying it now. I see my eight-year-old niece dressing up and playing Girl Power with her friends (see "Out of the Mouths of Babes" in the Epilogue). I used to play *Charlie's Angels*, which is comparable, really. In a way it makes feminism accessible to everyone. We may worry it's not "the right kind" of feminism, but you can't control that.

LARA: Like any new political awareness, it's not in and of itself anything; it's a step towards something. It's what people do with it that matters.

So what will you do with it?

— Lisa Mesbur

Part I

MY FIRST
FEMINISM

Since I am
a woman
whether or not
you are against me
I will braid my hair
even
in the seasons
of rain.

Audre Lorde

— Heze *She's Got Labe Zine* shegotlab@hotmail.com

ROBIN & ME

Mariko Tamaki

I've often told people that private school warped my evolution into adulthood. Nowhere is this more evident than in the story of my indoctrination into the world of feminist politics. It's a story I don't tell very often anymore, for reasons I'll explain later, but it is, I believe, the story of how I became a feminist.

A bit of history is required.

The year was 1992, eleventh grade, the year I gave my first blow job at a party in Forest Hill (that, in itself, is a really long story that should one day be published, but later), the year I had finally begun to consider myself a woman and not just some sort of biological acne-ridden mistake. By that time I had been attending private school for going on six years and I was, unfortunately, no closer to any vision of "Girl Power" that the school's original founders might have envisioned. There's a common myth that all private-school girls are feminists, which I have to say is far from accurate. Truth be told, the fear of being pegged under nerdy, virginal or lezzie stereotypes, at least in my day, had the majority of the student population insisting that they were against "that sort of thing."

At the time I was in no way above this green-blazer, short-kilt attitude. Having endured several years of peer bullshit, I was content to have a social life and would do nothing to risk my newfound quasi-decent social status. Even if it meant mixing with private-school boys, who knew more about Nintendo than human decency, I had no intention of blowing my situation by dissenting from the group.

27

Not that I didn't have complaints.

One of my larger complaints had to do with my new activity of socializing with boys. It was a task full of contradictions. For instance, despite the fact that all of my friends in school were able-minded, intelligent creatures with opinions (lots and lots of opinions) and goals, around men (boys really), these fabulous women turned into what I can only describe as mindless, butt-sucking flakes. Sitting around at local parties I couldn't help but think the only thing missing were the big lace fans and corsets. It was like living in a BBC period piece, in the early '90s.

Another part of living in that period piece, which would have been my other complaint if I could have admitted to it, was the tyranny of what Naomi Wolf would later call "The Beauty Myth." (You don't necessarily have to read Wolf to know what the beauty myth is, all you have to do is watch TV or pick up a magazine and it's right there in front of you. The beauty myth is that curious lie perpetuated by these, and other, media, which suggests that beauty is the distorted and ultimately unhealthy image of women they project.) I didn't know anything about Naomi Wolf back then, but I knew that it sucked to be a chubby, half-Japanese kid with glasses. It also sucked that, in order to keep my weight down to an acceptable level, I spent the majority of my time, post-meal, leaning over the porcelain bowl.

Still, because I was a sap with few original ideas of my own, I played along and said nothing about the things that bothered me. I was even getting better at my good girl routine when our local all boys private school held its annual political awareness convention. The title of that year's conference was feminism.

Feminism. No group was more afraid of that word than my friends and me. To be a feminist was tantamount to being a lesbian (goodbye social life). Being a feminist meant holding power. Power you would wield over men (again, goodbye social life).

Ironically, I almost didn't make it to see the guest speaker that would eventually change my life. I was making out with an ugly guy who, I was recently amused to learn, is now a dentist. Is that why his tongue was always brushing my molars?

I had never, until that point, heard a woman speak that way until I heard the guest speaker. Who knew that a woman could be like that, standing up on stage, in front of a crowd of snot-nosed private-school boys and girls, sending a message that no one in that audience wanted to hear?

> **My Definition of Feminism**
> For me, feminism is two parts definition and one part struggle — a constant process of defining, redefining and struggling against existing definitions.

Her message said that women and men were not treated equally.

That terrible things had happened and would continue to happen to women because of that.

That bulimia, anorexia, rape, abuse and other atrocities were as much our problem as anyone else's.

That women were angry.

And rightly so.

It is entirely possible that I had never considered the option of being angry before. I realized, sitting in my little plastic orange chair, that I, myself, was a little pissed. And maybe a little tired of pretending and trying to be someone I wasn't. Additionally I was pissed because my date and my friends were laughing at the woman up on stage. For the first time I felt myself separate. I pulled myself away from the group, slowly unhooking myself Velcro style, and leaned forward so I could hear.

As her speech neared its close, I ravaged my brain to think of something to say to the woman up on stage, who by that time was in the middle of Q&A period.

As an aside, for reasons I will never understand, the one question that sticks in my mind was the one where a boy asked the speaker if she didn't think that male pattern baldness could count as the male equivalent to anorexia.

A real thinker, that boy. I imagine he's now bald.

Wringing my hands as the speaker descended from the stage, I rehearsed my line. The speaker, glowing from her stage stint, smiled as I stood in front of her.

"Hello?" She said, smiling expectantly at me.

"Oh. Blessed be," I gushed.

I'm not exactly sure how the speaker, who I would later discover was Robin Morgan, feminist, activist, *Ms. Magazine* editor and writer, interpreted that expression. Perhaps she thought I was attempting, as some sort of amateur witch, to cast a spell over her to protect her from the mob of private school boys. Perhaps she thought I was saying a prayer. Maybe she thought it was, simply, the most profound thing I could think of saying.

In truth, I had searched my brain for the most feminist term I knew. I suppose, at that point, I figured all feminists were pagans. I have no idea where I came up with this theory.

Smiling, I received my first contact from what I saw as an honest to goodness feminist. She hugged me. "Blessed be!"

On the basis of that hug, I would later tell people that Robin Morgan inspired not only my dive into feminist politics but, additionally, my brief flirtation with paganism.

I think I even wrote a letter to Robin after that day, on stationery I found downtown that had little women's symbols on it. In that letter I vowed I would be a ruthless crusader for women's rights, even if that meant giving up my social life, even if all my friend's boyfriends were calling me a dyke because they saw me hugging a feminist. Robin Morgan, typical celebrity (even if she was a feminist celebrity), never wrote back.

I used to tell the story of this encounter more often than I do now. I stopped telling this story with such frequency about a year ago when I first saw the 1981 NFB documentary *Not a Love Story: A Film About Pornography*, featuring, you guessed it, Robin Morgan.

I did not know what *Not a Love Story* was about when I rented it at the library. It had been recommended to me by a professor for a project I was doing on images of sex work in film. I didn't know Robin Morgan was in the film either, until

I saw her, near the middle of the documentary, participating in a group discussion. *Not A Love Story* is a film that depicts a series of women talking about pornography. The argument of the film, and of director Bonnie Klein, is that pornography is ultimately degrading towards women, violent and wrong. As Robin Morgan put it, "pornography is the theory and rape is the practice." I, personally, do not agree with this argument, though I have heard it many times. I am a little more inclined towards Annie Sprinkle's theory, which suggests that the answer to bad porn is not *no porn,* but *better porn.*

It felt strange to see Robin in that film, to watch someone whose call to arms had been so instrumental in my own politics, argue the other side of a political issue (i.e., the right to freedom of expression, even if it is really bad porn) that I felt so strongly about. Unsettling.

My Robin Morgan story is a very different story now. It's an ironic one, about how sometimes sheroes get left behind, or traded in. Sometimes, depending on my mood, I try to make it a story about the value of a moment in history, a moment when I discovered the difference between the power they give you and the power you deserve. Other times it's a little more bitter, about how stupid you can be when you're a severely repressed sixteen-year-old. Still other times, when the topic turns to celebrity, it's my small "c" celebrity story, about how a semi-famous feminist celebrity who, perhaps misinterpreting my greeting, gave me a hug.

My Top 10 Feminist Influences

1. Adolescence
2. Prom night and all it encompasses
3. Sandra Shamas (who said, "You have to turn into a woman all by yourself, and you have to turn into the woman you were supposed to be, not the woman on the cover of *Cosmo,* not your mother, You.")
4. Janeane Garofalm
5. Margaret Atwood
6. Susie Bright
7. Every fight I ever had with my mother (for better and for worse)
8. My three favourite English teachers
9. The pair of jeans I kept for five years that didn't fit
10. My friends

My Bio

MARIKO TAMAKI is a proud card-carrying member of Pretty, Porky and Pissed Off, the Corporate Wet Nurse Association, Amateur Sexperts United and Airport Addicts United. Her goals are world peace and the invention of a bedside cupcake and cocoa dispenser. Mariko's first book *Cover Me* is available at a feminist bookstore near you.

ARROW SPACE

battling burnout: emotional renewal in

I worried all morning about coming to the skate jam. Not that I thought anything bad would happen, just the usual shyness. But everything turned out okay. First we watched a video on the history of women in skateboarding. Then we all took the bus to the Olympia Skate Park. I was getting really self conscious because I quickly realized that I was the only girl there in a dress. But those feelings were erased when, on the bus, coordinator Holly said, "I have to tell you that you're going to shred harder than anyone else here because you're wearing a dress!"

The skatepark was beautiful, all smooth concrete with different angles of incline. It was full of boys, but they cleared out fairly quickly. The coordinators got us to divide into two groups. Group #1 was for girls who had never skated before and #2 was for girls who wanted to skate at the park. The beginners were going to go to a parking lot. At first I was going to just be a beginner, but then I wasn't sure. I went up to Tracey who was leading group #2 and told her that I'd only been skating for about 3 months. She told me to come and join her group, which turned out to be the right decision. I learned something: it's better to over-estimate yourself than to under-estimate yourself. Very important. Anyway, I turned out to be really good at skating in the park. And my dress got me attention; people kept taking my picture. I got lots of compliments on how I was skating. I eventually thought I was going to die from the heat and the sun, so I hung out in the shade with two girls from Portland and L.A. and caught the bus home with them when it was all over.

MIDNIGHT SUN

12

tenant right training: yo live there

10

— Jennifer Whiteford *Matilda Zine* matilda@bust.com

ENCOUNTERING FEMINISM:
Stories from the Sandwich Generation

Susanne Luhmann

Circa 1978, I am fourteen and hanging around as women in purple dungarees, all twenty-thirty something, begin renovating a rundown downtown storefront in my North-German hometown. They are about to open the first ever women's bookstore here. On opening day, stars sparkle on the store's high ceilings. That same year, I watch the first ever "Take Back the Night" march. The marchers gather in the medieval marketplace and fill the winding street. Women are running, dancing, chanting, singing, noisily reclaiming the darkness while I, once again, watch on from the sidelines and dream of becoming a feminist activist when I grow up. For my fifteenth birthday, later that year, my brother gives me — hot off the press — one of the first new feminist novels published in Germany. The story, a hastily penned personal memoir of a woman discovering the women's movement and women as a way out of a restrictive marriage, leaves me with the impression that all women love women at some point in their lives. As I shyly continue exploring the women's bookstore, the earnings of my tutoring job buy purple women's symbol stickers. A special red sticker of two women's symbols intertwined is demonstratively placed on my school file folder for the remainder of my high school years; its symbol representing, as I believed then, the strength of women uniting.

Circa 2000, I am calling myself with slight irony a "professional feminist." I am training to become a Women's Studies professor. In some ways, I did fulfill my teenage dreams. Yet, for most of the thirty-six years of my feminist life — I do believe I was born feminist — I have not been able to fend off a feeling of slight disappointment. Born in the early 1960s, I missed by fate of belated birth my chance at partaking in the high noon of feminist activism in the early 1970s. Being too late also means missing out on the chance to share in the self-confidence that feminism seemed to ooze in its early days and means missing out on the self-assured buoyancy with which feminist social and political activism in those days boldly declared to "overthrow patriarchy, everywhere."

By the time I started university and was searching for a feminist community, the conservative 1980s had rolled along. By then, feminism had moved from the streets into institutions, and women in suits were busy creating equal opportunity policies in education and the workplace. As feminism went institutional, it seemed to lose its radical edge. An exception to this was my first Women's Studies professor, who introduced me to the expansive universe of feminist thought and to the practice of passionate thinking, of thinking up against what was then an entirely androcentric knowledge system in the German university. I guess it helped that she, the professor, already in her fifties and approximately the age of my mother, reminded us by way of her black leather outfits of her earlier days as the pianist in a women's rock band.

Today, as I listen to how second-wave feminism is talked about in the literature and Women's Studies classes, I come to believe that I must have been the only one who responded with awe when hearing that American feminists had publicly and defiantly burned their bras. To me, then a teenager with budding breasts that were to be reigned in to ward off unwanted attention, burning bras made immediate sense. No bras, yet dungarees, and, yes, Birkenstocks, were liberatory, small and yet worthwhile transgressions, forms of protests against capitalist and sexist fashion and body regiments. (Of course, we know now that the bra-burning feminist is entirely an invention of the sensation seeking media — too bad though, I still love the idea.)

I also wonder how my coming into feminism then, my feeling of coming too late for in-the-street feminist rebellion (and the adventures that vanguard politics promised), has a role in my particular attachment to feminist theory today. The way I continue to fall in love with books and texts is reminiscent of the excitement that I first felt watching purple dungaree-clad women opening a feminist bookstore many years ago. The theories that I read today — mainly critical race theory, postmodern feminist works and queer theory — share with early feminist activism a similar quality of critique and the promise of defiant intervention. Queer theory does this, for example, by bringing into focus sexual outlaws and gender rebels, critical race theory by questioning staid truths about universal gender oppression. Yet taken together, these bodies of theory produce a different experience than early second-wave feminism. Second-wave feminism appealed to me in its display of self-certainty and self-confidence, a position that it could arrive at by understanding itself entirely as outside the oppressive patriarchy that it opposed. By comparison, the work I read today does not afford me such a comfortable position. Instead, this work unsettles me by demanding radical self-questioning. The work destabilizes earlier feminist truth claims and pushes up against limits, ignorance and refusal — not only in mainstream thought but also in feminist thought. To call myself a feminist no longer affords me the safety of being "innocent," but asks me instead to consider how I too am implicated in the histories and present states of inequalities.

Circa 1994, once again, I find myself watching from the sidelines. This time, I watch in awe as young women reclaim culture and cultural production (not to mention the reclaiming of lipsticks, boas, miniskirts and push-up bras), pushing up against the feminism laid out by the feminists who came before.

In the process, young women today are demanding and shaping their very own brand of feminism. Not unlike women in the 1970s, who reclaimed the streets and storefronts to set up bookstores, women's centres, women's shelters and rape crisis phone lines, young women today are setting up shop. As writers, filmmakers, artists, zine publishers and activists, they boldly take on our culture, reclaim and subvert artistic production, assert and insert themselves defiantly as "girls" into society and representations. This

My Definition of Feminism

I think of my feminism as a practice of radical (self-)questioning that is skeptical of any kind of truth claims made concerning gender, sexuality and other kinds of social identities. My kind of feminism tries to understand (and hopefully intervene in) how gender, sexuality, race, class singularly and collectively are mobilized

time I bemoan the fate of being born too early, of not qualifying as a "young feminist" any longer, thus missing out on being the riot grrl kind of feminist that I secretly long to be. Yet, it is this context, as well as with the queer return of a butch-femme aesthetic, that makes it possible for me to reclaim the very garment I had wanted to burn earlier. I am well into my thirties when I first discover the pleasures of accoutrements that come with a feminist "fem(me)ininity."

Second- and third-wave feminisms look different. Yet from my vantage point as the member of an "in-between-generation," as Sharon Rosenberg describes so well in her contribution, I see strong commonalties. Both waves have in common their own versions of a "do-it-yourself" mentality; they share a similar kind of self-confidence and buoyancy. Looking from my position, looking with awe back and forth, I do see that different generations navigate feminism very differently, depending on how, when and where we enter and encounter feminist practices and theories. And, while I offer a generation-based model, I know that this is too simple; there is no generational unity.

Even those of similar generations might end up with very different feminisms. Yet, it is important to consider our attachments to feminist theories and politics in tandem with the specific psychosocial historicity of our encounters with feminism. It is one way to move beyond intergenerational and intertheoretical accusations, beyond the claims that certain feminisms are outdated and others are apolitical. Most importantly, it is one way to keep talking.

My Top 10 Feminist Influences

1. Genie in *I Dream of Genie*
2. Dolly in Enid Blyton's *Malory-Towers* series
3. Simone de Beauvoir
4. My girl/women friends
5. Alice Walker's literary protagonists
6. My feminist teachers, especially those wearing leather pants
7. Women with tools
8. Judith Butler
9. Femmes, then and now
10. Transgender boys

My Bio

SUSANNE LUHMANN is originally from Germany. She is presently finishing a doctoral dissertation in the Graduate Program in Women's Studies at York University, Toronto, where she also teaches "Introduction to Women's Studies." By the time this book goes into print, she hopes to be well on her way towards a stellar career as a Women's Studies professor.

i can't describe it so much of what i am doing lately, i am too busy running around and enjoying myself. i've been finding less time to think and write, my head is full of immediate thoughts, what to eat and when to sleep and shuffling between work and wherever else..

this part is more of a snapshot fof me in motion, it's harder to document what you do when it's mostly just running around.

— Sarah Evans *in morning clouds #14 zine sjevans@isz.dal.ca*

FROM CUTE & PERKY TO HARD-NOSED BITCH: The Evolution of a Feminist

Loretta Gerlach

I grew up as a working-class kid in the 1980s. For working-class girls, feminism was something that we didn't brush with much. Many of our mothers had traditional jobs and often did not have even a Grade-Twelve education. Many working-class families had ties to the trade union movement, making their politics usually more progressive than not. However, even one decade ago, women were largely invisible in the trade union movement. The closest thing to feminist thought permeating young working-class girls was the dominant idea that Madonna was cool because she didn't take any shit from anyone. Certainly, Madonna's "think of

39

me as your personal plaything" image did not make her a perfect feminist idol for young women, but she was a woman taking pop culture by storm on her own terms. I remember seeing Madonna's face and voice everywhere in those days, and I found myself thinking about the success and power of women for the first time. However, I still had a long way to go.

Like a lot of women from my working-class background, I did not go to university straight out of high school. My financial situation simply did not allow for it. As a result, I started a long painful stream of meaningless and degrading jobs. I was a sales clerk, a waitress and even a telephone solicitor. Sure it would have been great to go straight to university and get some academic exposure to feminism, but spending a few years working in crappy jobs also had some feminist lessons for me. For example, there was that job as a waitress where the uniform was a dress with a neckline somewhere around my navel (seriously!) and a slit that ran up to the very tippy-top of my thighs. It was held together by one snap. All the waitresses were self-conscious and uncomfortable about it, but we did not complain to our male boss. One by one, we just quit.

There was another waitressing job where the boss asked me out everyday. He would tell me what a loser my boyfriend was and ask me why I didn't want to do better, meaning with someone like him. Sexual harassment was not talked about as much as it has been in recent years and I had no idea that what he was doing was wrong or illegal—I just knew I could not stand him. So, I quit yet another low paying, degrading job and went on to the next one, where I had another persistent boss. He decided that I would be fun to date and bugged me until I finally agreed. Soon after we became a couple, he got into a big fight with the owner and quit his job with no notice. The owner wasn't too keen on the idea of having this guy's girlfriend around so I quit as well. I was off to another bad job, but I had my new boyfriend.

My boyfriend never really did get another management position. He joined the ranks of bartenders who go from job to job, from one trendy bar to the next. In public, he was funny and charming and everyone loved him. However, for all his highs, he had as many lows. Though he never once hit me, not a day went by without him telling me "You're lucky I love you because you're so ugly no one else would have you," or some other equally warm pillow talk. Day after day, year after year, I allowed myself to be brought down by him and threw away my self-esteem. I didn't know it then, but, sadly, this is a common experience among women.

> **My Definition of Feminism**
>
> Feminism is the context in which I choose to view the world and within which I make the decisions about my life and the actions I take.

Finally, after five years, I saw the light. Our building was taken over by a new landlord who decided we could not keep our cat. I decided that enough was enough and if I had to move anyway, I might as well go it alone. I packed my bags and my cat and went out on my own for the first time. Older and a whole lot wiser, I registered for full-time university classes. I still had the wretched part-time jobs, but I also had hope. I flirted with taking some classes in business administration, but then I realized there was not one single woman in the department. This outraged me, so I decided to pursue studies in human justice. It was in these classes that I first found a venue for speaking out. The students and professors in this area seemed to form a common front to seek equity and fight oppression. Women were encouraged to be leaders, speakers and teachers. I began to explore the idea that power did not have to oppress, that as progressive women, we could use our power and privileges to support one another and share in the many benefits and burdens of society.

Perhaps ironically, it was a male professor (one who has supported many a feminist) who gave me my first opportunity to stand strong in the face of oppression. We were involved in a struggle to protect our academic program at the university. This professor supported my participation, my values and ideas. He helped me to use my voice and gave me the support I needed to remain firm in my beliefs and demonstrate leadership for the first time in my life. Further details are irrelevant; the important thing is he helped me to bring my newly forming feminist perspectives to light. Almost without me knowing it, things mushroomed from there. Over time, I was asked to run (successfully) as an executive member of my students' union. I then became involved at the national level. Over the years, I have continued to take a strong feminist stand on many issues and have had the privilege to maintain a high profile in areas of trade unionism, pay equity and human rights.

I have certainly grown a great deal along the way. My background has been a benefit to me in my emergence as an outspoken feminist. I have had the privilege of having understood the concept of struggle from the perspective of a white working-class woman and have also had the honour of learning from many sisters who are single parents, lesbian / bisexual, of First Nations heritage, from different races, religions and lifestyles. They have taught me as much as I can learn about their challenges, their struggles and their gifts. Of course, I look forward to learning more in the future from my sisters. And there are so many other ways in which we continue to grow as feminists.

Becoming a feminist activist affects one's life in both the largest and smallest of ways. It affects what we wear and how we wear it, where we shop and what we buy, what entertainment we choose and where we get our news. I have been fortunate to find venues where I have been able to speak out and stand strong in face of patriarchy and oppression. I am certain that I have made many mistakes, some of which I am aware of and many more of which I am not. And, of course, as a lifelong learner, I continue to seek out other ways to effect change for the benefit of women and other oppressed people across the globe.

However, the gift of a feminist life has not been without cost. In high school, I was the girl who was constantly described as perky and pleasant. Today, you'd be hard pressed to find someone to describe me as such. In fact, you'd be more likely to have me described as a hard-nosed bitch. There are many people in positions of power in society that find it so easy to dismiss vocal feminists as women with personality flaws in order to avoid dealing with the issues that we bring forward. I have had male board members of my university tell me that I am "cute" when I am radical. I have been told by innumerable members of government that I am too young or too naïve to understand the real issues. I have had men walk out of meetings when I have risen to state a point. And I have been told by trade union men to keep my "personal" issues like childcare out of the trade union movement (I don't even have children). And of course, there is the chronic problem of men individualizing gender issues and feeling like they need to launch a personal attack against feminists to silence their perspectives.

And there have been the more concrete "penalties." I applied for a scholarship targeted for activists, for which I was far and away the most qualified but which was given to a male counterpart who had been the president of a social club — the professor in charge said he did not like my politics. I had another professor tell me he could not grade my work because he disliked my politics so much that he would prefer to just give me my average in the class. I did not pass a security check for a job that I wanted because I had a file with a national security agency, even though I have never been arrested for anything. (Apparently, being a feminist is some kind of threat to national security.) One employer I had tried to penalize me with a written warning on my personnel file for expressing "confrontational" viewpoints. The warning was removed when I successfully grieved this action with my union.

I became a feminist because of the injustices I witnessed and experienced, and I still see them all around me. I see young women working those crap jobs, stuck in those painful relationships, struggling to be heard in male-oriented systems and institutions, and I know I will be a feminist for a long time still. In the end, keeping my integrity is more important to me than not making waves. It's cliché but fighting back does make you stronger. I am proud of my journey as a feminist, and I am hopeful that I will continue to learn and evolve. Each time I meet another feminist, I grow from her strength and solidarity and she revitalizes my hope for change. I believe that if we stand strong in the struggles and support one another, wherever and whenever we can, our sisterhood will transcend geography, age, class and race. Every

43

time we speak out, we empower others and ourselves with the courage to stand strong.

My Top 10 Feminist Influences

1. My parents, especially in consideration of their struggles and strength as working-class people.
2. Madonna, she was the first woman that made me take notice that she took no shit and did whatever she wanted.
3. A series of bad waitressing jobs in bars and restaurants where I was objectified and mistreated badly enough to get seriously pissed off.
4. A male professor I had in university who not only talked the talk but walked the walk.
5. A wonderful community of feminist sisters who have become fellow activists and the dearest of friends.
6. The Canadian student movement, my participation in which allowed me to meet and learn from some key feminists in the country.
7. The working women of Cuba, whom I had the opportunity to meet and learn from several years ago.
8. The many teenage girls I have met who have led their lives on the street where they are afforded so few opportunities.
9. The Prairie School for Union Women — it has been an absolute privilege for me to study and work with women from all kinds of social, economic, cultural and employment backgrounds; they have taught me so much.
10. Maude Barlow, the chair of the organization for which I work, whose passion, integrity and dedication inspire me.

My Bio

LORETTA GERLACH is a Saskatchewan-based feminist who is active in a number of social justice groups. She is employed as a human rights investigator, a program worker with young offenders and disadvantaged youth and as an organizer with the Council of Canadians.

THE FORGOTTEN WOMEN

Jessica Lara Ticktin

When I was in Grade Five, my best friend Julie and I would take a twenty-minute bus trip every few weeks across the city to an apartment complex where her grandmother lived. We would sit inside her cozy little kitchen, our ten year-old-legs dangling off the chairs, and devour the cookies she had baked for us. She would be impeccably dressed, with her flawless makeup and gold jewelry on, looking like she was ready to go out for an elegant soiree. Her blue eyes sparkled with mischief as she looked at us and remarked with tactful sincerity on our childish attempts to look chic.

She spoke with a thick Norwegian accent, and I remember a calm and wonderful feeling would wash over me whenever I was in her presence. She fascinated me with her beauty, her accent and her charm, but it was more than that. It wasn't until I was older, years after she had passed away, that I realized her importance as an older woman in my life and how she, and the others who followed, came to shape my identity as a young feminist.

As a first generation Canadian, I did not grow up with extended family nearby, in fact, most of my relatives were in a different hemisphere. My mother's parents died when she was very young, and my father's parents lived in South Africa where he grew up. From time to time, I would write to my grandparents and thank them for the gifts they sent, but I didn't know them and they didn't know me. I remember meeting them only twice; when I was five, and then again when I was nine. My grandmother died of a heart attack a few years after that. I have very few memories of her and have always carried with me the loss of not knowing her.

From those early childhood visits with Julie's grandmother to my adult years, I had little exposure to older women. As a university student I needed a part-time job so I took one with the municipality where I grew up on the West Island of Montreal. It was a social program funded by the city to provide services to low-income and permanently or temporarily disabled seniors. I was hired as a summer student and then, because I loved the experience so much, stayed on and worked through the winter and the next two years.

I spent my summers and weekends with women ranging in age from sixty-five to ninety-eight. More than doing anything physical — mowing their lawns or cleaning their cupboards — the people I cared for wanted someone to speak to, someone to sit down with to share a cup of tea or maybe lunch. Mostly widows or single women who had never married, they filled my life with stories of their lives, their loves and their struggles. I found myself staying hours with some of them, going over photograph albums, listening to First World War stories. I fell in love with these women, their quiet strength, their humour. For the most part, these were women who were tucked away in one-room apartments with small pension cheques and, perhaps, if they were lucky, monthly visits from family.

I thought of them as the forgotten women. The women's movement came when many of them were in their forties and fifties and had raised children, served their husbands and owned nothing in their own name. Too old to easily reverse decisions made decades earlier, and yet too young not to be affected by the changing environment, many felt alienated and confused by women's liberation. Women of this generation, born in the 1920s and having lived through the Great Depression as well as two world wars, had seen many changes in their lives and had been forced to adapt to major world events.

They suffered losses of husbands, brothers, fathers and sons in the wars and had seen their roles as primary caregivers and homemakers as valuable. Yet the thrust of the women's movement in the 1970s turned on many of these women, rejecting their lives and what they stood for. Feminism in its early stages made some of these women feel as if their contributions were meaningless. Daughters who took up the cause chastised their mothers for the choices they made, for the lives they had "given up" and even for the way they had raised their girls. Where had that left them? And where did that leave me in relation to them? Both of our generations were born at radically different times within the feminist movement, and now we were both fumbling within its ideology. As I struggled with questions of identity and sexuality I wondered how these women could possibly inform my own nascent feminism. I even feared rejection — could they accept me if I accepted them?

I remember the first day of my job, I was sent to help a woman who was eighty-five years old. Her name was Rose. I was terrified. What could I possibly talk about with her? Rose and I sat in her living room. I inquired after her health, seeing she had just returned from the hospital. I was shaking. I was so nervous. I was nineteen years old and full of energy. As a first year literature major I was discovering works by women like bell hooks, Toni Morrison and Adrienne Rich, women who were carving out a whole new world of consciousness for me. It was a time of intellectual as well as sexual awakening. The prospect of sitting in what I imagined would be the stuffy, frilly, over-heated living rooms of frail elderly women every weekend was less than appealing. I wanted to get in there, do my job and leave. Although I only got to see Rose a few times before she went back to the hospital, she touched a part of me that had been dormant since I was in Grade Five. When she put her warm dry hands against my face, it brought tears to my eyes.

I didn't realize, until I had developed close and loving relationships with several older women, how much I missed having a grandmother, how my heart ached for that relationship. I felt a part of myself filled with joy, where previously there had been an emptiness. In dreams, Julie's beautiful grandmother came to me, her smiling face and her warmth gave me confidence in continuing on and forging relationships with older women.

At first it seemed like I was living in two opposing worlds. In one world, I was slightly wild, living with three other young women on the second floor of a house in downtown Montreal, going to classes at McGill University and throwing off the shackles of my very strict and regimented childhood. In the other world, I was the young responsible girl who cleaned, gardened and served seniors in need. I often laughed at myself, at what I thought was a dual existence, how the latter wasn't really me, but a part that I had to play for the job.

However, as the months went by, I started making the connection between the things I was reading and learning at school and the living, breathing, strong women I encountered every weekend.

One of these women was Sophie. Sophie was seventy-two years old and lived alone on the eighth floor of an apartment building. She had never married and had no living family or children. She suffered from diabetes and osteoarthritis as well as some substantial vision impairment. Sophie had a shock of white hair, deep laugh lines around her mouth and an ample figure. She always had a smile on her face and gave me a big hug when I walked through her door.

Sophie had worked her whole life as a secretary and had been the primary caregiver to both her mother and father during their ailing years. She had friends from all over the country and around the world and was only too happy to take the Christmas and birthday cards she received out of her old oak cabinet to show me.

I would come to help her out every other weekend, and I found myself looking forward to the visit more and more. We would trade stories about our weeks, talk about the latest events happening in the world. She didn't get out much as it was difficult for her to walk or stand for long, but she kept up with the news by watching television.

Her fierce independence challenged my notions about family, sexuality and what growing old meant. I thought she must be miserable without a partner, without children or grand-children, and yet every time we spoke about this she would tell me how all of her married friends would complain about their husbands or children. They all seemed to have so many more problems than she did, and she was thankful she had no one telling her what she could or could not do, that is how she put it. I started really thinking about what "a room of one's own" could mean and how solitude doesn't necessarily mean loneliness.

Here was a woman who had defied so many of society's rules, who had refused to adhere to standard notions of what a woman was "supposed" to do or be. She was not a mother or a wife. She was not even an aunt

My Definition of Feminism

For me, feminism is all about choice; the freedom to choose how to live one's life with respect, tolerance and compassion for and from others. It is about having multiple roles for women that are fluid and changing. It is about "ands" not "ors." It's being able to wear a miniskirt and study law, have children or have an abortion, be sexually active and not to be a sexual object. My feminism is about taking social action and striving for a society that is based on democracy and human rights. It is also about being inclusive and spiritually open.

or a grandmother. She was no one's lover, and she no longer worked. I began to understand that just because people make certain choices, it doesn't mean they should be defined by them.

In my mind I fought off the labels and stereotypes which surrounded women like her whose lives were dismissed by phrases such as "old maid" or "never married" and of course "poor thing." There was no acknowledgement by anyone, including myself, of her as a sexual being despite her choice to be celibate. But I would secretly wonder about her sexuality.

Initially, when I went to visit Sophie, she represented the death of sexuality to me, which was one of the worst things I could imagine. Although part of me felt shameful, thinking about the sex I just had or the sex I was going to have tonight, tomorrow, next week, I couldn't help but think of what was to me so painfully lacking in her.

As the months went by, though, I started becoming more perceptive. I noticed the Harlequin romance novels lining the bookshelves in her bedroom. Even though she presented herself as a "good Christian woman," I wasn't naive enough to believe that she was without sexual fantasies. I knew that capital "R" Religion could not and should not control one's sexuality or how one chooses to express it. After thinking so much about her in this way, I would then turn on myself, *how dare I be so presumptuous and intrusive?* Yet there was no one I could talk to about the older single woman and sex. When I listened to Sophie, I realized that in the stories or anecdotes she told me, she was expressing her frustration at being stigmatized, not only as "old and useless" but as asexual as well.

I became infuriated at the health professionals who, time and again, treated her like a piece of meat, pushing and prodding her without sensitivity or respect. I knew how strong she was, how much dignity she still held and how men like her doctor could constantly demean her and lower her self-esteem. If this was happening to her, then I knew it was happening to many other older women too.

My visits with Sophie and women like her fuelled my anger towards a society that discards not just older people but especially older women, sending them into institutions and foster homes where they are disciplined like children, their personal privacy is invaded and they are left to rot in front of the television. Is there no place, no meaningful role for older people in our society?

I began taking social work courses, which focused on the older adult, and I turned my attention to widows and single women in their seventies and eighties. I wanted to do outreach programs for these women, I wanted to design workshops for them and for the people who care for them. I wanted to talk openly about older women as whole people, which includes seeing them as sexual beings. I had never thought of myself as political or as an activist of any kind, but suddenly I found myself talking to everyone I knew about the reality of ageism and the need for social change.

I learned much about myself from my relationships with these women, and they indirectly shaped my vision of the world as a young feminist. While they would never call themselves feminists with a capital "F," their lives are testaments to what I would call a different kind of feminism, one that includes self-sacrifice as well as equal opportunity, that embraces family life as well as solitude, and finally that supports sexual expression as well as the right to be left alone. This is the kind of feminism I adhere to; it is all about choice, and not being judged for those choices.

During my visits with them, our discussions would always turn from their lives to my life and my future. They would encourage me to believe in my dreams and to always cherish my family first. They taught me education was important, but that so was love. I could feel a sense of urgency in their advice to me, they wanted me to know that they were not always like this, in a wheelchair, or using a walker, or unable to see. I recognized how much they still had to give, how valuable their contributions were and that they deserved a forum from which to speak.

Their voices were strong despite their ageing bodies; their eyes were bright with excitement for me and the opportunities which lay ahead for both of us, it seemed. While we would be physically separate, I knew we would always be spiritually bound. The difference they made in my life helped me believe that I could make a difference in others' lives as well.

My Top 10 Feminist Influences

1. My mother
2. My three older sisters
3. *The Edible Woman* by Margaret Atwood
4. *The Beauty Myth* by Naomi Wolf
5. Alice Walker
6. A Women's Writing and Feminist Theory course at McGill University, taught by Professor Sarah Westphal, 1996
7. *Not a Love Story,* documentary film on pornography by Bonnie Klein
8. Working with older women as part of the social program "Aid for Seniors" in Montreal
9. Libby Scheier (Toronto poet and teacher)
10. Recording the oral histories of six South African women anti-apartheid activists

My Bio

JESSICA LARA TICKTIN has found herself wading through a master's degree at the Ontario Institute for Studies in Education of the University of Toronto. She treads the muddy waters of public history, collective memory and testimony in post-apartheid South Africa. Jessica is currently working on a radio documentary for the CBC, has been published in *The Toronto Star* and has an article forthcoming in a book on arts-informed research. Jessica is also a member of the editorial collective of *Fireweed: A Feminist Quarterly.*

WHY AM I A FEMINIST?

Samantha Sacks

"Oh, so you're in university ..."
The eyes of those professing interest in my occupation light up; the prospect of an interesting area of study, maybe something they know, perhaps they think they can teach me a little, tell me what it was like in the good old days.

"What's your major?" asks my newfound friend.

And while the potential for sparkling conversation still lingers sweetly in the air (I can almost hear the clinking of good cutlery and wine glasses), I alone have the seasoned prescience of a thousand encounters of an identical nature to know that momentarily I will squash our titillating tête-à-tête with the oppressive weight of my major.

"Women's Studies."

And of course, the glassy-eyed stare settles over my partner's face. Sometimes the look conveys condescending humour, sometimes hate, sometimes astonishment, sometimes indifference spliced with ignorance. The combinations are endless. If I were to mix the ingredients of these myriad gawks and gapes and leers, I could make a vicious cocktail, as the one thing these looks have in common is their absence of genuine interest.

Regardless, I will still be asked to testify on my own behalf.
"WHY ARE YOU A FEMINIST?"

And this is what I will say:
Because at the dawn of a new century we have so much

death in our lives. Nature struggles to catch its breath, the earth heaves gently as the last drops of juice are sucked from its bowels. Sanitized lives hang leaden in the hot rotting air. Intolerance seeps into our kitchens through radioactive TV screens; breastless women, their faces lit with the gaunt glow of chemotherapy, cruise florescent supermarket aisles, where delicacies from the four corners of the earth, elegantly displayed on foam trays, offer microwave-ready cultural diversity. The first oxygen bar opens in Toronto and with AIDS comes the death of love.

Because the only security I feel leaving my home at night comes from countless self-defence courses. Because my body is qualified, quantified, valued and valueless, bought and sold on every street corner and television advertisement that invades my solitude. On purpose. Because where would we be without hysteria? Without anxiety, we may be able to get a grip, our claws, perhaps, into reality. Or the power structures that comprise it.

Because our lives are histories. The culmination of a thousand stories, myths and oracles. Recorded over many thousands of years by the most prestigious members of the most powerful societies, throughout time. As they see it. A myopic vision, a false prophecy. Where am I in your history? I look in the mirror, craning my neck to see past a distorted body image. A castrated, manipulated sexual identity. To see myself. But you built the chrome and glass and you can't see me. In this world I don't count unless I raise my fucking voice.

"WHY ARE YOU A FEMINIST?"

Recently I was asked this question in a very different context. I was in Honduras and had the opportunity to interview a group of women called "Las Amas De Casa," "The Mistresses of the Home" or "The Housewives." A community group comprised of single mothers whose husbands immigrated illegally to the United States to find work. For the most part they found work, and wives and new families. The single mothers secure latrines for their homes, build schools and organize technical training programs.

After I asked a thousand different questions about the role of feminism in Honduras, the relevancy of academics and who they would or would not accept money from and under which circumstances, the group leader, Gloria Reina Santos Montes, fixed me with a cold stare and asked me why I am a feminist.

And this is what I said:

Feminism is about change, about a redistribution of power. It is about challenging the status quo. A call for the redefinition of the family, the mosque, the temple, the church, the synagogue and love. Change is threatening to those of us who wield power and those who do not. And because it is threatening, it is electric and alive and powerful and I want to touch it.

> My Definition of Feminism
> A recognition of the social and economic imbalance of power between men and women and a commitment to change it.

And Gloria Reina Santos Montes stared at me, from her world that looked like Eden fixed between a garbage dump and a Coca-Cola billboard, and said, (and I paraphrase):

"I don't care what you call it, I just want to feed my babies and maybe someday shit in a toilet."

The world stands still. The earth stops spinning, the sun shines in one single long ray and except for my pulse throbbing gently in my ears, silence is everywhere. For a wrinkle in time I'm breathless and speechless and I want to puke because no matter how many post-colonial, postmodern binary pedagogies I wrench from some underexposed academic, YOU CAN'T THEORIZE BREAKFAST.

Hungry children are not concerned with political nuances. Theory is a luxury, the caviar of developed nations. Reality just stood on its head.

Where is the value of my course in Strategic Adjustment Policy in this land where the American owned Standard Fruit Company is mother's milk, the juice of life? Fuelling the Honduran economy while matricide pulses through the blood of the people. Who do I think I am in this Wild West armed only with a university degree?

And Gloria Reina Santos Montes and I lock eyes, and I recognize what it is I have seen in her stare from the moment we met. She knows me. She was expecting my armament of questions. My textbook sensitivity. She has merely been watching to see if I will recognize myself, if I will catch a glimpse of my reflection in the mirrors that are her eyes.

And now that I have, what will I do? Will I return to fill my head with someone else's words? Until I forget the hot green stink of the earth and those omniscient eyes? My thoughts sterilized and sanitized? My brain rocked into an academic stupor by the embryonic lull of Saniflush? Or perhaps I will go home to twist and bend and shape my words until, like a bulimic consumption and eruption of meaning, I can purge my mixed-up self. And pass it on to you.

So as I stand before you, my bones racked with the ache of what I don't know. Perhaps we can build a bridge, or do something lyrical and metaphorical and uplifting. That will make us all feel better. Conflict resolution. Or closure, or some such thing.

Or maybe, for a brief moment, we will take a breath between the spewing forth of academic bile. Because if somebody says the word "problematic" one more time, I'm going to scream. A silent beat between syllables. In our ugly language, our long vowels that reek of imperialism. We will stop and shiver as a gust of reality makes this comfortably heated room seem cold. And see ourselves.

And now the shimmering edges between questions and answers become blurred, wavering in the stifling heat of revelation. And I'm still wondering ...

WHY AM I A FEMINIST?

My Top 10 Feminist Influences (or almost)

1. My mother
2. My grandmother
3. My father
4. My friends

My Bio

SAMANTHA SACKS is a producer with CITY-TV in Toronto.

THE ELEVEN-YEAR-OLD FEMINIST

Megan Rivers-Moore

Introduction

I hadn't read this piece in years when it was sent to me so I could write this introduction. My first reaction was embarrassment. I didn't write it that long ago, only four or five years have passed. And yet my strongest desire upon reading it again was to crawl under the nearest rock or quick-change my name. The essay seemed so idealistic, so naively earnest, so angry. Since I've had a few days to think about it, my thoughts have shifted somewhat. What strikes me now is how profoundly sad it is and how sad it makes me to read just how much I was affected by my experiences in high school. I'm even a little surprised I was able to articulate anything at all about what was going on in my life at the time. I'm relieved and happy to report that I survived high school — long live the alternative school system!

Some of what I think and feel about feminism is the same. I continue to believe that I have to be a feminist because I don't have the luxury not to be one. I still believe that women do an excellent job of policing other women and sustaining oppression. I also believe in the importance of women-only self-defence and that high school is a terrible place for young women to be. But some of my thinking has changed. When I referred to radical feminism in the essay, I don't think I clearly knew what that meant from a theoretical or historical perspective.

Now that I've been exposed to radical feminist thought, and while I can appreciate its usefulness and contributions to feminist struggle, it certainly doesn't describe who I am or what I believe.

Through lots of reading and endless conversation I've come to what I hope should be an obvious conclusion (and probably should have been all along): that different types of oppression function as part of an integrated system and that all of them must be addressed and challenged in order to facilitate genuine change. This didn't come across in what I wrote, and I believe it's fundamental. Nevertheless, I was writing from a place of rage, isolation and, despite all my attempts to deny it, fear. It is precisely for this reason that I think what I wrote is fierce and brave. And that's why I'm working hard to stop feeling embarrassed and to start feeling proud.

***

I remember when I was eleven years old in Grade Six and a boy in my class asked me if I was a feminist. My answer was "How could I not be?" Looking back five years later, my answer is still the same. The difference in me now is that my feminism is more radical and I have fewer fears.

The only time in my life that I have ever experienced peer pressure was to shave my legs. Forget all the bullshit about my friends trying to sell me drugs, they were pushing razor blades. When I stopped shaving in Grade Nine I received many nasty looks and comments in the change room before gym class. I was crushed that I was being judged for being different, looking like a prepubescent model was not high on my priority list. Women policing women makes me angry; it's like we've fallen right into the five-thousand-year-old trap the patriarchy set for us. There's no hope for change if we're too busy hating each other. I think there's a lot less sisterhood than we like to think, at least in women my age. High school is a time of immense competition between women.

I used to be terrified of being hurt. Violence against women is so common in our society, I was paranoid that I was going to be kidnapped and murdered. Then I started taking Wendo, women's self-defence classes, and I realized that life isn't about fear. Wendo has given me a sense of safety and confidence that I never thought I had. My Wendo classes feel like really safe places; I find it comforting that for even a short time, I am surrounded by women only. There's no threat, only incredible support and power. I think a lot of my fear has been replaced by anger, which I have discovered can be a valuable tool. I have found a place in myself where I can use fear and rage to fight back.

A group of my friends and I get together every few months for what we call "bra parties." We sit around in our bras and talk about the boys or girls we're interested in, sex, our bodies, et cetera. I enjoy these times, yet they often frustrate me. So many young women won't call themselves feminists because they are afraid. Afraid of being called "man-haters," afraid of being unattractive, afraid of speaking too loudly or taking up too much space. I think it's really difficult for women to change what we are so subtly told from childhood, to be quiet and good and to keep our legs crossed. I'm not afraid of being called a man-hater, because I am quite willing to admit that there are things about men that I hate. I don't hate men, I hate what they do, what our society allows them to do. That girls and boys are socialized differently is painfully obvious. I think that singer/songwriter ani difranco put it perfectly when she wrote "women learn to be women / and men learn to be men / I don't blame it all on you / but I don't have to be your friend." Even the young women I know who do call themselves feminists only tend to go part way. I've had wonderful conversations with friends about feminism and then watched them begin to blur when their boyfriends are around. As far as I'm concerned it's all the way or nothing. Radical feminism or why bother? I think this probably gets me some enemies but I really don't care. Being able to say fuck it and carry on is one of my strengths. As

Robin Morgan said, "If you can't stand the heat, step down from the stake."

High school is the worst place for women to be. We're unimportant in class and worthy of interruption and ridicule from other students. It's been proven that we learn better when we can see reflections of ourselves. When the only mention of women's contributions to anything is most often a few remarks on the side, is it any surprise that all our education system teaches us to do is hate ourselves? Last year a group

> **My Definition of Feminism**
>
> Feminism is many things for many people, but it includes a revolutionary movement dedicated to dismantling oppression based on sex, class, race/ethnicity, sexual orientation, age and ability, among others. It's also a lot of fun.

of students at my school organized a series of meetings to try and establish a Women's Studies course or, at the very least, incorporate Women's Studies into the already existing history courses. Teachers and administration listened, made a few condescending comments, put up a few miles of red tape and told us to try again next year. Complaints of all kinds are often ignored.

Many young women I know have been harassed by teachers and other students but seldom request help anymore, choosing to ignore unacceptable behaviour. I decided to leave my east-end school last year when I was forced to give a warning before I did a seminar on homophobia for one of my classes. I had been verbally harassed many times in that school, so I knew firsthand that the students could use some education against homophobia. When I was told to warn people that my subject was offensive I knew that continuing at that school was a bad idea. It didn't feel like a safe place for me to be anymore. I now attend an alternative school.

I've said it before, life isn't about fear. I'm sitting in my room again writing and yelling because it's all that I know how to do. And even sitting here, I'm starting a revolution. I'm writing because I have no choice. My words take up space that I have a right to. I yell because I can and because I deserve to be heard. Like all women do.

My Top 10 Feminist Influences
(in random order)

1. My mom, whose example has taught me everything I know and then some
2. bell hooks
3. Hothead Paisan
4. Wendo Women's Self-Defence and the fabulous Deb Chard
5. Anne, the smartest person I know
6. My cousin/sister/friend Valerie Eisenhauer
7. Alice Walker
8. Grupo Venancia
9. Emilia Méndez Calvo
10. My Grandma Dorothy, an extraordinarily committed feminist, activist, organizer and grandma

My Bio

MEGAN RIVERS-MOORE is a Latin American Studies major at York University. She has no definite plans for the future, apart from changing the world.

SMASHING THE ONION

Ana Ratcliffe

An Onion sits on the window ledge
Drenched in buttery sunlight
It sits for days and days and a green bud appears
The sign of new life
I walk over to it and roll it in my hand
Its papery skin crinkles and a piece falls onto the linoleum
floor
I put it back on the ledge and it looks out on the world with
child-like curiosity
Time steals two more days
Another green bud emerges
I stare at it for two and a half minutes
Then my jealousy boils over.
I run to it and rip off its outer skin.
I can feel its humiliation.
It does its best to protect itself, and it tries to sting my eyes.
It's powerless against my force.
I raise the cleaver into the air
Smashing it into a million pieces.
With mad fury, I throw the tiny demolished
pieces into the frying pan, they sizzle.
Their sizzle is them screaming,
they are screaming because of what I have done to them.
They scream because I cannot.

My Definition of Feminism
The dictionary defines feminism as the advocacy of equal rights for women. However I don't consider myself to be a feminist, I consider myself to be a humanist. To me that means there is no definite line between males and females and all humans should have equal rights.

My Top 10 Feminist Influences
(in no particular order)

1. My parents
2. My teachers
3. Ms. Burns
4. Ms. Craig
5. Ms. Robinson
6. My friends: Andrea and Anne
7. The women of the Davidson household
8. The Unitarian Church
9. Tank Girl (from the best movie ever made!)
10. The girls at Trafalgar!

My Bio

My name is Adriana Nelleke Ratcliffe, aka Ana. I am seventeen years old. I am a Grade Eleven student at Trafalgar Castle School, an all-girls school. My favourite things are bright colours and people who hold their cups with two hands. I didn't write "Smashing The Onion," the poem wrote itself. It was a manifestation of all the frustration I was feeling.

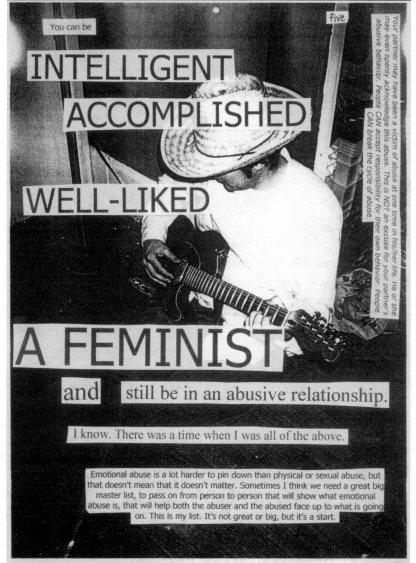

five

You can be

INTELLIGENT
ACCOMPLISHED
WELL-LIKED
A FEMINIST

and still be in an abusive relationship.

I know. There was a time when I was all of the above.

Emotional abuse is a lot harder to pin down than physical or sexual abuse, but that doesn't mean that it doesn't matter. Sometimes I think we need a great big master list, to pass on from person to person that will show what emotional abuse is, that will help both the abuser and the abused face up to what is going on. This is my list. It's not great or big, but it's a start.

Your partner may have been a victim of abuse at one time in his/her life. He or she may even openly acknowledge this abuse. This is NOT an excuse for your partner's abusive behavior. People CAN accept responsibility for their own behavior. People CAN break the cycle of abuse.

— Jennife Whiteford *Matilda Zine* matilda@bust.com

POSTCARDS OF A
WOMAN LEARNING

Shelly Abdool

& when i hear Sunera's voice wrinkle, tears well up in my eyes
let me sit and digest this work this class her words
let me look into myself, find the reason
i am a feminist

***

hey paki, why don't you go home and help your mother clean the house?

tarry's voice shouts across the schoolyard.
it is the first day of kindergarten, and i am alone on the tarmac.
3:30 has come and my sister is not here to walk me home. i sit and wait, listening to tarry taunt.
i am five years old. don't know what a paki is.
tarry runs over, sticking her tongue out. throws sand in my hair

paki paki, she jeers.

before i can stop them tears run down my face. brine and sand mix in my mouth as i try to explain to mrs. castle what happened. she is my teacher. she tells me to go home and forget about tarry.

where is your mother?

she is at work. my sister is not here. who will i go home with?

i am five years old.

***

ten years later, i learned a paki is from pakistan. but i am not.

***

grade 2

mrs. b was my baby-sitter. she gave me a lifesaver duffel bag with silver ends. just like the candy roll. it was my favourite bag. carried minimal homework proudly.

until shawn bruised my back with a metal baseball bat. kicking fragile foil wrapping on my life-size roll of candy, the bag crumpled. deflating before my wailing back, it whimpered softly in the wind.

school principal schauss asked me why i didn't want to come to school anymore.

I'm afraid.

quietly told me it was okay. said shawn would never touch me again. no one else either, said they'd have to deal with him.

though he leaned down and taught me how to whistle, i learned fear of violence.

***

grade three

my timid brown hand raised, trembling, to answer the question.

what are your family traditions?

mrs. m did not want to hear mine.
she told my mother to speak english at home so my spelling would improve.

67

my mom is unilingual. her only language is english.

my hand shivers in dead air as strong ones are answered. boys talk about chopping firewood with dad, fishing with grandpa. girls talk about sunday school, doll houses daddy built them. my hand remained still.

i want to tell her how i hold the trouble light for my dad while he fixes our basement. how my sister takes me home 'cause my mom is a nurse. i am proud of her. she left me when i was a baby to go back to school. Canada didn't think an rn from trinidad was smart enough. even though she was a nurse before, wore a white cap too.

but mrs. m does not see my hand. she is busy smiling, nodding at chris talking about the time he went hunting with his dad.

i want to ask why he hunts animals when my turn comes.

my arm began to tire in the stillness of the class though it never lowered as mrs. m shut the lights to show a movie. finally, in the dark room drowned out by shouting on the screen, i proudly gave my answer.

no smile. no nod of approval. a pat on the hand and

we're not talking about that anymore, shelly.

***

grade five

mr. r and his pristine choir were too good for my tenor voice. a public school choir must be very selective. only the best voices for their numerous concerts.

i wanted to be a singer. but mr. r said maybe i could volunteer in the class for disabled students. my talents would be better suited there.

it was a grade five choir.

yet i was already in this role. this silent, self-sacrificing role that has become known as woman.

my friend jenny got to sing. every day. and loud right in the centre of the front row. pale hand clutching a puffy little doll she wore a gingham dress and bouncy pigtails. her voice drowned out the pianist. she often forgot the words to the songs while i sang them softly in the audience.

my hand would never be that pale.

i never wore gingham.

but i learned what role to play.

***

> *My Definition of Feminism*
>
> feminism, for me, is a societal d&c scraping out unwanted hegemony and oppression. to do this, the curette is filled with women's voices and struggles to carve out social, political and economic space for women and all of their differences to BE, replacing hegemony with consensus and oppression with justice.

my entire muslim life, i have never eaten pork. this isn't allowed. mrs. s, with her puritan cluck of tongue, disapproved.

you have to try a piece, shelly. we've worked on it all day.

french tortière. made with pork.

i can't mrs. s. I'm not allowed. i can't eat pork.

everyone needs to try new things, shelly. just try one bite.

other kids snickered.
throat constricting heart breaking, tortière made its way into my stomach. i thought about what i would say to god, how i could apologize.
i learned something new.

i learned shame for my difference.
i learned hate for myself.

***

grade eight

mr. c liked to tease girls. wasn't embarrassed to touch them either. he taught gym class, picked little black hot pants as female uniforms.

lisa and i were badminton partners. we were also gungas, a club michelle created for 8 of us to be forever friends. we were waiting for a court and mr. c was talking to us in a grating voice. maybe he thought it was sexy. he said we were too self-involved to include anyone else in our club. i roll my eyes at lisa. he pretends not to like us. but we see him watch us as we run track and field, do open-leg stretches on the lawn.

lisa drops the birdie she was bouncing off her racquet. i bend over to pick it up and mr. c swats my behind. bolting up i say

don't touch my bum.

waxing apologetic, he walks away.

we smile at each other. high fives and pinkie swears of friendship.
i learned where to find my voice.
and it came from within.

***

it's ten o'clock and I'm in mr. y's office. he's my high school guidance counsellor. we're choosing my courses. i want to take world issues and study politics.

he suggests home economics. says i will learn how to keep a house according to a budget, to care for children and cook. says i will like the teacher. she really knows her stuff.

i tell him i already have a teacher for that. my mother. i've been cooking since the age of thirteen and i know how to do it. my mom also knows her stuff.

i can clean a house. a course on how to do things i do everyday is a waste of my time.

i will take world issues and study politics instead. that will be
more worthwhile.

he shrugs. looks away. says it's up to me.

i walk out of his office, head high.

i have learned what it is like to be heard.
damn right it's up to me.

***

york u — years 2 & 3
al writes, all women are flaming cunts of glory.
defends it by referring to my story on breast cancer. i don't see
the connection.

later, he yells and screams and tells me I'm a feminist. he
doesn't like my writing and all immigrants are useless drains on
society. my grandfather shouldn't have died in a hospital if he
didn't pay taxes.

my stomach turns and class is dismissed. libby comes to give me
a hug but i don't know what to say. she will call me.

we decide to report al's comments as unacademic. inappropriate to the classroom. he is not happy. booming voice over me
asks,

why didn't you tell me you were offended? i am not racist.

for weeks libby and i lost security. parking lots loomed scary.
skulking shadows filled ttc subways. al's credit is in jeopardy.
this is what t.s. wants to talk about.

libby loses her office.
he gets an A.
i have learned who has power
and it is not me.

71

***

i listen to Faith Nolan sing and we cry. me and mic, helena and leianne. we talk about my friend who was hung by her lover. about my prof who says i'm not important.

i look down on the crowd in vari hall and i see a woman i have learned much from. i turn to my friends and say,

that's not true. I am important. We are important. see that woman? She taught me that.

pinkie swears of friendship and

We pledge to remind each other of Our importance.
We pledge to remind others of Our importance.
We pledge to teach Our daughters
and Our sons
of our importance.

I have learned.
I am not playing someone else's role anymore.

I am Shelly
and I am a feminist.

My Top 10 Feminist Influences
(thanks to those people from whom i have learned and continue to learn)

1. My mom (who teaches by example)
2. Janice Newton (who taught me how to "learn")
3. Public policy (which often pretends that women exist in singular and homogeneous realities ... if it acknowledges their existence at all)
4. The chilly climate (which is sometimes frozen ... thawing only long enough to magnify sex difference)
5. Rhea Tregebov (whose scribbled comments across my poetry opened a door in my mind that i have yet to close)
6. Libby S (who stood beside me in the fight)
7. Traditional ir discourse (for its unabashed male bias)
8. Trish Mcfarlane (who learned with me)
9. Margaret Atwood (who was one of the first authors i read who wrote about women and their lives and not about bra size)
10. Rigoberta Menchú (whose story should never have happened in the first place)

My Bio

SHELLY ABDOOL has never been good at writing bio statements for herself for fear that she will etch out a contrived identity that merely represents her productive role in society. That being said, she currently lives in Montreal where she works as a research assistant. After a four month contract in Gujarat, India — where she learned from rural women about the relationship between autonomy and health — her political science background has transmogrified to include the intersections between gender, migration, health and public policy. Her poetry is her refuge and is often inspired by events from her life, or those around her, in addition to the nightly news when she witnesses the paradox of society and the irony of our leaders.

YOUNG WOMEN AND DISABILITY

Alessia Di Virgilio

I remember the first time I knew that life was going to be a constant struggle. I was in Grade Eight and, like everyone else, was anxiously awaiting the coming of our overnight trip to Ottawa. As a physically challenged student, I knew that it was going to take a lot of planning to get there, but how could they say no? Guess what? They did. I couldn't believe it. I was told that it would be too difficult. One teacher told me that I was the first disabled student to want to go, so it was my job to lead the way for others by finding a way to get to Ottawa. She encouraged me to fight back. I phoned the tour company and told them my needs as far as accommodation and transportation go. They told me they would look into it then call me back. They didn't call me back. They called my principal instead. He hauled me into his office and lectured me on why I couldn't go. My teacher told me to give up. All I wanted to do was go on our class trip to Ottawa. It was the first time I had gone over someone's head and taken control of the situation. In the end, I didn't go. This experience made me realize my life would consist of people telling me I couldn't do things, and my endless fight for the respect I knew I deserved. I have never understood why people discriminate, especially against women. Why judge me because I am a woman? Why not see what I have to contribute to society?

Everyday I am bombarded with images and words that push women lower and lower under the hands of men, and it is not easy to resist what is accepted by most. I see women being judged on their appearance and not by their words. I see women portrayed as sex objects on so many billboards and in so many magazine ads. I hear comments being made by men and women that categorize others on the basis of their exterior. I try to look at the larger picture, though, at what the women of the future will have to endure if something is not done.

Ever since I was little people told me there was no such word as *can't*. I guess they wanted to motivate me. But when I looked around I saw that people were being told they couldn't do things and I didn't understand why. As I got older I grew more confused and angry. I began to notice the way men looked at women and didn't pay attention to what women said. I wanted to be heard.

If you call yourself a feminist, you are automatically a lesbian or a man-hater. I am neither. I'm just a woman trying to survive. I'm just a woman trying to be an equal. Being a feminist means different things to different people and each interpretation is not right or wrong. Feminism is that part of you that gets so furious every time you witness the subordination and degradation of women. It's that part of you that doesn't understand why difference is a bad thing. Most importantly, it's that part inside you that is willing to help and change.

My Definition of Feminism

Awareness and acknowledgement of women's struggles in past, present and future challenges and the on-going fight for equality.

My Top 10 Feminist Influences
(or almost)

1. My friends
2. *Body Image/Body Politics* by Donna Ciliska and Carla Rice
3. *A Vindication of the Rights of Women* by Mary Wollstonecraft
4. Oprah
5. Rosie O'Donnell
6. Whoopie Goldberg

My Bio

ALESSIA DI VIRGILIO is a first-year student at York University. She has not yet decided on a major but would like to work in human rights law (someday!). Alessia is a general membership director at Able York. In 1998 the Starlight Foundation sent her to New York City to meet one of her heroes, Rosie O'Donnell. When she graduated from high school, Alessia was given a Principal's Award for stellar participation in student government.

HIGH SCHOOL FEMINISM 101, OR "For Every Lie I Unlearn I Learn Something New"

Lara Karaian

I often sit among my fellow graduate Women's Studies students and wonder how it is that we arrived at this place, "Women's Studies." And apparently I'm not the only one who's baffled. This is best exemplified in Samantha Sacks' essay, "Why Am I A Feminist?" (earlier on in this section) where she describes how the "titillating tête-à-tête" she's engaged in is "squashed" when that question of questions, "What's your major?" comes up. When she answers "Women's Studies," she's asked to testify on her own behalf and braces herself for the next question, "Why are you a feminist?" This is the question that many of us self-proclaimed feminists must answer on a regular basis, and the answer is never straightforward nor the same from one individual to the next, even one moment to the next. A less frequently asked question, however, is *how* did we all become feminists? What was the process, the turning point, the epiphany or the "click," to borrow Gloria Steinem's expression, that defines when our consciousness connects to this non-dominant social and political movement? Or, since there is no one single definition of feminism, what was it that fostered an identification with a strand of feminism that reflects our own personal politics?

I have often found myself reflecting on the origins of my feminism as well as those of other young women. With this in mind

I undertook a research project to help me understand how five young women had come to their feminist identities. In my interviews I asked open-ended questions about who or what may have encouraged or discouraged their adoption of a feminist ideology, including school, family life, peers, relationships, religion and cultural productions. I wanted to identify what the young women perceived to be the most important influences in their decisions to become feminist and what barriers they faced. I was determined that the voices of these five young women be heard and I hoped that by doing so they would shed some light on my questions as well as destroy some misconceptions about young women's rejection of feminism and fear of identifying as feminists in today's society.

So, I approached a bunch of funky women at the release party of *Revolution Girl Style,* the issue of the feminist journal *Fireweed* that was created by, for and about young women. I anticipated that women attending such an event would identify as feminist, but I didn't come right out and ask them. All of them were really interested in the project and agreed to be a part of it.

Joanne, Marie, Catherine, Sara and Amia were seventeen, eighteen, nineteen, twenty and twenty-one years of age, respectively, at the time of the interviews.[1] Joanne, Marie and Catherine, identified as white and were attending high school; Sara and Amia identified as women of colour. Amia had recently graduated from high school, and Sara was in her second year of university. Catherine and Amia claimed no religion; Marie and Sara identified themselves as non-practising Catholics; and Joanne identified as non-practising with no reference to a particular religion. No specific questions were asked about their class position, however, the neighbourhoods and schools that many of the women lived in and attended suggested they came from middle- to high-class backgrounds. Specific questions about sexual orientation were never asked.

Before I started my interviews I thought that I had identified the driving forces for, and barriers against, my adoption of a feminist identity. I say "before" because during the course of the interviews I came to recognize the complexity of a process that I had wrongly assumed would be rather straightforward. I thought that I had identified my university undergraduate education as the major catalyst for my adoption of feminism. Many of my fellow classmates had also expressed to me how they felt that Women's Studies in their undergraduate career had changed their lives. At the time, I was adamant that nothing else could have played as important a role, certainly not my traditional Armenian family background or my friends who were as ignorant as I was about feminist thought. But even though I quickly became aware of the claim that "feminism is a movement, not a scientific theory,"[2] I had hopes of singularly explaining my feminism and so I heralded undergrad Women's Studies as *the* determining factor. That said, in light of the current absence of Women's Studies in high-school curriculum, I assumed that education would not be identified as a major influence in the construction of a feminist identity for these young women. Well, I was partly right, but for all the wrong reasons.

So, I want to share some of what I learned from these young women, and while I explored with them the many different influences and barriers to becoming feminists, I've chosen to highlight the role that their education played in their adoption of a feminist identity. What struck me was how big an influence the education system had in their decisions, but the reasons were completely opposite to what I expected. Some of the women identified the alternative woman-centred school they attended as fostering the adoption of a feminist identity. For others, the experiences of sexual harassment, racism and homophobia at the hands of the public school board and its staff acted as a major catalyst for their feminism. But even then it wasn't that simple.

Catherine, Marie and Joanne all attended a woman-centred school in Toronto. This particular school is designed and staffed by feminists who practise a feminist pedagogy. This differentiates it from a school with mainstream subject matter that is taught to a solely female student body. Of these three, Catherine and Marie had attended a public high school before transferring to the alternative school. Joanne had been there for her entire high-school career, except for some time spent at another alternative school where she completed courses through correspondence. Amia had attended numerous public high schools, and Sara had been at the same public secondary school until she graduated.

Louise Althusser's reproduction theory sees schools as socializing agencies that reproduce the norms, values and ideologies of the dominant culture by outfitting students with the skills for appropriate roles that perpetuate the social inequalities on which capitalism is built.[3] However, I soon realized that the women I interviewed, like many of the women in other studies of identity, were "actively engaged in counter-hegemonic moves both in accommodation of and resistance to school structures and sex stereotyped messages."[4] The school, I soon found out, is a dynamic lived experience and many of the experiences of women within it acted to complicate the reproduction of a dominant ideology.

According to Antonio Gramsci, hegemony is a condition that secures the consent of the exploited. It is a process that serves the ruling class and institutionalizes its values and goals.[5] This dominant value system and its integrative effects penetrate everyday practices — all aspects of the social order. Hegemony then is secured in religious groups, the law, education, the media, in everyday events. Moreover, the ideological positions are not static but have to be consciously accepted by people before they become part of the cultural practices of various groups and subgroups within society, even though the particular ideological position in question may go against their interests. Gramsci's position is that people have to be continually won and rewon to any ideological position. "The work of ideology however, is rendered invisible because it is so overdetermined or comes from so many different sources that it seems like commonsense. It seems natural."[6]

Young women today struggle with the dominant ideology of patriarchy and the non-dominant ideology of feminism — an ideological position that is in their interest but goes against many of the values and goals of the ruling ideology. The struggle to adopt a feminist ideology is in part conditioned by social place and power. As young female students, their power is minimal and their knowledge is partial. As a result, these young women often struggle with feminism and their acceptance of a feminist identity. Power, or a lack of it, is key to the acceptance of a feminist belief system. Without power, young women are frequently discriminated against in society and especially in the education system. It is this discrimination, however, that acts as a major catalyst for the acceptance of a feminist identity, according to the women I spoke to. This lack of power also rendered my interviewees susceptible to backlash and stereotyping, which often led to confusion, conflict and rejection of a feminist ideology. Similarly, the major source of their knowledge, the education system within which they are engrossed and which makes up most of their experiences at this point in their lives, plays a contradictory role.

Mostafa Rejai identifies a number of functions of ideology that are important to acknowledge when researching why young women adopt or fail to adopt a non-dominant, feminist ideology. First, he claims, "Ideologies propose to 'explain' political reality to us, give meaning to the ambiguities of the world around us, and give order to our lives."[7] For young women with little power, who attempt to embrace feminism as an ideology, disorder is what they can often expect. The doctrine of feminism is fragmented and distorted by the dominant culture's institutions so that, for these women, order is not often the first thing they experience when they are introduced to feminism. Similarly, what has often been portrayed as disunity and tensions within the movement add to an appearance of an inconsistent feminist ideology and may add to young women's experiences of confusion.

High School Experiences: Tales From The Dark Side

Discussions of these women's experiences in public schools were filled with stories and accounts of discrimination. Joanne, the only woman who felt she had not been discriminated against, had attended a feminist woman-centred school since Grade Nine. Nevertheless she recognizes that her rather sheltered existence may be one reason she does *not* identify as a feminist to a greater extent. The women who had previously gone to public schools had this to say about their experiences there:

MARIE: They [the teachers] were unbelievably sexist, it was just disgusting. I think that that school should be shut down and all the teachers should be fired. My homeroom teacher, who was also my math teacher, had a women's symbol and a man's symbol for the bathroom hall pass and he'd say that the women's hall pass, the symbol on it, was like that because women are so vain and that's a mirror so women could look at themselves! And I totally believed that. And he would say how women shouldn't be able to drive. If you were in his class and you answered the question wrong he'd say, "Oh and she's not even a blond!" Or if you were a blond he would say, "Well could we expect anything less?" And the boys would applaud; they loved him so much and they looked up to him, and he was so disgusting. Eight girls went to the principal, who was a woman, [to complain]. She said that he was just joking around, and that was really upsetting.

CATHERINE: I'd been the first chair [in the school band] and I was undoubtedly the best and the most reliable [player], but [one year] I was not put in it. Instead one of the boys was put in it. My teacher who worked with the music teacher said to me, "You know it's nothing personal. He never puts a girl in first chair." I was really mad. I felt completely powerless. I didn't really know what to do and I ended up not doing anything because what could I do, you know?

SARA: I think probably my first form of activism was Grade Nine, it was right from the get go. We had a gym teacher who kept making really inappropriate comments. She was doing role call and this one Asian student was just stretching her hands, she was yawning and the teacher was like, "Oh she must be doing her Tai Chi." And we were like [makes a shocked expression] what did she just say? So we put that aside and said okay, she's nervous. We figure we might as well give her a chance ... And then she was telling us about the importance of gym class and about the importance of wearing a good brassiere yada yada yada, [and says], "You don't want to be like those African women in [a glossy travel magazine] who can throw them over their shoulders ..." Then this poor girl, she didn't want to do stretches, she was having cramps and so she just sat there, you know, stretching with her legs closed. So when we were doing open leg stretches the teacher said, "Well, how come you're not doing stretches? Aren't you open for business?"

Marjorie Ingall, a contributer to *Click! Becoming Feminists,* an anthology of women's writing reflecting on how they became feminists, talks about discrimination by her high-school teacher who told her that she was a two-cylinder engine while a male classmate of hers was a six-cylinder one. He went on to say that she could never be a six-cylinder engine but that she could be the best damn two-cylinder one that she could be. She left and wretched in the girls' bathroom. She says, "I changed; I stopped buying in. It was quite liberating, in a way. Hey, I'd tried to challenge the bubble-world of high school injustice, and it was bigger than I was, and that freed me."[8]

Ironically, it is the inequality experienced by the women who attended regular public schools that reproduced relations of exploitation that "freed" or forced women to react in a retaliatory manner to sexism and exclusion of women by internalizing a counter-hegemonic ideology. "Making sexism real" was identified as a major influence in the adoption of a feminist identity. Catherine claims, "I think I did think about [discrimination] and it probably did have some sort of influence, just because it made sexism really real for me and, you know, once it's real you kind of think well, you know maybe feminism is a good thing (laughing)."

When I asked Marie what she thought it would take for her sister to become a feminist she said, "I think that she would have to be in a situation where she'd be discriminated against because of her sex and be made very aware of that. And that might be a starting point." Similarly, discrimination did not have to be experienced personally for it to have had an effect on the women. Marie claimed, "I think I've experienced a lot of discrimination maybe through other people's experiences. You know, it still touched my life. One of my friends, she's gay, and she's been beat up in gay bashings ... [and] that really saddened me, you know?"

These negative high-school experiences are echoed by Christine Doza in *Listen Up:*

High school is the single most dangerous place for a girl to be … Male teachers treat girls like property, like victims, like last-class citizens and no one seems to care … Nowhere is competition between girls more intense than in high school … After twelve years of learning that we don't matter, what else can you fucking expect? The "education system" has taught us little else but to hate ourselves.[9]

Sara concurs: "I mean high school, I hated it, I mean really, really hated it. I could not wait to get out. I felt more oppressed because I didn't meet the lowered expectations these people had set out for me because I was a woman."

School, then, can "be a sight for autonomous identity structures where social actors do more than simply mirror and accommodate themselves to dominant structures."[10] Claire Renzetti, in her study of attitudes towards feminism in college women, found that "specifically, respondents who have personally experienced sex discrimination possess a higher level of awareness of gender inequality and show a stronger support for the women's movement than respondents who have not personally experienced sex discrimination."[11] She also found that as students progressed through college, their support of feminism and the feminist movement increased, in part by the liberalizing attitudes one can be exposed to in college and in part because of the experience of discrimination in their college career. Noella Taylor makes the excellent point that while those who were discriminated against were more likely to consider themselves feminists, "it is also possible that women who identified themselves as feminists are more attuned to sexual discrimination and more aware of gender inequalities than those who do not identify themselves as feminists. Hence their being feminist may have given them the awareness and language to identify their experiences as discrimination."[12]

For two of the three who attended the alternative high school, it was their attendance there that was instrumental in their adoption of a feminist ideology, but for completely different reasons than those mentioned above. Marie said, "I think that my school has just made me a lot more aware of political issues on the whole. Once I got there I realized ways that my gender had kind of belittled me in my public school." Catherine pointed out, "Once I got to my school and I kind of realized [about gender inequality in language] I read more books and realized the power of language. I realized language is very powerful and so I thought that whole thing out. Oh, and one of things I really loved about this school was finally loving the fact that I was a woman."

While school is the major lived experience of the young women I interviewed, the alternative woman-centred school experience espouses a non-dominant ideology and fosters non-consent to the status quo. Taylor points out that "feminist education often allows women to recognize alternative choices and consequently to move a step closer to true liberation."[13] This ideology is compounded and strengthened by the inclusion of women in the curriculum, as Catherine explains:

> I think that what you need to do is really change around what people are studying so that women are seen as much in the text books, for example, as men … and when you're studying things like the eighteenth century you also learn about the problems that women faced like, poverty and prostitution, and you learn about what women were using for birth control and you learn about what the Pope was saying about population control — all of which at this point in time I don't think most people learn about in the average high school.

One of the most important influences for the adoption of a feminist ideology was the feeling by women that feminism was not being forced upon them by the school. Interestingly, the reasons for attending the school had little if anything to do with its feminist ideology. Catherine picked it because "it's a small school, has really good teaching, and small classes." Marie shares the sentiment, "I went there because it had small classes and I had just come from a huge, like really big, junior high school and I really, really hated it. I applied to … all the girls schools I could think of because I just wanted to get away from the boys cause they were taunting me so much." When I asked her if her parents had picked it specifically because it was woman-centred she repeated, "No, just because it was small."

Aside from the physical atmosphere, both Catherine and Marie talked at length about their school's faculty and its pedagogical structure that appeared to advocate the notion of educating rather than simply schooling its pupils. Instead of demanding unquestioned acceptance and memorization of knowledge, the staff encouraged critical thinking and decision making. However, Joanne thought that, to a certain extent, the alternative school had contributed to her becoming "less" of a feminist:

> Well it's a feminist school and we've been doing so much reading of women's literature and women's roles in all sorts of historical events that in a lot of ways I've been a little bit turned off feminism. I haven't been doing anything [outside of school]. I go there and that's my feminist experience for the day, and that's it. (laugh) Now I'm sort of thinking that because I've grown up with [feminist ideas] and they're so involved with my education that I find them old hat, kind of. It's like I [already] know about this.

Ironically, when I asked Joanne what she thought was a barrier to women identifying as feminist she responded, "Well, I think it's what I said about having a lot of privilege, in that a lot of young women don't suffer from too much discrimination on the basis of their gender [if they have privilege]. But also I think in some public school systems there really isn't access to those ideas."

Therefore, when the ideology is not that of the dominant class it does not necessarily mean that a non-dominant feminist ideology will be adopted, much like the dominant ideology espoused in public schools is not mirrored by many young women that attend them. Rather, the relationship or process must be seen as multifaceted and complex. The adoption of a feminist ideology is just as much about learning as it is unlearning, and one's education is very much intertwined with this.

Regardless of my emphasis here on the role that education plays in the adoption of a feminist identity, the reality is that, for many, coming to feminism is a complex journey. What I found out from these women was that the unravelling of all our influences after the fact is a difficult thing to do. In a recent review of *Click!,* the reviewer rightfully observes that after reading the collection one recognizes that it is the "little day-to-day events that turn us into feminists."[14]

I wanted to better understand how I came to think the way I do and during the course of talking with these five women I did gain many insights. Often this introspection proved embarrassing and even painful and other times it was quite touching. Yes, I remember the male high school English teacher who told me I had penis envy because I played rugby. I also remembered getting my shoes shined one day and suddenly wondering what I was doing in a high chair while someone scrubbed my boots for pennies just so that I could see my own reflection. I remembered the ubiquitous and gratuitous movie rape scenes that would move me to tears and infuriate me time and time again. I particularly remember the time I witnessed a man hobble up the theatre aisle, barely able to hide his erection. But, I also remember the independence and strength of my mother, who left her family and her country at age nineteen to come to Canada to continue her nursing career. I remember the many words of praise and encouragement from my dad, who always supported me in whatever fight for social justice I was involved with. It looks as if I'm bound to keep learning and unlearning and that's just fine with me because as I grow so does my feminism and, hey, all I have to fear now is my high-school reunion!

Notes

The quotation in the title is from ani difranco, "My IQ" from the album *Puddle Dive*. Righteous Babe Music, 1998.

1. The names are pseudonyms chosen by the participants or me, if requested. The interviews took place in Toronto between December 1997 and January 1998.

2. Nancy Mandell, ed., *Feminist Issues: Race, Class and Sexuality*, 2nd ed. (Scarborough: Prentice Hall Allyn and Bacon Canada, 1998), 199.

3. Louise Althusser cited in Amira Proweller, *Constructing Female Identities: Meaning Making in an Upper Middle Class Youth Culture* (New York: State University of New York Press, 1998), 4.

4. Ibid., 8.

5. Livy A. Visano, *Crime and Culture: Refining the Traditions* (Toronto: Canadian Scholars' Press Inc., 1998), 170.

6. Michael Barrett, "Ideology, Politics, Hegemony: From Gramsci to Laclau and Mouffe," in Slavoj Zizek, ed., *Mapping Ideology* (London: Verso, 1994).

7. Mostafa Rejai, *Political Ideologies: A Comparative Approach,* 2nd ed. (New York: M.E. Sharpe, Inc., 1995), 17.

8. Marjorie Ingall, "Why Mr. Levesque Sucked," in Lynn Crosbie, ed., *Click! Becoming Feminists* (Toronto: Macfarlane Walter and Ross, 1997), 82.

9. Christina Doza, " Bloodlove," in "Generation F–Excerpts from Listen Up," *Ms.* (1995), 38.

10. Proweller, *Constructing Female Identities,* 6.

11. Claire M. Renzetti, "New Wave or Second Stage: Attitudes of College Women Towards Feminism," *Sex Roles* 16, nos. 5/6 (1987), 271–272.

12. Noella J. Taylor, "I'm Not a Feminist, But ...: Young Women's Attitudes Towards the Concept of Feminism" (master's thesis, University of Toronto, 1993), 119–120.

13. Ibid., 139.

14. Kerri Huffman, "Using the F-word," *The Varsity* (University of Toronto), n.d., 17.

My Top 10 Feminist Influences
(in semi-chronological order — more biographical
than bibliographical)

1. Emily Murphy. My sixth grade introduction to first-wave Canadian feminism. I was young enough to start thinking about what it meant to be a woman, not so old to be able to be critical of what type of woman.
2. Judy Blume. Wow, teen angst, what a life altering thing.
3. Madonna and Cindy Lauper. I wanted to have fun too.
4. My high school English teacher who told me I had penis envy for playing rugby. Once I figured out what that was (though I had a pretty good idea), I got mad.
5. My high school rugby coach for starting the women's rugby team, being a kick-ass coach and for chewing out the English teacher who told me I had penis envy.
6. *Sassy Magazine.* Because even though it put out some pretty screwed up mixed messages (conform/love yourself the way you are), it was my only source of alternative thought, at the time.
7. My undergrad profs who opened up a whole new sphere of thought for me and encouraged me to become a critical thinker.
8. My girlfriends, especially the grad school gals.
9. My mom and dad — Mom, for being my first example of an independent and intelligent woman. Dad, for being my biggest fan.
10. Chris Kinkaid, my partner and best friend. My true example of how men can be feminists and someone with whom I have grown as a person.

My Bio
See Editors' Bios

Part II

WHAT'S BIG
AND HAIRY:
Expanding
Identity

— Allison Jack *Can you see yr self: zine* allithena@hotmail.com

Ms. Fit

stylish fake dreads
(also disappear when
she makes the squad/meets the boy)

sarcastic remarks

lipstick

tight shirt
(just like everyone else's
but in camoflauge)

keys to fancy, yet quirky, car

GIRLS ROCK!

RAY GUN

semi-obscure rock magazine

wallet chain
(she's tough!)

baggy pants
(change into a skirt
after she's been "accepted")

shiny combat boots

— Jennifer Whiteford Matilda Zine matilda@bust.com

LIPSTICK

Leah Rumack

It was an ani difranco concert that made me. ani had just finished her abortion/fuck you/ my heart is broken (again) show on a sweltering night in 1996. It was drippingly hot, and I was crouching at my friend's foot trying to hide the fact that I was slyly putting on a fresh coat of lipstick as she chatted with one of those alarming creatures — her "Women's Studies colleague." I was hiding because I couldn't, after all, be seen as hopelessly co-opted at an ani concert of all places for goddess-sakes. It was the era of Naomi Wolf's *The Beauty Myth* and hairy armpits as a political ethos. I was definitely the odd tart out. But as fate would have it, at that very moment, my friend's colleague (who turned out to be one of the editors of this book) was pumping her for young women who could write for the collection of young women's thoughts she was putting together. My friend generously offered my services. "Oh, I wouldn't know what to write. I don't do that kind of stuff," I protested meekly, imagining pages full of dense deconstructed gender theory. But then it struck me like a bolt of sparkle eyeshadow. I could write about the thing most dear to my heart and in my hand at that very moment ... lipstick. I could get those mean, self-righteous womyn who quietly discounted me (some in my very own "vegetarian, feminist" co-op home) because of my hair removal obsession and makeup adoration.

And so "To Coif or Not To Coif" was born.

To Coif or Not To Coif

I'm a feminist. I'm a feminist and I have some painful confessions to make. I wear makeup. I also remove my body hair. I am a very bad feminist.

Or am I?

I have been plagued by this question ever since I met my first organic lesbian. It has grown to epidemic proportions now that I am the only socially conscious woman I know who has an eyelash comb. I live in a household full of furry feminists. I swear I slink to the bathroom shamefacedly with razor in hand. I cowered at the ani difranco concert when I wanted to put on lipstick (my lips were dry, okay?!). It may sound trite, but I am beginning to feel oppressed.

I think this is an issue the feminist community needs to address. Really. I have been thrown dirty looks at Rape Crisis meetings and had eyebrows raised when I said I wished I'd taken Women's Studies instead of, um, humanities. I think there is a growing silent bias in leftist circles against women who, as the rhetoric goes, attempt to conform to male standards of beauty. These women obviously aren't liberated/intelligent/pimple-free. (If she dresses like that she deserves to be oppressed! Pass me my tofu.)

I guess the first battle cry I can make is one in defence of choice. The women's movement is meant to, as I understand it (but I do have eye shadow dust seeping into my brain), widen the scope of women's lives so that they are free to define their lives for themselves. In this respect, I don't see how any standard of beauty that is defined by others is acceptable.

Choice, however, is a dangerous word. Can a woman really have choice when totally immersed in a patriarchal culture that defines, among other things, the parameter of the question? If I choose to wear makeup and submit my body to Hair Management 101 does that mean I'm choosing or does that just mean I'm choosing to give in? If you can't beat 'em, manicure!

 There is another school of thought that supports anything women do to make themselves feel good about themselves. Okay, so I slap on a bit of mascara and feel just that much more ready to face the cruel world, that much stronger, that much more smear-free. I do ask myself why it makes me feel better, but if I don't do it, I feel like — like textured veggie protein bits. So when I wake up in the morning and look in the mirror and say "Oh, you again," what do I do then? Just keep mantraing Naomi Wolf's *The Beauty Myth* under my breath as I slink through my day?

The answer to this is a resounding "I dunno." I am not looking forward to an illustrious career as a feminist scholar. Naomi Wolf and I will never be close. However, since much of feminism questions the white middle-class ivory tower and accords value to women's own experiences, there are a few things I do know. I know what I hate, so for all those aficionados of hairiness et cetera, who may question my commitment to the women's movement, I have compiled "My List of Things I Hate That Make Me a Good Feminist":

My Definition of Feminism

Understanding that the way the world is structured socially and economically has historically served to keep women and girls as second-class citizens.

White Guys who say things like "they discriminate against us now you know" (wank wank whine whine) family gatherings where women always do the dishes while the men discuss Important Things in the next room that when my father does housework he's "helping out" but he's probably planned four meals in twenty years (average = omelette, year one; roasted potatoes, year two; omelette, year three; omelette, year four. Aren't I great? Aren't I great?) that the fucking (can I say that?) the fucking religious right are still under the impression that their schizophrenic, insecure God the Father the Son the Holy Ghost is Everyone's God and that therefore they can bomb abortion clinics and kill doctors in the name of saving lives and still think that denying women choice is fun when really all they need is a good social club (scones anyone?) that when the cooks at the restaurant I worked at told me I had a nice pussy I complained to the manager who said that he didn't like me anyway (bitch) that Disney heroines have waists the size of their necks that since women can vote we must be equal and since oppression and sexism are now more subtle but most people are too blind/stupid/self-satisfied to look. When men want to march in Take Back the Night (We will support you! We will support you! We say so!) that because Christy Hefner is president of Playboy we're obviously emancipated now because the fucking (can I say that?) the fucking computer guys at the local computer shop are so mean and treat women who aren't hackers like that little girl in *Jurrasic Park* like they're stupid because my ex-boyfriend thought he was a feminist but had two emotions (lust and panic) because Barbie is still suffering under the weight of severe physiotherapy bills ...

For many many other reasons I am a feminist and I am going to click my platform heels and smack my glossed lips and grind my manicured nails all over the face of patriarchal institutions/ideas/people until they are a quivering mass at my well-dressed foot promising to make me an omelette.

***

By the time this book is published, that brief rant will be almost six years old, a lifetime in terms of political environments. And I think the discussion about beauty and politics has changed since then. It feels like battles over how your politics are reflected or created in your personal presentation are not as much of an issue as they once were, at least when you're talking strictly about "feminism." (The anarcho-vegans whose politics lie in their commitment to sunflower seeds and hemp clothes are another discussion altogether.) Some of my dearest, most ardent non-shavers no longer see hairy legs or unlacquered nails as a measure of your commitment to the cause and have even ventured the occasional romp with a Ladyshave themselves. Maybe we have bigger things to worry about or, alternatively, maybe we've started to own the discussion.

Third-wave feminist magazines like *BUST* have "reclaimed" wanting to look hot or feel sexy as an important moment of personal confidence. And I would hazard a guess that with the growing cross-breeding of feminist thought into a wider arena of gender studies, with all its trannies and drag queens, the new message seems to be that its okay to be fabulous, as long as you're ironic about it (at least a little), and that beauty is okay as long as there's a wider, more active definition of what it is. Which brings me to the cutest grrrl in the world. Grrrl. Once the ultimate as-bitchy-as-I-wanna-be word, it began with the Riot Grrrls of the punk movement and spread into the zine-land of chick writing in the early 1990s. But the rising use and the now-sanitized popular associations with the word tell me that beauty is still very much a feminist issue. Let me illustrate.

In the winter of 1999, activists from all over the world converged on Seattle for the third ministerial of the World Trade Organization. As a writer for a local paper, I was one of a handful from Toronto who got to go and witness the mass protests. When I returned, I got a call from the editor of *This Magazine,* a long-running lefty rag. She had this amusing tidbit for me: *Glamour Magazine,* a glossy American fashion publication, had called a Toronto activist group to see if they knew a young anarchist woman who had been in Seattle whom they could profile. Now, the thought of any self-respecting anarko chick giving the time of day to *Glamour* was funny enough in itself. (We ended up writing a spoof of *Glamour's* dream activist girl, complete with her own line of clothing stores like Prole Panache and Urban Sloganeering.) But what was disturbing is that we knew immediately exactly who they wanted. They wanted a grrrl. The year 2000 version. With a snarl on her lips, some chunky boots on her toned legs and a sassy thrust of her slender hips, this random hot-but-smart twenty-one-year-old could grace their pages. You could almost hear the editorial meeting: Maybe her hair is blue. No! Better— Pink! (Pink photographs well.) She's political, but not too political. She's alternative, but fashionable. You know the kind.

From the Spice Girls to the latest in change purses at Le Château that proclaim "Girls Rule, Boys Drool," it's now cool to be a grrrl. Fashionable. Sassy. Very millennium. But what is really going on is that it's cool to be a grrrl, as long as you're cute. If you're pushy, loud, sexually aggressive, political or angry, fat or plain or hairy or old, then you're so not a grrrl. You're just ugly. Feminists are ugly. Grrrls are hot. The if-you-want-to-be-a-grrrl-you-better-be-pretty aesthetic was brought home to me by the *Glamour* episode and by observing my reactions to two political women I knew. It felt weird that my reaction to the thin pretty one was: She's blond and thin. She's such a grrrl. My reaction to the less fashionable chubby woman was: Gee, she's not very good looking, is she? My affiliation to grrrl was also affected by a fluctuation in my weight. For a couple of years I was suddenly transformed from someone who was always relatively small into someone who was carting an extra 25 pounds, and it completely changed my life. The way I was treated, not only by potential sexual partners (though that was absolutely immediately obvious) but just in general was turned on its head. I've never forgotten it. It didn't dawn on me what had changed until I was thinner again.

But I know that somehow, subconsciously I guess, I didn't feel like I had the right to call myself a grrrl until I could fit into those baby tee's with the women's bathroom signs with horns on them again. I didn't feel like a grrrl until I looked good in little pink kitty cat hats, which everyone knows look dumb on you unless you're either twelve years old or weigh 8 pounds. I didn't feel like I knew what that kind of grrrl meant until all the "political" men I dated literally didn't even notice I existed until I was 110 pounds again. I didn't feel like a grrrl again until it was obvious that I was a feminist by choice, not because I couldn't get laid or whatever other unspoken but assumed slag the not-cute-club receive every day. It's entirely possible that this was all just my personal neurosis, but I don't think so.

This isn't to say that women who fall outside of a narrow range of physical definition don't still self-identify as grrrls or value the term in its original politicized state. But personally, I'm starting to value the reclamation of harsher terms like bitch, whore and slut as epithets of affection rather than grrrl. I mean, if the local fashion kitten thinks she's a grrrl just because her panties say "pussy power" on them, then forget it. I'd rather be a fucking bitch.

The pussy-power-panty phenomenon brings up another issue around the word grrrl and around what is being called "third-wave" feminism. The third wave, generally the territory of women twenty-five and under, has been characterized by an emphasis on pop culture, individualism and, above all, sex. Now, I have loved this kind of grrrlness. It was so much snappier and hip than being a run-of-the-mill Simone de Beauvoir feminist. Besides, we know all that *The Second Sex* stuff already, we thought. Let's get laid, tie up our girlfriends and go sex toy shopping. But the problem with the sexual empowerment of what I call "vibrator feminism" is this. While it's important for a young woman to feel entitled to a full, hot and self-directed sexuality, it also paradoxically makes it easier for the mainstream culture and media to eat her out, if you'll excuse the pun. That's because some dried-up shrew who just won't shut up about things like national childcare or rape or poverty is not very titillating or media-friendly, but everybody loves a grrrl who masturbates while laughing her ironic head off at *Buffy the Vampire Slayer*. And this sexualization of grrrlness is also connected to beauty. Women masturbating for other's eyes is a common fantasy. And you can bet that when people think of empowered chicks jerking off, they aren't going to want to imagine someone who isn't attractive.

In the middle of thinking about this essay, I opened my *Globe and Mail* to see a full-page article on a group of young women who have started a Web site devoted to straight women's sexuality. As someone who works in the media my first thought when seeing the piece (and the accompanying photograph of the four winsome Web mistresses) was "Great picture. Cute girls. Sex. Cute story. Damn. I should've written it myself." Even I have bought into the easy sell of grrrl. I got the right writing voice. I got the clothes. I got the vibrator. Let's sell my sisters for all they're worth (until they're too old and ugly to be cool anymore, or I'm too old and ugly to be cool anymore, whichever comes first).

My Top 10 Feminist Influences
(in no particular order)

1. My creepy millionaire Reform-voting uncle, who had me in tears at age eight when he told me women make half of what men make, and that it's gonna stay that way.
2. All the awesome groundbreaking women who have gone before me and have made it so I don't have to worry about so many things.
3. My best friend Steph who, even though on our first date went with me to a Catharine MacKinnon lecture, now gives me rings with the word "hussy" on them and books like *A Woman's Right to Pornography* as gifts.
4. Two years on the Rape Crisis Line.
5. *BUST* Magazine.
6. Realizing I hate women who are male-identified and whose energy is always directed towards the men in the room and in their lives and who ditch their girls for a second of male vibe.
7. Wanting to have a child one day but knowing there still (surprise) isn't any national childcare and worrying that the financial and time stresses of motherhood would ruin my career, but never imagining my male partner would have to make the same choice.
8. My intro Women's Studies class at York U.
9. The porn-making, S&M-working lesbians who live upstairs. (They really don't identify as lesbians anymore 'cuz really they're transgendered now but they were lesbians when I first met them, so there.)
10. Chantal Daigle's boyfriend who tried to stop her from getting an abortion in 1989.

My Bio

LEAH RUMACK is a freelance writer for the likes of *Toronto Life Magazine, The Globe and Mail, The Toronto Star, Now Magazine, Chatelaine* and *The National Post*. She is also a contributor to *Bust, Elm Street, This Magazine, Shift* and *Xtra*! In 1998, Leah won the *Rolling Stone Magazine's* North American-wide campus journalism award for her thesis project on feminist columnist Michele Landsberg.

ODE TO OUR CLOSETED SHEROES

or To Be Young, Out, Black and Bitter

*T.J. Bryan
aka Tenacious*

One
freelance
corporate ho
drops off time sheet.
A week's work
for multi-national
corporate pimp
with offices in
Canada, the US, the UK
and South Afrikkka.
A week's pay
for a week's worth of
fried hair
curled to perfection
demure wool slacks,
skirts
and long-sleeved tops.
No sign of flesh.
Meant to disguise

the inky permanence
of her
family connection.
Sensible shoes
don't please
or tease.
Good for walking
and playing
steppin' fetch'it
to yet another
flaccid, white
male prick.
This one ain't
so bad.
First in a string
of many
who don't
treat her like
she just got a total

lobotomy.
Over-educated
but under-utilized
freelance corporate ho
for hire
fears becoming
a has been
before she gets
to just
BE.
She hears
her words –
powerFULL,
hybrid
chit chat,
music –
begin to ring hollow
in her ears
with two years
of memos,
may I help you's,
email
and acronyms
for every
capitalist abomination
under the sun.
Freelance corporate ho
remembers times when
places when
she was
a fine, young,
arrogant,
spit in your face
and dare you
to do something
about it
out, Black dyke.

Freelance corporate ho
puts food on her table
instead of manuscripts.
Pays the rent
instead of waiting
on pins and needles
for acceptance letters
from hamstrung councils
riding high
on the Green Peace
list of
endangered species.
Corporate ho
came out naive,
optimistic.
Dancing to the
tune of that old
familiar song –
the promise of
something betta.
The advent of a
phoenix femalia.
Corporate ho
feels bitter, hardened.
Wonders why she
came out at all.
Came out to loose
herself.
To find herself
answering to this
hypocritical crone tribunal
or that.
Expected to kow tow
to yet another
formerly closeted,
still closeted,
in public gotta

BE
closeted
visiting
fat cat
sheroe.
Herstorically large,
rich, famous and feminist.
Still selling the published
promise
unfulfilled.
An anthologized
collection of
socio-historical
stupidities
to be consumed
by the unsuspecting
and genuflecting.
Corporate ho's
pickled in her own bile.
Sees the dream
unrealized.
Wishes the old girl bibles
had never been written
or read.
Maybe SHE
should'a stayed in
'til she got too large
to hide.
Maybe SHE should'a
got tenure
or the much-longed-for
first book
before she thumbed
HER nose at
all things het.
BUT,
there will be no more

tears shed
over spilt milk or blood.
No more tears wasted
over coming out stupid.

Coming outta the feminist
fold
out into
the cold
a whole world
unfolds.
One bold
Corporate ho
comes into
her own.

Here,
one corporate ho
comes into
her own.

My Definition of Feminism

I no longer define as feminist. Felt too much like being stuck in a very small room with people who would like to see some parts of who I am wiped off the face of the planet. True feminism for me was always a utopian ideal that I held dear. It was about transformation, the challenge to learn more and stretch farther. It was also about wimmin coming together unafraid of each other or themselves. Looks good on paper, don't it?

My Top 10 Feminist Influences

(some of whom may not/do not even define as feminist, some ain't even wimmin, some may not even appreciate the significance of being [theoretically] brought together in me, but are all powerful, shit-disturbing folks who embody what feminism has been about for me)

1. Audre Lorde
2. Sappire
3. Rozena Maart, South African Poet/Activist/Professor, author of *Talk About It!*
4. Marlene Nourbese Philip
5. Lilith Finkler (see her courageous poem in *Fireweed's* Jewish Women's Issue)
6. My grandmother
7. Pat Califia
8. bell hooks
9. Rupaul (a femme(inist) can never have enough lipstick)
10. Lisa Jones, author of *Bullet Proof Diva: Tales of Race, Sex, and Hair*

My Bio

T.J. Bryan aka Tenacious is a black conscious, first generation immigrant West Indian, queer, femme, polyamourous slut on sabbatical, writer/artist. She has been published in eight different black/wimmin's/queer/lesbian/erotic anthologies and in magazines including but not limited to *On Our Backs, Mix, This Magazine, Fuse Magazine, Matriart, Fireweed* and *Canadian Woman Studies.*

I'D THINK OF A CLEVER TITLE IF THE BABY HADN'T JUST POOPED ON ME

Sophie Tamas

I burrowed into Women's Studies from an adjacent tunnel four years ago, when I began graduate studies at Carleton University. I was somewhat clever then; what I lacked in skill I made up for with verbosity. I read convoluted theorists as easily as one might read a cereal box. I felt informed. I could deconstruct. I knew who said what that anyone cared about, who thought what and, more to the point, I knew what I thought. Opinions beamed out of me like sunshine. I was Feminist.

But that was then. Now, while my toddler sleeps (no two hours of the day are shorter than those at naptime), I am not sharp, I am not beaming, I am not even remotely clever. Looking through my sheaf of old feminist articles and assignments, I see words read by another, written by another. Those voices no longer speak to me. And something about this compels me to write, although writing itself has grown difficult and requires a forgotten language.

I am twenty-seven years old and religious. I have been married for eight years. I am a stay-at-home mother. At school, we read and discussed black women, native women, lesbian women, disabled women, socialist women, working-class women, prostitutes, privileged women, academic women, third-world women, single-parent women, fat women, starving women, old women and, even occasionally, men. Married, religious, full-time-mothering women were most likely to appear in the discourse as victims, representing our ongoing and multi-layered oppressions, or as the anti-feminist emblems of false consciousness.

Unlike Adrienne Rich, I am not enraged by the limitations that motherhood imposes on my personal liberty. (At times, surely, frustrated. But rage? No.) Joanne Kates, writing on the heterosexual feminist experience, has said that being "constantly furious, out loud, for hours" is the only way for her to be a "woman of honour" and that "anger is a constant companion in a feminist bed."[1] Yet I have no desire for war with my husband and take pains to avoid it. So am I a woman of honour?

The fact is, I work hard to promote equality. I run workshops, give talks and perform in my faith community. I write plays and more-or-less academic essays on equality issues. I raise a confident, competent daughter. I volunteer with a group of women who provide essential social services in our area and almost all of us are married and have kids. Many are church-goers. None (to my knowledge) read feminist theory. I do more now for feminism than I ever have; but is there a voice for me and others like me in the feminist discourse?

The women's movement I studied in school sought to be open, to recognize and celebrate difference, or at least it tried to. The result-

> ## My Definition of Feminism
>
> Belief and action in the promotion of gender equality and the elimination of gender-based prejudices.

ing emphasis on pluralism has spawned a brave foray into iden-tity politics, with much heated discussion of "women's experi-ence" and who can speak for whom. It is a crucial and troubling debate; but will basing one's identity on how one differs from others inevitably draw attention away from points of unity and amplify our differences? I do not want a separate shelf in the feminist bookstore devoted to my distinct experience as only I can describe it.

But I do want to feel that my work is recognized as legiti-mately feminist. The assumption that I have been unwittingly co-opted by masculinist structures because I am happily married and devoted to an organized religion insults my intel-ligence. The idea of false consciousness must be handled with extreme caution; mistakenly applied, it becomes blinders, becomes arrogance and deprives the women's movement of the insights and activism of the women thereby "othered."

If it is to continue to create social change, the women's movement must inspire and catalyze the activism of a broad range of Canadian women. In order to do so, old prejudices may need to be reconsidered. Religion may not be so ubiqui-tously patriarchal after all; we do not live on a monoreligious planet, and all "organized religions" are not the same. There are few motivating forces more powerful than belief in a Divine decree; Baha'is and others whose faiths place an emphasis on the establishment of gender equality may constructively collaborate with the women's movement if not put off by suspicion and skepticism. While many Marxists, socialists or materialists may maintain that religious belief is inherently oppressive, not all feminists are socialist. It would be refreshing if this were reflected by feminist literature, if equality could be primarily about principle rather than politics.

The literature of the women's movement must also develop a more nuanced treatment of motherhood. I do not fret all day in a housedress, flirt with delivery boys, make jellied salads or fix myself up at five so I'm pretty for my man. I am not full of repressed desire and thwarted ambition. I do not perceive the rationing of my artistic and intellectual pursuits during my childrearing years as a grave injustice or the waste of a mind, nor do I think I would be more liberated if I paid someone else to raise my child. I know many young feminist women who have made similar choices; after so many years of fighting for the right to work in the formal economy, do we now have to fight for the right not to? The women's movement can ill afford to lose the resources and support of this demographic group.

I have not had my fill of academia. In time, I hope to pursue doctoral studies and make my own efforts to grapple with the issues I've mentioned. My mind is still in there, somewhere; it speaks to me sometimes, at the edge of sleep. There will be other chances to be clever, but for now I believe this is the greater work. The women's movement seems to consist of simultaneous processes of action and reflection; I intend to continue to contribute to both. And in the meantime, I'll be saying my prayers and making playdough. Just please don't write me off.

Notes

1. Joanne Kates, "Once More With Feeling," in Maureen Fitzgerald et al., eds., *Still Ain't Satisfied: Canadian Feminism Today* (Toronto: The Women's Press, 1982), 81.

My Top 10 Feminist Influences

1. The Baha'i Faith. Its presentation of gender equality as an essential component of a broadly based social and spiritual transformation of humankind, practical guidance on how to promote this transformation and incredible history of feminist activism is my number one inspiration.

2. Pregnancy and childbirth. It may sound corny, but these processes completely changed my relationship to my body and my sense of self.

3. Motherhood. Ditto above. Through it I have learned about female community, about partnership and the mysterious relationship between self-sacrifice and self-love.

4. My parents. Their implementation of gender equality is by no means perfect, but all my life my dad and mom have both really busted their butts to be egalitarian.

5. Living overseas and in remote parts of Canada. The world is a big and diverse place; it's easier to believe this when you've lived it.

6. My mother's bathroom scale and its tyranny in her house. I intend never to own one.

7. Carleton University's Canadian Studies/Women's Studies MA course. All those authors, all that anger, so much defining the problem, and so little suggesting solutions.

8. Jane Siberry and k.d. lang's "Calling All Angels." Soothing when you've got that powerless feeling.

9. Marion Woodman's *Addiction to Perfection*. A little deep-woods Jungian in places but darn interesting.

10. My husband. Theory is nothing without practice. There are good men out there.

My Bio

SOPHIE TAMAS is a mother of two daughters. She has lived all over Canada, mostly in the North, and presently resides in small-town Ontario. Currently, she volunteers in her community, keeps house, raises kids and does an incredible amount of laundry. In her previous life, she earned an MA in Canadian Studies/Women's Studies at Carleton University (1998), a Bachelor of Independent Studies at University of Waterloo (1993), and was an award-winning playwright. Her hopes for the future include more writing and an uninterrupted night's sleep.

A QUESTION FOR FEMINISM

Cat Pyne

So the question is ... is feminism dynamic enough to respond to the tranny movement? Lesbians have established a place for themselves inside feminism but trans identities are separate. Queer by gender but not necessarily by orientation, our identities do not centre around the gender of those we love or how we relate to them. We create identity in how we relate to ourselves.

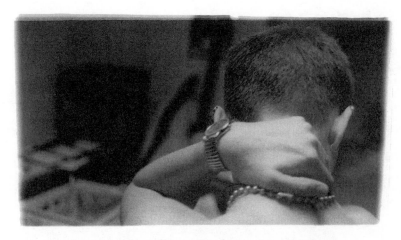

Transgendered: *Anyone who breaks the rules of gender.*

Gender: *A mucky malleable substance found between the ears (as distinct from "sex," which is found between the legs).*

Real: *What your gender is until the moment you realize you've been performing it ... then it becomes drag.* *

*Credit to Rikki Ann Wilchins for this one.

Can feminism see more than two genders? Can I? If I already know that there are boys with cunts and chicks with dicks ... and people with both ... If I already know that man and woman are impossible to define ... then how can I draw strength in a movement that relies on the existence of, and difference between, boys and girls?

In trying to live as genderless as possible, I've asked people in my life to use the only non-gendered pronoun available ... the plural "they" or "them." Some people say this makes them "gramatically uncomfortable." Some people don't admit to what actually makes them uncomfortable.

Does "not woman" mean "man"?

Am I still a feminist if I'm no longer a woman?

What does it mean for patriarchy if I can bind my breasts and stuff my pants and have instant access to male privilege? Am I the only one who finds this exciting?

Can I locate myself inside a binary?

Can I build my identity around something if I'm not sure it really exists?

In this society, daily interactions are played out against a backdrop of hierarchy. We meet someone, assess their status and treat them accordingly. In this environment, gender becomes a class system. When people aren't sure whether I'm a man or a woman, they don't know how to treat me. When they think I'm a woman they treat me worse. This is the point where trans liberation and feminism intersect ... and this is where they diverge. Trans people fight a binary, patriarchal system that is handed down and acted out by both men and women. Some feminists have reacted with hostility to the trans movement and put up "womyn-born-womyn-only" signs for their events. Some feminists have been as limited as they are liberated. And as Rikki Ann Wilchins says, some feminists want to know what's in your pants and how long it has been there.

Everyone's gender is subject to change in their lifetime ... just like everything else about them. This scares patriarchs and feminists alike.

I was born female and sometimes I call myself a boy, and wear boys' clothes, and use the boys' washroom. This needs no more explanation than someone who is born male. Everyone's gender is an expression of self ... a performance ... a show. We are all in drag.

Can feminism celebrate with us when we have the courage to transform?

My Definition of Feminism

A definition for feminism? Christ! Who knows? There are, however, some things I do know. I know that gender is a regimentally organized yet infuriatingly inconsistent and often violently enforced (but well meaning I'm sure!) class system built upon shifting sands of assumptions and status-quo maintaining (but mostly renegotiable) assigned characteristics. I know that this affects men, women and me. I know that our genders are subject to change in our lifetimes and that this is deeply threatening to patriarchy and even, sometimes, feminism. I know that without defined polarized roles of "men" and "women," men could not dominate. I know that currently, they do. And that this really sucks.

My Top 10 Feminist Influences

1. *The Sexual Politics of Meat* by Carol Adams
2. *Gender Outlaw* by Kate Bornstein
3. *Stone Butch Blues* by Leslie Feinberg
4. Daneila Lechet, who first showed me the poem "This Bridge Called My Back"
5. ani difranco (how embarrassing)
6. *Sexual Subversion and the End of Gender* by Rikki Ann Wilchins
7. Kandis Cyndi-Ly for saying "my survival needs no apologies"
8. My mom (sigh)
9. *Feminist Theory: From Margin to Center* by bell hooks
10. Audre Lorde for saying "we must do battle wherever we are standing"

My Bio

CAT PYNE is a photographer, queer invader and radical cheerleader, currently working in high schools as a sexual health educator and dreaming of being a constant thorn in the side of the binary.

NOT POST-FEMINISM

Christina Ahn

Young women interpret feminism in so many ways. For some, feminism can mean exploring one's identity in relation to other women, defying conventional views of women or advocating women's rights. But other women associate feminism with outspoken, bitchy, butchy, hair-legged, men-bashing, bra-burning, PMS-ing, shit-disturbing lesbians. It is evident that the latter opinion, which generalizes the term "feminism" into personality and image, is more prevalent in my generation. The media does an excellent job of toying with feminist ideology as well as publicizing women's advancement that has already occurred, making it seem like women have achieved all feminist goals. This strongly influences young women today and affects their perceptions of feminism. Misconceptions about feminism have sparked the emergence of a post-feminist era in which there is a noticeable lack of social and political change for the advancement of women.

The media often contribute to a cloudy, unfavourable perception of feminism that today's tweens and teens assimilate. A highly commercialized, "teeny-bopper," so-called-feminist culture marked by exaggerated "Girl Power" has erupted in North America recently. This trendy "in-your-face" culture is not only superficial, like Spice Girls' paraphernalia or Tommy Girl perfume marketed as "a declaration of independence," but also unrealistic. Television shows like *Xena the Warrior Princess*, *Buffy the Vampire Slayer* and *Sabrina the Teenage Witch* portray female role models who are entertaining, yet whose power is fictitious. The characters' girlish onslaughts cannot be applied to help young people deal with the problems they face in the real world: a young woman can't use Sabrina's magic to zap away an abusive family, nor can she use a stake and a clove of garlic like Buffy to drive away a sexual harasser at school. This shallow notion of female empowerment leads young women to believe that feminism is about purchasing the right "gear," like liberating short skirts and sequined halter tops, and projecting a self-absorbed, kick-ass image. Lesser known is Simone de Beauvoir's idea that "feminists are women, or even men too, who are fighting to change women's condition, in association with the class struggle, but independently of it as well, without making the changes they strive for totally dependent on changing society as a whole."[1]

Angry, aggressive women are also portrayed as feminists by the media. For instance, a caption on the front cover of the book *Bitch,* by self-defined feminist Elizabeth Wurtzel, reads "In Praise of Difficult Women." Wurtzel also poses on the cover topless with her middle finger raised defiantly. The hit single "Bitch" by Meredith Brooks, who joined the all-female Lilith Fair tour, features the lyrics, "I'm a bitch/I'm a lover/I'm a child/ I'm a mother/ I'm a sinner/ I'm a saint/ I do not feel ashamed!" While some feminist movements, like SCUM (the Society for Cutting Up Men, which no longer exists), are driven by this rebellious image and attitude, other feminists do not embrace these ideas at all. Betty Friedan, a so-called conservative feminist asks, "If that rage and bitterness is discharged in blind reactive hatred against men, personally and politically, must it not create a backlash from men, and ultimately, outrage, disillusionment and bitterness from women? Has the rhetoric of sexual politics blinded us to the real political actions and the allies needed to actually open new options in women's life?"[2] The media often neglect to address such valid questions; instead, fashionable, celebrity-saturated, feminist spectacles like Eve Ensler's *The Vagina Monologues,* a play about female genitalia, and Vanessa Beecroft's *Show,* a live showcase of bikini-clad models representing female power, capture the most attention. This results in young women associating these one-sided representations with all feminists but falling short of also seeing feminism as "any attempt to improve the lot of any group of women through female solidarity and a female perspective."[3] North American young women can easily absorb and accept socially constructed realities about feminism, and about almost anything, in search of their identities.

It is undeniable that the world has awoken since the

My Definition of Feminism
A social and political movement for the advancement of women.

feminist movement first arose during the French Revolution, and "in this century, feminism has achieved striking successes in gaining women access to education, political rights and jobs and in eliminating laws enforcing a double standard."[4] Numerous bureaucracies, laws, policies, conventions, declarations and institutional mechanisms exist for the advancement of women. Although the progression of women's status is widely publicized and known to young women, many do not realize that these bureaucracies and policies are useless "paper tigers" unless they are implemented, acted upon, constantly monitored and evaluated. For instance, the *Employment Equity Act,* introduced in Canada in 1986 is supposed to ensure that women achieve a level of employment equal to their representation in the workforce, as defined by qualification, eligibility and geography. It would be rare that one would meet somebody that didn't know that it is illegal to hire (or not hire) someone based on gender. However, most people wouldn't know that in 1993, the average annual pre-tax income of women aged fifteen and over from all sources was $16,500, just 58 percent the average income of men ($28,600).[5] These seemingly miniscule injustices are easily ignored by young women who live in a society that lives comfortably with all the favourable changes the women's movement has brought about.

How is it that the *Beijing Platform for Action* and the *Convention for the Elimination for All Forms of Discrimination Against Women* (CEDAW) have been adopted by so many nations yet atrocious violations of women's rights still exist in those very nations? In North America, young women enjoy the right to vote, the right to control our sexual reproduction, the right to an education and more freedom than many of our international counterparts. The fact that in at least fourteen Central and South American countries a man can escape rape charges by agreeing to marry his victim[6] or that genital excision or infibulation is a brutal reality to 80 to 100 percent of women in Somalia[7] may not seem to affect young North American women directly; however, the injustices that women face worldwide affect the identities of women everywhere. Young North American women need to realize that if they become contented with the advancement in women's status that has occurred, they will become self-absorbed until they are oblivious to the ever-constant need for the progress of today's women globally. Feminism as an international movement for social and political change fostered by young women is still alive today and needed more than ever!

An increasing number of young women are blindly accepting the media's ideas of feminism and getting comfortable with the idea that there isn't anything they can do to further advance the status of women. This has resulted in the term "post-feminist era," which is used to describe the time period in which we currently exist. Some women believe that post-feminist "implies that women have already won their rights and currently enjoy absolute freedom ... we are 'post' that brief period of time when the media found feminist views fashionable ... but only as entertainment without any feminist political analysis."[8] Popular television shows like *Dawson's Creek* and *Buffy the Vampire Slayer* are "becoming emblems of postfeminist girlhood,"[9] and as young women misunderstand the meanings of feminism, they become disinterested in exploring feminism as the spirit of women uniting for a common political or social cause.

Notes

1. Alice Schwarzer, *Simone de Beauvoir* (New York: Pantheon Books, 1984), 32.
2. Betty Friedan, *The Feminist Mystique* (New York: Dell Pub. Co., 1963), xiv.
3. Marilyn French, *The War Against Women* (New York : Summit Books, 1992), 12.
4. Ibid., 12.
5. Minister of Industry, *Women in Canada: A Statistical Report,* 3rd ed. (Ottawa, 1995).
6. Eric Nonacs, "The World According to Women," *Jane* (August 1998), 46–47.
7. Joni Seager, *The State of Women in the World Atlas,* New Edition (Toronto: Penguin Books, 1997).
8. Phyllis Chesler, *Letters to a Young Feminist* (New York: Four Walls Eight Windows, 1997), 24.
9. James Poniewozik, "Their Major Alienation," *Time* (September 20, 1999), 58.

My Top 10 Feminist Influences
(or almost)

1. My ninth grade religious education teacher at school taught a class about female genital mutilation. The thought of this practice existing and occurring to girls my age horrified me. I telephoned the public health department asking what I could do. They were very polite, although I didn't understand the political, social and cultural implications of FGM. Eventually, they sent me an information package about FGM and I became more knowledgeable about it. This led me to read up on other current women's issues.

2. I read *The Edible Woman* by Margaret Atwood in Grade Ten which made me think about sources and images of female empowerment.

3. My English teacher, Ms. Yorke, in Grades Ten and Eleven really encouraged me to become an independent thinker. With her encouragement, I wasn't afraid to venture out on a limb and explore feminism for myself.

4. Singers like Tori Amos and Sarah McLachlan who incorporate feminist elements into their music and support women's causes. I went to the first Lilith Fair concert in Toronto in August '97 and the positive female energy from the crowd and performers was inspiring.

5. I love Maya Angelou's poetry: she draws so much strength from the female identity. "Phenomenal Woman" is one of my favourite poems.
6. I heard Germaine Greer speak at a Women of Influence luncheon when her newest book was released. Her writings along with Gloria Steinem's are always so elucidating and driven that one can't help being inspired.
7. In Grade Eleven, I had the amazing experience of attending sessions of the Commission on the Status of Women at the United Nations as a guest of Canadian Voices of Women for Peace. The group of amazing women I travelled with included Lara Karaian and we all learned a lot from each other. I learned about the Beijing PFA and CEDAW and familiarized myself with existing policies and conventions to help women. The women who spoke on the panels in sessions and workshops were also an amazing resource as they all came from different backgrounds and perspectives.

My Bio

CHRISTINA AHN is a seventeen-year-old peace activist and feminist. She enjoys taking on leadership roles in her high school and is dedicated to making a difference.

— Nicole Fram *She's Got Labe Zine* shegotlab@hotmail.com

THE GOOD GIRL
AND THE BITCH

Angie Gallop

I was about eight years old when I discovered *Hot Stuff* in the record cabinet. The jacket cover was bright yellow with orange flames and a smiling, earnest-looking cartoon jukebox on the front. I opened the jacket, slipped out the LP, gingerly placed it on the turntable and put the record needle in the first groove. "Ooooooooooooooooo … Love to love ya, baby," groaned a breathy, almost desperate-sounding Donna Summers. It was like she had cast a spell. My back straightened, hips jutted out and I slithered around the room moving my hands up and down my body. I jumped up on the stoop in front of the fireplace and gazed into the mantle mirror, hand on my throat, cheeks sucked in, lips pouting.

"She sounds like she's having an ...," my mom never finished the sentence. Instead she watched me with concern, stuck with the dilemma of whether or not a "good mother" should prohibit *Hot Stuff.* I was oblivious to her struggle. Instead I basked in the music and my reflection in the mirror.

Then came the night of the dinner party. Friends came over, daughters in tow — Andrea, five, and Sarah, three. I decided to "put on a show" and excitedly led Andrea and Sarah up to my mother's closet for costumes. I chose a black spaghetti-strap dress; for Andrea, a gold-lamé knit dress; and for Sarah, a silk blouse did the trick. When show time came, I dropped the needle on *Hot Stuff* and the three of us took off. Andrea jumped up and down wiggling her bum and Sarah got so excited her blouse fell off. I twirled my skirt until people could see my underpants then dropped to the floor and crawled seductively.

"My, she's developing quite the body," one saucer-eyed guest exclaimed to my mother.

After that evening, *Hot Stuff* was put in the record cabinet to stay and I was told that "Someday I'd understand."

Fast forward to age twelve.

Guiltily playing Barbies (pretty soon it would be really uncool). Crystal (my Barbie) is about to give birth in the midst of great intrigue. (Crystal was constantly pregnant.) The evil Marie (the Marie Osmond Barbie doll) is posing as a nurse to come and steal the baby. Then she is going to kidnap Crystal and seduce Ken. Ah, but Ken is so in love with Crystal that he braves great danger to save her just in time, foiling the plot of the evil Marie. Innocent delicate Crystal, a perpetual pregnant victim, kisses her saviour. Her power is in her beauty and delicate state. And the neat thing is that she doesn't have to lift a finger. All she has to do is wait ... but the wait was excruciating.

Two years later I started a high-school career that I spent waiting, all the while trying to appear "cool." Wanting to be beautiful enough so that the football jock would come over and ask me out. When he did try to make conversation, all I could do was blush. I couldn't talk. Couldn't appear to want. So he went away.

Almost twenty years later, *Hot Stuff* is a campy relic and, for me, a sad irony. I've dropped the Barbie-inspired "cool" façade and have been in a relationship for four years where it is appropriate, even expected, that I strut my "Donna Summers" now and then. Only I'm stiff. These days sexual power for women is "in." So, what has come between me and that hollow-cheeked pouty vamp in the living-room mirror? As a straight woman (at least up until now), I've spent my sex life bouncing between two extremes. Kelley Aitken describes it best in her essay about women and writing:

> Somewhere along the line, she lost a child's sense of confidence, a sense of herself at the centre of things. What replaced it was not of her own choosing, a maddening self-consciousness that has her swinging between the twin tyrannies of media femininity: the good girl and the bitch.[1]

We are still living in times where, for those of us who were lucky, sex and learning about sex was relegated to the realm of the health classroom, where my teacher passed around a condom but refused to show us how to put it on even a wooden penis. Those of us who were even luckier graduated to "girl talk" to share experiences and compare technique. Yet, let's face it, when we girls talk about sex, it can still be difficult to let ourselves admit and explore just how much and how often it just isn't working for us in an honest, authentic, vulnerable way. When I'm smacking my partner's ass or riding him, "on top," emulating the strong sex-positive women I read and hear about, I'm really acting no differently than the wilted wallflower in the high-school gymnasium dying to be asked for a dance. In the back of my mind, there is this nagging consciousness that I am playing a role, swinging between the wilful ignorance of health class to a "put on" daring in the bedroom. These are roles I hold in my head, intellectually, rather than inhabit in my body, physically and spiritually.

As is often the case in life, a serendipitous moment came

127

along. I was asked to write for a sex Web site for women and men. In the course of researching an article on "How to Lap Dance for Your Lover," I decided I had to see a female "exotic" dancer in action. I had never been to a strip club before. My stomach was in my throat as I stood outside the cheerfully painted red-and-yellow doors. I hesitated. A picture of a cigar-smoke-filled room of men with sweaty, sticky hands staring at mean, Barbiesque women who would scoff at my naïveté dominated my headspace. I opened the door. Inside, the club was a sea of empty chairs. Blue -gelled stage lights shone on an empty stage. Ambient black light gave the air-conditioned room a purple haze. Two crisp white tuxedo shirts seemed to float behind the bar in the sepulchral darkness. I welled up my most sensible, confident persona and approached the bartender. His glowing shirt reflected on his face and he had the tight muscled physique, manner and speech of an aged jock. He told me that after many years in the business he could "sense" that I really wanted to be a stripper.

I looked to my left, a woman I assumed was a stripper was sharing drinks with two male patrons at the bar. She looked at me as she answered a suggestion that she get a "boob job" with the refrain that she liked her body the way it is. To this the bartender piped up, "You're perfect, baby, you know why?"

"Why?"

"Because you swallow, baby. Because you swallow."

She laughed caustically then turned to me and asked, "So you want to be a stripper?"

I explained that yes, I do, but in private. She encouraged me to watch the next show. I took a seat, next to my partner, whom I had brought for safety.

Suddenly, the dancer I had spoken to at the bar took my hand and said, "Come on, I'm going to give you a dance," she said leading me to a booth at the back of the bar.

"Pardon?" I didn't understand.

Thrilled by the prospect of watching me, "a good girl," be "educated" by the stripper, the men at the bar dared her to perform for me, upping the price until she agreed. A little skeptical about the situation, she told me she had never danced for a woman before and asked if I was "into" women. I said I loved women but had never had sex with one. She said she had never either.

We then shook hands and introduced ourselves. Her name was Diane. She had the protective, street-smart aura about her that I had anticipated a stripper would have, fortified by long black hair, gold jewelry and thick black eyeliner. Yet she was quick to bond with and easily shared a giggle.

As she slipped off her wrap top, I was struck by the confidence and smoothness with which she presented and handled her body. She caressed and licked her breasts, then unwrapped her skirt, danced and caressed some more before turning her back, straddling my crossed legs and bending over right in front of me to unhook her black G-string. I could smell the sweet of her perfume mixed with body scent. We giggled some more as she flaunted a leg, a thigh, a butt cheek vaguely following the music pounding in the background.

Then, she stepped up onto my seat and extended one leg over my head, resting her foot on the back of the tall booth to stand above me, fully naked, flaunting to the men who had paid for the performance. When she got back down, she sat on a chair across from me, crossed her ankles in the air, my eyes went to her spiked black heels. She then spread her legs, fingered herself and to my complete surprise, put her finger in her mouth to taste.

Although I was sweating nervously, I felt a safe, fun rapport with Diane and was excited by the pleasure she took in her own body. The song ended and she smiled as she wrapped herself back up in her clothing. We talked. She told me she has three children and a boyfriend she met at the bar, who gets jealous when she

> ## My Definition of Feminism
>
> Feminism is about balancing honesty with compassion in your daily interactions with the people and ideas that surround you, and it is about listening and stretching your mind to honour the realities of the new people you encounter.

works. I gave her an extra tip for her beautiful dance.

We were interrupted by the bartender.

"Now it's your turn to dance."

I wanted to dance for Diane. To return what felt like an incredible gift. My mind was swimming.

Diane stood up, protesting with the bartender, who looked twice her size. He eventually walked away.

The safety was gone. The environment around us started to close in around me.

"If the cops came in and saw you naked without a licence, you'd be hauled away, not him," she told me.

I worried that I had caused trouble for her. She assured me she could take care of herself. On leaving the club, I was overcome by sadness. Diane's dance was a beautiful experience yet was I perpetuating the objectification of women? I believe I was.

Catharine MacKinnon writes that in the case of sex workers in strip bars and pornographic magazines, their consent is masked because of the economic oppression they face. Diane strips, or her kids don't eat. Yet, is it that simple? Lily, a former stripper and feminist academic who teaches "Lap Dancing for Your Lover" at the Good for Her sex shop in Toronto, had an interesting comment on this:

> I am not disputing the fact that this happens a lot and that women are victims of low-paying jobs in all sectors of society and that women face harassment in all different workplaces on a large scale. But I think that it is problematic to say that ending pornography is going to change that. I wish it could be that simple. But it is not that simple.[2]

With Diane, I was able to see a woman enjoy her body. For the first time, I was able to *feel* that enjoyment physically, in the way her dance turned me on. And, when I performed for my partner, I drew on the memory of her spirit. As I pictured Diane's confidence, I was able to really feel and understand the power of the gift I was sharing. Sex and the sharing of sex are sacred. Sex-related words that have become taboo, like "cunt" and "bitch," are derived from the names and titles of goddesses. Prostitution was originally practised in holy temples, as a way of dispensing the grace of the goddess. The Great Goddess Ishtar was called the Great Whore of Babylon. What made me sad, and now angry, is that Diane performs her sacred gift in a seldom-aired corner of society thick with "you swallow, baby" jokes. She's offered advice about "boob jobs" rather than the respect she deserves for the gift she puts herself at risk to offer every time she goes to work.

****

Everybody is doing it. I swear. Classes on sex tricks and techniques fill up the classifieds of the newspapers, at least in urban centres. In the last couple of years, Web sites offering "respectable" and "intelligent" sources of thought and conversation about sex for women and men have popped up and are thriving. Traditional media outlets are plastering their pages with stories about sex to attract readers. Last summer, *The Globe and Mail* declared that young women, even self-described feminists, are going to watch other women perform in strip bars. Discussion about sex is everywhere and women are moving into corners of society previously frequented exclusively by men. This is a start. But I think we have to go further, deeper. As Audre Lourde says in her essay "Uses of the Erotic," in an anti-erotic society where women are surrounded by images of "gorgeous" but unreal women and "good" but unreal sex, connecting with that "sense of ourselves at the center of things" and bravely acting on inner knowledge and feeling instead of external directives is a potentially powerful, transformative force that can give us the energy to pursue genuine change within our world.[3]

Instead of merely engaging in intellectual discourse about how daring we can be sexually or visiting male-centric clubs to watch women dance, I would love us to create spaces — common, well-accepted spaces — where women of all different backgrounds, body types and levels of comfort can give to each other the pleasurable and erotic display of sex and arousal. Whether stoic and passive, aggressive and dirty, or somewhere in between, I would want us to feel and understand erotic arousal and power and fill in the spaces between the "good girl" and the (sacred) "bitch." I would love us to have a space where women could learn the sense of confidence and body love that I saw and felt from Diane that day. And, I would love to dance for her to my favourite Donna Summers tune.

Notes

1. Kelley Aitken, "Writing Versus Talking," *Resources for Feminist Research* 21, nos. 3/4 (Fall/Winter 1992).
2. Lily, interview with author, Toronto, August 12, 1999.
3. Audre Lorde, "Uses of the Erotic: The Erotic as Power," *Sister Outsider* (Trumansburg, NY: The Crossing Press, 1984), 59.

My Top 10 Feminist Influences

1. Mom, Kathy Gallop, best friend, biggest foe and the first feminist in my life.
2. Dad, John Gallop, who taught me that big is beautiful.
3. Great-grandma Mildred Mitts, who is reflected in the shape of my eyes and independent spirit.
4. My two grandmothers, Myrtle Gallop and Eileen Coulter, whom I've been privileged to know in adulthood.
5. My partner Eric Squair who taught me to ask for help.
6. Wise older women who have inspired me: Alice Doi, Jan Miller, Deborah Barnett, Andrea Moodie, Lynne Van Luven.
7. Soul sisters, fellow explorers: Treesa Cowan, Val Leinan, Paula Gilmore, Karen Renzoni, Judith Rupert, Laurie Thompson, Jen Febbraro, Stephanie Anderson.
8. The many people I have been privileged to meet, interview and work with as a writer.
9. Music by ani difranco and one concert that rocked my world at a difficult time.
10. Works by Audre Lorde, bell hooks, Alice Walker, Toni Morrison and Irshad Manji.

My Bio

ANGIE GALLOP is a writer and editor living and working in Toronto.

SHE

Crystal'Aisha PerrymanMark

She is Truth
and Passion
and marvelous sound persona

She is Temperance
and Warrior
and the heart of
a Mighty Revolution

She is manna and milk
Breast and body
and Mind and Soul with Spirit

She is Movements
and radical
and that calm silence before
and after the storm

She is Black
and maiden
and conqueror of downpression(s)

She is Integrity
and Dignity
and Honour to her peers

She is All
and More
claiming Divine-Trinity-Goddess
salvation

She is the Many
and the One

Whose tears cleanse, purge, renew

She is Faith
and Trust
Healing and Redemption

She is the Coming
and the Present
with all its hopes and fears

She is Wisdom
and Johara
an epiphany coming of essence

She is Resistance
and Fury
A tumultuous combine
of Justice and Action

She is Knowing.

She is all that I have desired
All that I have sought
and thirst for,
She is my hunger and a quest –

A longing ...

She

Is the Woman I want to be.

My Definition of Feminism

1. Feminism is the collective movement of justice to affirm and ensure the inherent rights of women as equal beings, socially, politically, spiritually and economically within society.

2. Feminism is the daily revolutionary practice to engage and destroy the system of patriarchy and all its interlinked systems of oppression in an effort to free women, children and men everywhere and in every capacity.

3. Feminism is anti-oppression in its truest meaning: anti-oppression for women, races, classes and sexualities. A collective title for all that embodies the integrity of total freedom for all.

My Top 10 Feminist Influences
(They can never be ordered or hiercharized)

1. Audre Lorde. She revolutionized poetry and my thinking. A fearless genius.
2. Sojourner Truth. Her life is a testament to integrity and truth. She walked the path to freedom for many.
3. Angela Davis. Revolutionary bravestar and Intellectual weaponress.
4. Dionne Brand. Poetess, revolutionary and writer; my personal example that it can be done.
5. Alice Walker. Her books enrapture, her politics bleed through every page.
6. Angela Kyodo Williams. Spiritual warrior, enlightenment author and entrepreneur.
7. Maya Angelou. A woman who has been through everything and has had the courage to "tell it," write it and continue to love it.
8. Mariama Ba. Poignant novelist who illuminates the plight of women in Dakar, Senegal, about polygamy. A poet and a paper revolutionary.

9. Gloria Steinem. The brave well-known founder of *Ms.* and revolutionary of the streets.
10. Oprah Winfrey. Though not a self-identified feminist, her work speaks to my definition. A philanthropist and another example that for black women, anything is attainable.

My Bio

CRYSTAL'AISHA PERRYMANMARK is a poetess, writer and revolutionary. She is committed to anti-oppression and social justice, believes in everyday revolutions and the strength of spiritual internal power. A Bachelor of Arts student at York University and a young mother of two (Sable is four and Sojourn is due at press time), Crystal'Aisha is dedicated to the principles of truth, passion and integrity and explores this in her creative and academic work. Believing, as Lorde said, "Poetry is No Luxury," she identifies writing as her greatest calling and thrives in a life where this has become her sacred vocation.

FULL FRONTAL CONFRONTATION

Maren Hancunt

This piece is a behind-the-scenes look at the first (and only) book I've ever written: *Lady Lazarus: Confronting Lydia Lunch.* The subject was Lydia Lunch, a key instigator of the post-punk, No-Wave music/art/film movement in the late 1970s, who is considered by many to be the one of the "original Riot Grrrls," being one of the first performers to don a baby doll dress and scream lyrics about sexual abuse whilst brandishing her guitar like an Uzi. That is but one of her many claims to infamy. She was one of the first musicians to get into spoken word (inspiring and influencing imitators such as Henry Rollins and Jello Biafra); her pieces such as "Conspiracy of Women (COW)" and "Uncensored" were groundbreaking works awakening thousands of "alternative," alienated teenage girls and women.

Lunch was, and continues to be, controversial, not only because of the content of her work but also because of the various modes of artistic expression that she uses to challenge ideas about femininity, poverty, rage, power, violence, sex, everything. When I was in my late teens, I read an interview with Lunch in Andrea Juno's *Angry Women* and began to see how my desire for feminist justice and S&M with male partners weren't necessarily incompatible; there could be some room for contradiction. I also became fascinated with how someone who is so prolific and influential could so be totally unknown to the public in general and academic feminism in particular. How could Lunch simultaneously express her desire for a female planet whilst remaining a promiscuous heterosexual sociopath? I chose Lunch as the topic for my undergraduate thesis, and away I went.

During my research and our correspondence, my "theories" of feminism, anti-racism and censorship came into full confrontation with the realities and the pluralisms of just who Lydia Lunch is — a real person with as many dimensions as her art. During the initial stages of my research, I realized that I didn't agree with everything that she said, and a situation arose in which I had to confront her with my opinion on some aspects of her work. Not only that, but to voice my criticisms of Lunch's work to Lunch herself meant that I had to really, really interrogate where I was coming from. The challenge I faced in confronting one of my feminist heroines, and myself in the process, was confusing, somehow delicate, challenging, contradictory and infinitely rewarding. The following are excerpts and full reproductions of our actual e-mails to one another.

"No names have been changed to protect the innocent. They are all guilty ..."
— Lydia Lunch, *Paradoxia*

September 23, 1997

Dear Lydia Lunch,

Greetings from Victoria, BC. I would like to thank you for taking the time to read this letter, as I'm sure you receive many. My name is Maren Hancunt, and I am a BA Honours student at the University of Victoria. I am currently embarking on my Honours paper, the subject of which is yourself. First I would like to say that I got this address from one J— R—, an acquaintance of mine who interviewed you in Calgary when you played there. I saw one of the shows, and it blew me away. It blew the whole audience away apparently, as no one spoke or moved for the whole hour you were up there. I remember at one point you asked if any of the females in the audience felt safe in our society. You had to repeat this question several times, because we couldn't answer you. We were frozen, embarrassed and pained.

But I digress. It is too early in the game to say exactly what angle my thesis will take, however I am particularly interested in exploring the impact that you have had on feminism, the Riot Grrrl movement and the art of spoken word. I understand that you don't identify as a feminist. I do, strongly, and in many ways I came to embrace feminism because I loved your art.

You taught me that I could wear makeup and fishnets while doing it doggy style and still be a feminist. I was just discovering my sexuality during my self-conscious teenhood and I wanted to work it, I didn't want to be raped, harassed or afraid because of it. I was sick of seemingly asexual feminists who were for censorship. I was looking for the opportunity to express my own anger and wield my own power — I was more "manly" than many of the guys that I hung out with — and I saw you doing this in the public arena. Yet nowhere in academic feminism does your name surface, and I feel that you have made a significant and unique contribution to feminism.

I would love to be able to do an interview of some sort. I understand if such a thing is not possible, however I still wanted to write to you to tell you about my thesis, in hopes that when it's completed you might be interested in reading it. I am hoping to have it published as well.

Lastly, I am wondering if you could tell me where I might find some missing items of research. I encourage you to contact me if you wish. I have enclosed my phone number, address and e-mail. Thank you for your time.

Maren Hancunt

DATE: *Tue, 30 Sept 1997 13:20:10 -0400 (EDT)*
FROM: *lydialunch@cow.com*
TO: *maren@uvic.ca*
SUBJECT: *Thesis*

Maren,
I'm flattered to be the subject of your paper. I agree I have been

denied lip service in the feminist community due to my ribald nature and tendency to promote pornography, etc. I'm here [in the US] for the next month and then gone for a month. I'd love to do a phone interview ... tell me when to call you (you'll need time to prepare no doubt) and what materials of mine you are familiar with. I'll try and fill in the blanks.

Lydia Lunch

DATE: Wed, 1 Oct 1997
TO: lydialunch@cow.com
FROM: maren@uvic.ca
SUBJECT: Re: Interview

Lydia,

I'm flattered that you're flattered! My thesis is causing quite a stir in the department, all the instructors are very intrigued with you. If you are planning to be in Canada anytime this year, the department has $$$ to bring in speakers. Why not Lydia Lunch?

I am so happy that you agreed to an interview. I would rather do it in December or early January, because you see, I have to attempt to be familiar with all of your stuff, and I am currently in the process of ordering it, and it's coming from Florida, California, Wales, etc. There are all the secondary sources that I need to read, as well as this huge ethics application that needs to be approved by the "powers that be" at this university — "Interviewing Human Subjects" or something — so the university is assured that they won't get sued. This is an eighty-page paper, it's more like a book really, and as you know, your creative output since the seventies is quite extensive. I just hope that I can get it all over the border!

I will be in the vicinity of the East Coast over Xmas holidays, I could do the interview in person, if you would be comfortable with that. I can't tell you how ecstatic I am to hear from you, it's hard not to be a little "star struck," so excuse the gushing tone of my correspondence.

Maren Hancunt

I was happy, because I had gained access to my "subject." To make matters even happier, a publishing house I had contacted in order to obtain a zine they published on Lydia Lunch e-mailed me a reply, generously offering their assistance, as well as stating that they were interested in seeing the completed thesis for possible publication. I was stoked

My Definition of Feminism

Feminism is one word that indicates the desire to eradicate oppression — your own and everyone else's.

beyond belief and proceeded to order all the Lunch I could find, devouring it ravenously. Surprisingly, some of it didn't sit well.

DATE: Mon, 6 Oct 1997
TO: lydialunch@cow.com
FROM: marenh@uvic.ca
SUBJECT: Remember Nardwuar the Human Serviette?

Lydia,

With regards to our earlier e-mails discussing the possibility of you performing in Victoria, I thought that you could do two shows, one on campus and one off. There is a delicate consideration, however; it's sort of vague, so do bear with me. The show that I saw you do last year rocked, it was great, and a show like that or whatever would be delicious. I have begun reviewing your stuff, and it would be a really bad scene for me in the department an in the feminist community, and indeed with many of my friends and lovers, if anything that you espoused would be interpreted as racist. Now the key word here is interpreted. I'm speaking particularly about the use of the word "nigger" that pops up frequently in some of your stuff. It is unclear to me what you are saying with that, but that's not the point, the point is that it is such a loaded word, etc.

I don't know if I'm making sense, I feel really stupid trying to describe my concern. I would love to have you on this campus, I'm quite comfortable with your controversy, however I'm not comfortable about racial controversy because as a white women, I can't make decisions about what is going to be taken as what and piss off a person of colour, that's not how I would want to learn either. Anti-racist activism is something that I've become more and more involved in, and it's quite confusing but very necessary because this continent is extremely racist, etc., and all oppressions are linked, and the women's movement has a history of being really racist and if that doesn't change nothing will change. I have no idea what your views on racism are, although I'm sure you think that it sucks. However your descriptions of black people in some of your stuff seems very confusing to me. Is this making any sense? It sounds like I'm trying to tell you what you can and cannot say at UVic, and that's not it at all. AT all. However, if I am the one setting this thing up, I am going to be held responsible if anything around the issue of race relations goes bad. Obviously, I don't care if any men or anti-porn activists get pissed off. Does this make any sense? Feel free to tell me to fuck off.

I wish I knew your work better at this point, then maybe I wouldn't sound like such an idiot or even have this vague, indefinable concern that I have. It basically stems from one incident last week. My lover is black, and when we were watching your video *The Gun Is Loaded* and the word "nigger" came up, he flinched, and we stopped the tape because I didn't know what was "coming next" and I was afraid of hurting him. That word has been used against him so many times, that even the mention of it, regardless of the intention, can hurt him quite deeply. I felt responsible at that moment for exposing him to something that he interpreted as hurtful, and this is a really small community. I would feel responsible if any other people of colour found your performance problematic around issues of race. If this just sounds like total bullshit, fair enough. I can totally help your agent with doing a show downtown, and we could just skip UVic on the account that I'm paranoid. Thank you much for your time and co-operation, it's truly amazing and beyond appreciated.

Maren

DATE: Tue, 7 Oct 1997 06:27:02 -0400 (EDT)
FROM: lydialunch@cow.com
TO: marenh@uvic.ca
SUBJECT: Remember Nardwuar the Human Serviette?

Maren,

Of course I'm not prejudiced. I hate everyone equally (that's a joke). The word nigger is a loaded word, that should cause no more controversy (re/fine for black people to use it, not white) than fuck, redneck, bitch, slut, whore, big dick, macho asshole, white trash (which for some reason is never as loaded as NIGGER. WHY??? PLEASE READ "THE REDNECK MANIFESTO" BY JIM GOAD).

The line that best defines is "sin is a trick on niggers & we're all niggers broken by the wheel of fate" (from UNIVERSAL INFIL-TRATORS). I HAVE SPOKEN OUT about the incarceration of black men/called up welfare for who is really on it (white women with two kids) and have NEVER DONE ANY MATERIAL BLA-TANTLY RACIST. SEXIST YES (against men) ... when I use that word it is usually as a quote by someone else, or to diffuse, remind people how truly insulting or not that word is ... it is ridiculous to censor such a strong word from one's public speaking if the issue you are addressing is larger than the connotation of that one word. I grew up in black ghettos for thirteen years and understand the plight of poor people, the underclass, poverty and lack of opportunity. I also completely understand scapegoating and have addressed this repeatedly in some of my works. I am not prejudice and understand your concern. I wouldn't be doing a political speech on this tour, I'd be reading from my book *Paradoxia: A Predator's Diary (Sexual Horrors and the Psychic Repercussions)*.

Finish watching the gun is loaded w/or without your boyfriend and see if the bigger picture is not addressed. Realize that it was made in the early '80s when that word was even more taboo re/before rap co-opted it into every song. It's unfortunate to me that i have not had a bigger effect on the black community when the issues I have dealt with, poverty/incarceration/the haves vs the have nots, speak directly to any oppressed people. Could it

143

be the black communities' blatant racism that divides them from me???? When I have more in common as a journalist w/rap than with bush or hole??? The most black people that have ever at one time attending a show of mine totaled four!!!!

So do not trip out on one word when the whole picture is so much greater. And tell your boyfriend to loosen it up and dig the picture ... especially in *The Gun is Loaded.*

Will review the list you sent me and see what I can fill in/thanks for addressing this/it does not disturb me at all and I truly understand your concern.

Lydia

DATE: *Wed, 8 Oct 1997*
TO: *lydialunch@cow.com*
FROM: *marenh@uvic.ca*
SUBJECT: *Re: Censorship Sucks*

Lydia,
Thanks so much for your illuminating e-mail. The person I viewed your video with never said anything, I just got the sense of him flinching. As you may have noticed, I am one paranoid motherfucka.

That sucks that there aren't more black people at your shows, maybe they are confused (as I was) as to what you're saying, although it must seem obvious to you, as it does to me now that I read your e-mail. I can't stress enough that if I were further along in my research I could have figured it out for myself, however thanks for clueing me in.

DATE: *Wed, 15 Oct 1997 06:05:27 -0400 (EDT)*
FROM: *lydialunch@cow.com*
TO: *marenh@uvic.ca*
SUBJECT: *Re: Re: Censorship Sucks*

Maren,
I'm glad the e-mail I sent made things a little more clear. You may be paranoid (and I believe paranoia is justified) but I am one contradictory motherfucka, which often leads to mass confusion

since I purport to have no dogma or philosophy that lies under the root of what I espouse and love to rattle the bird cage, insisting on covering taboo concepts, how could I expect anyone (and I DON'T) to truly get or agree with everything I say (never my intention anyway). MY goal is to force others and myself to question ... question, question both their own response and what it is exactly I am espousing. I have always eschewed responsibility for my work, the power of my words, because you cannot control what others interpret or misinterpret.

Lydia

Looking back at my e-mail to Lydia describing my discomfort with the discussed aspects of her work, I am disgusted with my pathetic, two-faced, bullshit approach to a very important issue. I so badly, for my own benefit, wanted Lunch's co-operation for this project that I was willing to compromise my own personality and feelings by downplaying my own strong reactions to what I feel to be her misguided use of the "n-word" and instead hide behind the fear of my lover's and other's objections to her work. At the same time, I did not want her to think I was calling her a "racist." I was not calling into question her character or core beliefs, only her use of language and foggy subtext. Also, just from seeing her live, I knew how fucking scary her presence and personality can be — intentionally. In both of the interviews which informed my study, I would bring up examples of what I felt to be racist content in her work, and our resulting discussions are printed in full in *Lady Lazarus: Confronting Lydia Lunch*. I cannot stress enough how this one disconcerting aspect of Lunch's work became a wonderful mind-fuck, and thinking through it was of the utmost benefit. This experience held true for all the themes that came to prominence in *Lady Lazarus,* of which racism and uncertainty are two of many. One of my professors remarked upon the irony that I, a wanna-be confrontationalist and avid admirer of Lunch's rantings and wisdom, was "pussy-footing." Another contradiction.

When I initially took Women's Studies, I don't think that I spent too much time thinking or learning about the artificial separation between "isms." Several classes that I took at UVic brought this issue to the forefront for me. These classes, in which I became aware of and tried to deal with my own subconscious racism (made even more subconscious as I thought I was not "a racist"), I'm sure were a far different experience for me than for the Women of Colour who had to listen to the Women of No Colour vomit up their racist socialization. In addition, many incidents that occurred within the department and the Women's Centre brought the issue into centre stage. Looking back it seems that I came out of Women's Studies having learned far more about "racism" than "sexism," but what really happened was that I began to learn far more about "sexism" once I began to recognize my white privilege and apply it to an exploration of "racism." I had begun my endless journey towards becoming an anti-racist feminist, an ally.

Although I don't remember when I first used the word to describe myself, by the age of twelve I self-identified as a feminist. So by the time I went to university and took some Women's Studies classes, I thought that I had my shit sufficiently together as a feminist. Like, "I know who is oppressed and who's not." Embarrassingly, I had not grasped the concept that I could be involved in oppressing people, even though I was white, came from an upper-middle-class family and looked really "heterosexual"(blondwithbigboobs). I assumed that sexism was way more tolerated in our society than racism (probably because my white privilege ensured that I didn't notice it going on or notice myself engaging in it). I never sat around and tried to rank oppressions in my head or anything, I knew that all oppressions were based on the same BAD stuff, but I would get really pissed off when I saw how some of my guys friends (many of them black and brown, some white, some Jewish) would get so wickedly pissed and AWARE when it came to racism. It would anger me, not because I wasn't totally DOWN WITH DISSING THE RACIST BULLSHIT, but because they were so there for each other when it came to articulating the experience of racism, so good at calling it and allying themselves with each other to face it. Yet they were not there for me when I faced sexist crap. They didn't perpetuate it, but they did little to acknowledge or confront sexism, and I had a hard time getting them to discuss it with me. This, and the fact that I heard "Bitch!" more at my college than "Nigger!" somehow led me to believe that sexism was more socially acceptable than racism, instead of just realizing that there were more "bitches" in Calgary than "niggers." This example of utter stupidity led to something terribly embarrassing.

At a Montreal Massacre memorial in 1995, I stood on a platform in the Student's Union Building and ranted about sexism at the college, about fear, about bullshit, and then I spewed forth: "And what I don't understand is why YOU PEOPLE will tolerate sexism but you won't tolerate racism ... why is so it so much more socially acceptable to be sexist than it is to be a bigot?" It was almost five years ago and I confess to prolonged pot smoking; however, that is the gist of what I said. And not only was I totally sucking, no one called me on it. Everyone, my instructors, the members of the feminist group I was part of, guys, girls, everyone thought it was such a great speech. "Great speech, Maren." Nobody said to me "How the fuck would you know if racism is more tolerated than sexism, Whitey? And what about the experiences of Women of Colour, do you think that they get to separate the two — racism and sexism??" No one called me on it. And of course, it hadn't occurred to me that, just because I didn't see my brown friends' oppression manifest itself in the same ways that I saw sexism manifest itself to me, didn't mean that racism was happening on a less frequent basis. This flashback to a hurtin' oratory moment makes me feel like a hypocrite when I delve into a critique of how another white woman discusses race. Does a budding awareness of your privilege and position as a woman of pallor allow one to judge others from the same racial category on their racial discourse? How can you call someone on something without judging them? This was and is a big question for me with regards to *Lady Lazarus*.

Things were complicated throughout the whole writing process. At first I was cautious because I wanted to obtain an interview with Lunch and because I was in awe of her. As things progressed, and my manuscript was accepted for publication by

Questing Beast, I understood that things would be much more successful if Lydia lent her hand and her name to the project, by providing an afterword and agreeing to have our interviews printed. So again I struggled with trying to ignore the effect that the knowledge that this book probably wouldn't get published without Lydia's approval was having on me. Would I downplay my criticisms of her work in order to advance my literary career? Furthermore, I had hung out with her twice, talked on the phone and been in constant contact via e-mail. I really liked Lydia. And even though I knew that I would gain Lydia's respect by exhibiting intelligence, I was hesitant to criticize her too harshly and fearful that people would view Lydia a "racist." My fears were confirmed after friends who read my drafts asserted that I did indeed position Lydia as the ubiquitous "racist." This was the impression that she got as well.

DATE: *Wed, 14 Apr 1999 08:45:06 -400 (EDT)*
FROM: *lydialunch@cow.com*
TO: *maren_hancunt@bc.sympatico.ca*
SUBJECT: *Re: Changes2Lazarus*

Maren,
Loved the book ... the problem I have with it, and I hope your amendments clear it up somewhat, is your conclusion of my racism, while at the same time insisting white women have no right to speak of/for minority concerns. This is confusing and contradictory, and I think you make a bigger deal of it (perhaps there is a larger context) than the few examples (damn! they must be strong) of my use of "racist slurs" merit. For instance, the American Indian in "The Beast" is referenced in the story exactly as he appeared in the real incident which makes it racist??? because he was drunk??? or had a speech impediment??? or because I didn't use it as a forum for declaration of their plight??? I spend far more time insulting the white race (and in that sense, I have a reverse racism, which I wouldn't mind if you inserted) than ANY MINORITY WHOSE STEREOTYPING IS A REFLECTION OF THE AUDIENCE'S AND WHITE AMERICA'S ATTITUDE which

is still the final taboo. I still find this a sore spot which I feel you exaggerate, or perhaps it is simply a reflection of the power of a slur. I feel it paints the wrong picture, makes me appear almost neo-nazi instead of feminazi (a joke sister) when it is ALWAYS THE WHITE MAN WHO IS MY TARGET. Also since I am speaking about personal issues, for the most part my exclusion of queer issues (and again, claiming we should speak only from our own point of reference and not adopt the "others" predicament, or appear to pander), I think it is a strange point. Just my feelings ... get back to me on them.

But I do love the book. Thank you for all the research and I do not expect you to simply kiss my ass and swallow. I am certainly not above criticism. I just don't want to be accused of what I do not feel guilty of (right, like I feel guilt). Call me if you want to clear anything up.

Lydia

I rewrote the last chapter, clarifying my position and ensuring that it centred around Lydia's discourse and not Lydia. I tried to do this by positioning the really strong content, her words which I had found problematic, alongside an articulation of my own uncertainty and guilt as a white women seeking to be an ally in the struggle against racial oppression, and how these feelings informed my reactions to her work. This took a lot of time, most of it just thinking and talking to friends and peers. I came to really appreciate this amazing dialogue that I was having with this amazing woman, her honesty and her attempts to take my feelings into consideration. She was sweet, and took the time to check in to see how I was doing.

DATE: *Wed, Apr 21 1999 EDT -400 (EDT)*
FROM: *lydialunch@cow.com*
TO: *maren_hancunt@bc.sympatico.ca*
SUBJECT: *Re: Re: Yourtheshitthathitthefan*

Maren,
You must be puking Lunch for breakfast and shitting it out for

dessert ... sikofme yet???

Lydia

I was getting kind of sick of the project, but my overwhelming feeling was one of gratitude for being "pushed" into thinking deeper and harder about what I was saying and where it was coming from. My understanding that I as well could be called a "racist" for the assumptions that I articulated in public in my aforementioned speech, if I subjected myself to the same criteria, served to remind me that "racists" and "racism" exists in many degrees and many spheres. All my criticisms remained, but without their previous context of "objectivity." I didn't merely stand back and "judge" but instead tried to implicate myself in my analysis, and upon reading my adjustments, I realized that by dialoguing with Lydia on a continued basis, I had avoided a pat, smug "objective" judgement of her work. Instead I told a much more holistic story. I had successfully attempted a subjective objectivity and the after-Lunch manuscript was much truer to truth, and pleased us both.

DATE: *Thu, 22 Apr 1999 17:46:04 -400 (EDT)*
FROM: *lydialunch@cow.com*
TO: *marenhancunt@bc.sympatico.ca*
SUBJECT: *Re: Re: GoldenChubby*
LOVE IT
YOU AMAZE ME
LYDIA

In the "Introduction" to *Lady Lazarus: Confronting Lydia Lunch,* I wrote: "Fortunately, Women's Studies has never claimed to be objective." I am forever grateful for that.

My Top 10 Feminist Influences
(plus one)

1. My mother, Susan Olivia Hancock
2. bell hooks
3. Marilyn Monroe
4. Gloria Steinem
5. Andrea Juno
6. Marjorie Garber
7. Betty Carter
8. Fish Creek Provincial Park
9. Kara Keith (aka Sailor)
10. Lee Bolton-Robinson
11. Lydia Lunch – of course!

Bio

MAREN HANCUNT lives in Vancouver's West End with her dog Carter. She altered her last name from Hancock to Hancunt upon learning that the word "cunt" is etymologically related to knowledge, sexuality and creation. *Lady Lazarus: Confronting Lydia Lunch* is her first book (Questing Beast, 1999), and is available from Questing Beast (questing.beast@virgin.net) in the UK and Scratch Records (commerce@scratchrecords.com) in North America.

Rianne MacEachern Age 9 October 1998

BOY FEMINISM:
Looking Up to
Little Sister

Sean MacEachern

Before my sister was born, I didn't see myself as a feminist. I don't mean that feminism didn't agree with me (or that I didn't agree with feminism), just that I didn't feel it was a part of me.

Sometimes I don't know how I feel about an issue until I'm inspired to figure it out. Having a little sister has done that for me. She is almost a generation younger than I am, so she's growing up in a different environment than I did. It surprises me to see her doing things I thought only boys did — she kicks ass at video games and is more of an athlete than I can ever imagine being. I would like to think that she will find more opportunities and face fewer obstacles than women I grew up with. As optimistic as I am for her future, however, I know she will experience challenges that I never had to. Realizing that someone I love so much may be mistreated, abused or denied opportunities because of her gender has helped me to see how much of a feminist I really am.

> **My Definition of Feminism**
>
> I'm sure my definition will sound less academic than most. Simply stated, it's the belief that women should be allowed to reach their potential and be recognized for their enormous contributions.

My Top 10 Feminist Influences

1. My sister
2. My mom
3. Lynn (a dear friend)
4. Studying dentistry. I was surprised to how well-balanced the class is gender-wise and, in my eyes, gender seems to matter very little as far as being successful is concerned.
5. Being inspired by female classmates who manage to do all the work that I do, and yet still have time and energy to be terrific parents.
6. Being raised in a religion that stifles women's roles in the church.
7. Being raised in an environment with very poor male role models.

8. Managing to obtain a BA in philosophy without studying a single female thinker.
9. Having the opportunity to live in a country where women experience much more severe prejudices than women in Canada.
10. The life and work of Frida Kahlo has also been of special influence on my views.

My Bio

SEAN MACEACHERN lives in Halifax, NS, where he is presently studying dentistry at Dalhousie University. Former pursuits include a BA in Philosophy, some dabbling in black and white photography and teaching junior high school in Mexico.

— Jessica D. *Because We Matter Zine* womyn_riot@femail.com

I LOOK *FAT* IN THIS!

L i s a   A y u s o

When I was a baby I barely fit in to my mothers' belly; I sat tight waiting to find room. I became too big for my crib, too heavy for teeter-totters, too full for words. Stuffed to the gills with nothing left on my plate. Then I turned twelve and fifteen and twenty-one still looking for that room; trying to fit into a space that was not quite ready for me, still not ready for me. What was available was instability, contradictions and the notion that I was an "other" in a world with standards where I had no fighting chance. The word FAT replaced my name, my body and the future of normality. FAT as a noun, adjective, definition was the one thing I could hold on to. I kept this with me all through growing up, finally creating a space on my own terms with enough room for me to move, jump and run so that the world was big enough to fit my own standards.

To understand sizism, one must understand its roots. I think those roots lie in sexism. It may seem foreign and trivial but the fact is "sizism" is a term rarely used when discussing oppression. It's a term that exists but has not yet been justified in a society that still relies on medical journals and scientific data to prove the weight and worth of a human being. Even spell-check in Microsoft Word has warned me that sizism is the incorrect spelling for sexism. The term size does not stand alone but is combined with "ism" to define the struggle with size as a women's issue. Interesting if you think about it — sizism and sexism have taken over runways and magazines with an ideal beauty and body standard that reduces the value of women solely to appearance. This has had a profound effect on the self-esteem of women and girls.

I'm not saying that men do not deal with body image because I know men that do. However, the reality is that larger sizes for men in the average unisex retail stores are available in sizes up to 48, whereas women's sizes rarely exceed size 34. The message is clear; there are fourteen sizes between what is acceptable in a man's world and what is considered obese in a woman's world. Hence, the need to shop in specialty stores where clothes cost more than the average size 14 and where there is less selection. For women, this hinders a positive body image. If a woman wants to be fashionable, she has to reduce her size in order to obtain what has been deemed acceptable for females, size 14 being the cut off point.

But it's more than just bathing suits cutting off circulation, sausage legs and squeezing into newly shrunk jeans that make it hard to breathe. FAT activists have a bigger challenge. We must endure feminist's and women's groups who support "celebrating our natural sizes" and "non-constrictive standards of body politics" without truly understanding FAT issues. They support, in words, women who are size 14 and over. But it is a different world from the outside and a lot easier to be supportive when your pants aren't growing tighter and tighter — one more Thanksgiving dinner can change everything. As soon as FAT becomes personal and an individual is bigger, the struggle turns into losing weight to reclaim the body we once had or resuming self-hatred.

My Definition of Feminism

Feminism is a term without definition. It is defined by person and experience, by adding, subtracting, altering, redefining an identity that reflects a person's being, beliefs and lifestyle.

Self-pity versus self-empowerment. Feminist books don't tell us "How to stay FAT and still be loved for being loud." In fact, popular feminism's bigwig spokeswomen have done little to relieve FAT oppression. These women are supporting FAT on their terms only and as their feminism deems fit. For example, mainstream feminists I've talked to often have a problem with even using the word fat (stick it into the same category of words like girl, chick, dyke and so on that are often seen as "too" political or "militant" by different generations.) It's very unlikely that generic feminism will ever empower the word FAT. To FAT activists it's the only word we can define on our own terms. Everyone knows what to say to make a girl feel pretty, or thin — but not FAT!

Even the most confident of FAT girls have to struggle to keep every ounce of FAT intact. The truth of the matter is that many FAT activists hold a small and guilty desire to be skinny. The longing to be thin, to be accepted and fit in to such a stereotype of thin is what fuels the struggle. It is true, FAT activists can be sizist. Dreaming to be thin and hoping to wake up with less is sizist.

Shame has everything to do with FAT, in more ways than one. Very few people want to identify with the category FAT.

The point is that those of us who don't fit the accepted body image (even a slightly overweight image) have to find ways to live as we are. Our bodies are always changing and will never stay the same. Coming to terms with this is never easy. It's never a stagnant decision to embrace one's FAT self and be done with it. One can't have a "love it or leave it" attitude because "leaving it" is not an option. Shame plays the part of doing the next best thing, which is finding a way to leave FAT behind, to focus on loving a body. Shame and "you've got such a pretty face" are one step behind each other. I've had the experience of people singling out my beauty as starting at the top of my head and ending at the bottom of my neck. They want to erase the rest of my body. Or they could never imagine incorporating it into my beauty. Then I fall into the trap of doing the same thing. It's a way of settling. It can be a defence mechanism. I use it to arm myself with enough gumption to look in a full-length mirror and have it pay off.

So why do we do this to ourselves? For starters, beautiful and FAT have never painted a pretty picture in popular culture. The corruption of beauty stems from the minds behind the glossy magazine ads and the media, which continually reflect a formulated beauty on runways and in advertising. It would be false to say we are innocent bystanders of this corruption. Our minds are certainly influenced by a standard of beauty, and as a society we have more to do with the consumption of beauty than its creation. We are participants, reflecting the marketed version of the female body, the end result being the product of thin.

Now, the media is changing to meet the demands of mothers and their childbearing hips; advertising is recognizing the need to change beauty standards. In the media, body image has been something that recent ads on TV have half-heartedly tried to acknowledge. Granted there is some effort here but there are no women in these commercials who are FAT and seen as "ordinary people." Most FAT women a portrayed as some schtick selling a joke or a product. The "It's OK to just be you, no matter what" scenario is played out with new marketing ploys that "care" about consumers and their choices. This is a pathetic attempt at using emotional appeal to market products that represent society as a martyr with good caring intentions. This is what we are made to believe, and it works. I mean TV and marketing are perfect examples of mixed messages. We have talk shows with FAT people as guests where people in the audience say "What matters is in the inside" (or some catch phrase like "all that and a bag of chips") yet the next episode on the same show is a "Look At Me Now" segment where women show off their slimmer figures. After the show, these same people clap their hands loud for The Body Shop and their Size 18 campaign. People may know what they want to believe, but they don't have any faith or trust in that belief. They too drop it easily when beauty in the size of a slender and tall size 6 takes the stage.

Women are constantly bombarded with contradictions that, quite frankly, take longer to filter out than digest. At work and in the media, the PC ethic has scripted a person's vocabulary and thought with little, if any, sincerity. The anti-diet and the size 10 are back (supposedly runway models are bigger). But why, then, is FAT still a bad word? How does this ideology meet in the middle and remain real to the women who have to work around all this crap to survive it?

Today I heard "Any more of those cookies, Richard, and you're gonna get FAT." I heard someone say to a pregnant woman, whose bulging stomach is legit, "When I had my first one I gained 50 pounds and I was so FAT and embarrassed, even after it was almost impossible to get back to normal." And there are people I know (size 6) who say things like, "I feel FAT today," or "Does my ass look FAT in this?" These are statements made by women, feminists, friends; people who support a world where individuals create their standard for self-worth but do little about helping us FAT girls stay above water.

What it boils down to is judgement and validation, which may have improved slightly, but please, there is no GAP/Club Monaco/Urban Behaviour that has my size at all. So this whole line of being more inclusive of body shape and giving out women-positive messages as a society is just full of half-assed merit. As far as I know, Jenny Craig and Weight Watchers are still sky rocketing in profits and those profits have little to do with health and everything to do with skinny. There always seems to be a perfect opportunity for people to turn a blind eye to body image issues. The whole "heard that before" attitude replaces addressing the issue because it's an issue deemed as nagging and redundant. Acknowledging and sharing women's experiences have also become futile and negative. So now what? It's frustrating living in a world that constantly tries to look responsible rather than being responsible.

For me the desire to stay round is all relative to size. It's not about getting rid of the size 8's of this world but rather taking away the fear of size 9. Freedom comes from the support of other FAT friends looking great, sharing experiences, writing and being active, organizing clothing swaps and potlucks, joking and enjoying real life, trying daily to make real body sizes the standard for all women. Trust me, it is not easy being FAT and taking all that you have to create an individual standard, which for me is a reflection of my genes and my love for food. Are you kidding? You try feeling good about yourself in a society that continually degrades and shuns your size through a lack of clothes and role models. The only FAT people on TV are loud, obnoxious and sexless, sometimes all together nuts!

As a FAT activist, and I am one, I feel the way to survive is to acknowledge I am sizist, that I want to be thinner, maybe not thin but thinner, and why. Thus, my FAT becomes feminism, just like sizism is sexism in a Microsoft world. With every word there is another branch to swing from, I suppose. How I approach my activism dealing with FAT politics relates to all this. Activism that legitimizes both the not-so-good days of being FAT as well as the days where surrounding myself in a FAT world is sometimes the best medicine for a broken heart.

It's the honesty in FAT that makes me strong — the willingness to survive as is, to continue to find and respect the genuine support that keeps my body from melting. I may never be rid of the guilt and shame of being FAT, but I know I have more than just a beginning to work with and a body that is willing to stick it out.

My Top 10 Feminist Influences

1. Joan Jett & The Runaways
2. Kathleen Hanna
3. *Rubyfruit Jungle*, R.M. Brown
4. Esther Choi
5. bell hooks
6. Dorothy Allison
7. Huggy Bear
8. Nomy Lamm
9. Kelli Williams
10. *Foxfire*, J. Oates

My Bio

LISA AYUSO, aka Luvmuffin, is a girl with a heart for rock, food and Smooches the cat. She keeps her head high above water by performing air guitar and rock moves in front of a mirror, writing e-mails at work and playing it up on stage with her co-conspirator Traci Rock. She longs to travel more and date her vet. Currently, she works at CBC Radio.

FEMINIST INVITATIONS

Kristen Warder

There have been some complaints
about the lesbian content in this class
she said lumps
forming deeper than throat
quickly washed away by walls of
water dripping
wells of anger filling over-
flowing
spilling
indignation
Rage
Yes I am enraged –
because it is easier than hurting
today
I refuse to be absent
to distort
conform
pretend
reform
no performance
not today.

II

There have been some complaints ...
and I look at the ceiling, the floor,
my empty hands filled
with hatred
hiding

and I want to hide with them
but I can't
I Refuse.
Those words relentless
like water pounding stone
rhythmically surging wearing leaching
mining
under this porous limestone
rind
composure cra ckin g
crumbli
n
g corners of
Eyes peering embarrassed
for me Themselves this world
which does not yet satisfy me
(which instead almost daily
forces me to withdraw my-
selves and regroup)
but I am glad that *this* does not
and I would rather *Them* not
because betrayals whispers erasure
exile
can never be rectified by guilt.
Never.

III

This class
full of feminist
invitations to pretend
thinking up quick tales of boyfriend and
van
on the spot
I'd rather die than belong
to this world
because not belonging to this

is something to be proud of.
It really is.

IV

And there have been some complaints ...
but not *ONE* has been mine
in *Your* special world of
mini vans gum commercials billboards beer commercials
movies soap-operas sit-coms romance novels talk shows poetry
bus advertisements greeting cards newspapers theatre art shows
clothing advertisements fashion magazines airport embraces
pictures in the office posters on the walls songs on the radio
couples on the train sermons in the churches stories heard in
coffee shopsholidayseasonshighschoolreunions40thanniver-
sariesweddingsweddingsweddingsweddings ...
I know it's hard for you
to hear occasionally
that lesbians exist
I *know* ...
You have not heard *me* complaining
and I haven't
because love is something to celebrate
and not just Your love.

V

In one class visible
not invisible
not even for You scared
to face me see me LOOK AT ME GODDAMNIT!!!!!!!
But I know that You do sometimes because
I can feel Eyes boring into back.
Some days this is fine with me
and other days other days ...
dripping off cheeks onto chins onto
reaching hands

that match my own
and understand ...

we just can't understand this ignorance and *hate* doctors and
Oedipal conflicts labelling and asylums rejection and disowning
unless *It's just a stage so We'll get you some help* because *Trust me
honey, you just haven't slept with the right man the right way* – spit
and *Who's the man anyways?* –grin *You must be lyin' because yer
too good-lookin' to be one of them dykes* and GOD, *that's such a
waste of a body like that* because *Girl, the things I could do to you*
but *Ya know, there's really nothing for me to worry about because
everyone knows that all the lipstick lezzies straighten themselves out
and get married someday anyways.*
Someday.

VI

Oh this has been one of those days
when i need to know
where am i are we are you
i can't find
since we can't see
or be seen or know or
let Them know who and what we know
because there is *already* too much
lesbian content in This world –
but where it is today
when i need to find you
and you are hiding
in a dress
at the back of the room

silent.

My Definition of Feminism
A movement that strives to empower all types of women all over the world. Any other agenda is not a feminist agenda.

My Top 10 Feminist Influences

1. Audre Lorde
2. Adrienne Rich
3. Judy Grahn
4. Pat Parker
5. Simone de Beauvoir
6. Virginia Woolf
7. Judy Rebick
8. Susan Gingell
9. Dionne Brand
10. Dorothy Livesay

My Bio

KRISTEN WARDER finished her Master of Arts in English at the University of Calgary in September 1999. She is currently travelling through Asia and preparing to enter a PhD program in English in the fall of 2001. "Feminist Invitations" is the first poem she has written, now over six years ago. Kristen's master's thesis was nominated for a Governor General's Award.

NERVOUS GIRL

Zoe Grace

Drumming my chewed-down fingernails on the counter at work, I'm trying to not to let on how I feel inside, like I'm faced with a fast approaching bus. My heart is racing, my legs are giving out, I feel terror and dizziness, speedy and breathless, lungs like lead and fingers numb. I am certain I might go crazy or collapse. The worst part is that although I am aware that I am being irrational, every moment of this attack feels acutely dangerous. Somehow I am still moving this body that doesn't belong to me, punching numbers on the cash register, trying not to let on how terrified of losing control I am. My neck hurts. I think I'm dying. My bones are de-attached floating under heaps of my skin forgetting to do their very skeletal best. I am jelly and exhaust fumes, scattered bits of memory and fabric. After I hand over the change, I sit down on the milk-crate seat behind the counter, pulling my knees to my heaving chest. I want nothing more than to just run out the door, get in a cab and get home fast, under the covers with my girl-friend, where I am safe.

The worst thing is that after all of this, I won't even have a scar. No proof. I could walk beside you on the street and you wouldn't know that I almost died. I have panic disorder and ago-raphobia, a condition that, like many mood disorders, is misun-derstood and stigmatized. After years of dealing with frequent panic attacks, everything came to a climax that night at work and I knew I couldn't just keep on keeping on without seeking help. What's particularly difficult to handle is that all of my life I've been told that I'm tough. From my grandmother to people I lock eyes with on the street I've been read as independent and capable of a lot of things. I don't like to let many people know that sometimes I'm not able to deal with everyday responsibilities due to an invisible disability. My frustration is paralyzing and affects the way I move around in the world, literally.

Sometimes panic attacks last just five minutes and sometimes five days. They might creep up unsuspecting during an otherwise normal walk about town or I might feel them lurking like a low-grade fever for weeks. Today it's day eighty-five-in-a-row of off-centered panic-ridden weeks. I'm at a breaking point. Leaving my co-worker with a line up of cranky tofu-buying Annex-dwellers, I sprint out the door, attempting to breathe. I need to work more than full-time hours to pay rent, but in this moment I can't see beyond thirty seconds. I know this is the last straw for my boss. She thinks I have cancer or that I'm really irresponsible, constantly giving me looks that are alternately pitying and angry.

When I'm home and safe, I bask lifeless in the glow of *Entertainment Tonight.* John Tesh and Mary Hart put on their sombre face and talk about a serious problem facing many of today's stars. I learn that it's now hip to be diagnosed with panic disorder. Just like borderline personality disorder was in the '70s. Break out the Ativan flavoured lipsmacker. It's the new Gap catch phrase: Everybody Indoors. The only thing Ally McBeal and I have in common. Anxiety disorder. My boss calls and fires me. I don't try to explain, I'm too embarrassed. Secretly I am relieved that I don't have to go back there. There hasn't been a job I haven't had to leave because of my disorder. There are barriers specific to my disability and I've learned to cope with them with the support of invaluable friends and lovers. Along with being queer, it's something I have to contend with in terms of being out.

Sometime people think I'm unreliable because I can't always know ahead of time how capable I'll be of things until the day of. When times are really anxious I need to know that I can leave somewhere if I need to, which can make school and shift work a problem. When I'm planning to take my band on tour, when everyone is making lists of places to play I'm mentally listing off

where the hospitals are in the middle of the Prairies and if someone I'm travelling with can be understanding of my condition.

Most panic attack sufferers eventually hole themselves
up in their house because they associate the attacks with wherever they happen to have them most often: at school, work, in
restaurants, eleva-
tors. So they avoid
taking elevators,
driving, going to
the grocery store. It
gradually moves on
so that they have
them almost every-
where. People who
suffer from panic
disorder usually
develop depression.
The two go hand in
hand. It's awfully
sad-making to be in
your house all the
time, all of your
goals on hold and
your relationships
strained.

My Definition of Feminism

Feminism, in my everyday life, is
something that doesn't often come up
as a word but is always present, lying
low, subtle and challenging. As I grow
older and farther away from Women's
Sudies, my place within feminism
blurs. It was a jumping off point for
the ways I've chosen to live in the
world and the battles I've chosen to
fight. I don't often shout about it
anymore but it's a part of the way I
became who I am. Maybe I'm just
taking a post-teen break. I'm still
planning to be a "Raging Granny."

So I am without a job, waking up briefly to calls from credi-
tors, selling my CDs and books and musical equipment. I stay in
bed. My lover talks me through terrifying moments, and I feel as
though she holds me together. Friends and family lend me money
to stay afloat. I try to find a therapist. I discover that all three of
the sliding-scale therapists I'm referred to don't know what panic
attacks are. I get an art therapist, who looks like Mary Tyler
Moore and suggests drawing in crayons. I sit silently scoffing but
start drawing. I will try anything at this point to avoid feeling this
way. Ms. Art Therapist insists I am dealing with old demons. I
insist my demons are all in check. This is about Now. Getting to
therapist's appointments is a problem. Taking the bus to school is

a problem. It feels physiological, like something in my bones and blood is stopping me from functioning.

I get a student social worker in training at the Gay and Lesbian Youth counselling centre. She is sweet as pie and trying very hard, but she doesn't really know agoraphobia. She says I am brave and I don't believe her. Meanwhile, most days I'm unable to leave the couch until my lover gets home and she takes me to my appointments as though I am four years old. Afraid of the dizzy feeling I get when I open the door, the slanted sense of ill reality I get when faced with my moving body in the world outside my bed.

Ultimately, it's do or die, literally. I owe everybody money, and my lover is as exhausted as I am. More than that, I want to have my life back, the one that didn't terrify me. I seek out everything I can read on panic disorder, braving the self-help aisle in the women's bookstore, once I am calm enough to read a paragraph without pacing. I learn that maybe I am genetically predisposed to it. Maybe it is post-traumatic stress. Maybe I did some questionable drugs once and ever since I can't sit still. Maybe it's a thyroid condition or hypoglycemia.

Whatever it is, it will have to stop because hiding is no longer an option, taking a giant chunk out of my self-esteem, my self-worth and my normal tenacious angry-girl self. I seek out medication and go on welfare; last resorts that help me get out from the worst part of my illness. Psychiatry, which I was formerly against, as a feminist, turned out to be the only thing that was covered by OHIP and as it turned out, was somewhat helpful. Not that I'm going to praise Paxil or my semi-useless homophobic doctor, who said, in a deadpan voice, "People either take medication or they kill themselves." But, in my particular case, the drugs did work in the interim. They gave me back the little jump-start of willpower I needed to make it on my own again.

Evenutally I no longer need Paxil and I can function again without constantly policing everything around me. It's always in the back of my mind though, that it could all just fade fast. That nothing is permanent. After I get a new job, one that I can keep, I hoard all my earnings to cushion myself the next time I fall. Every time I get on the subway and my heart doesn't race I take notice and am thankful. Maybe dealing with homophobic doctors, frustrated teachers and bosses, well-meaning but clueless therapists and, most importantly, my own pride made me stronger in my will to survive. Perhaps I could say this experience showcased the triumph of self-determination. Maybe I might feel even tougher because, other than my incredibly supportive partner, no one made it particularly easy for me. Though I am proud of myself, I do not give into those thoughts. I miss the time I could've had to myself in the last two years. I wonder what I could've accomplished had I been more present and fearless. I wonder if that expensive psychotherapist specialist would've made any difference. I wonder about relationships that could've been different if I wasn't constantly sick. I am amazed to not be afraid of my own life when I wake up, or terrified of the open sky when I walk out my door. I am thankful I am nothing like Ms. McBeal.

My Top 10 Feminist Influences

1. My mom, because in Grade Two I asked her what the word "revolution" meant and she said, "It's what we need, dear."
2. Dorothy Allison, whose book *Skin* made me think I could really be a writer.
3. Amber Haullibaugh, Joan Nestle, Minnie Bruce Pratt, Leslie Mah and all the other femmes who wrote femme history so fierce and whose writing, art/music and activism have allowed me to proudly strut in heels and be powerful and queer.
4. The band Fifth Column, especially their song, "All Women are Bitches," 7 Year Bitch "Dead Men Don't Rape" and Bikini Kill all

turned me on to feminism when I was seventeen and ready to rawk.

5. Hothead Paisan.

6. Spike and Lucy from *Degrassi Jr. High;* Jo from the *Facts of Life;* and *Roseanne.*

7. The teachers at the New School of Dawson College in Montreal who made me read both Andrea Dworkin and Annie Sprinkle, leaving me confused but sharpening my debating skills.

8. Thelma and Louise.

9. All the grrrl collectives I ever grew to hate but that taught me a lot in the process.

10. The zine *Doris* by Cindy Gretchen Ovenrack.

My Bio

ZOE GRACE is the semi-alias for a Toronto journalist and fiction writer who is working on her first book of poetry and constantly rewriting a novel in the works. "Nervous Girl" is dedicated to Willy Scott.

PRANK CALLER

Sarmishta Subramanian

The prank caller is Sri Lankan. I know this because he asks if I am. It's the flash of recognition I know from encounters on city buses, trains and hinterland malls in this home away from "the country." There's also the accent he wears, perhaps shamefully, perhaps proudly, like a flag. He tells me his name (unusual in a prank caller), first only. I don't tell him mine, but he already knows it, of course, last only, pried from the pages of a phone book, a long line of Subramanians from which I don't come.

Really, he is not a prank caller. He makes harassing, though not obscene phone calls, but this sounds more sinister, and so I think of him as a prank caller. His dialogue is familiar. Hi. How are you? Not a very rude caller, he asks the same questions always. Hi. How are you? What are you doing? *Enne seyerengo?* Sometimes he talks to me, sometimes he leaves messages, the soft, barely audible messages of a tentative prank caller, usually in Tamil, sometimes in English, but always with the cadence of his own language. Like a Bollywood playback singer, switching tongues for each lip-synching film actor, Hindi to Tamil, Tamil to Telugu: the transliterated words can be read but the cadence gives her away.

I half wonder if my cadence gives me away. I have no accent, of course. I have been fully assimilated for thirteen years now. I came to Canada when I was fourteen, lost my accent by fifteen. I was easily suggestible and possess a good ear for sound. Now, even the giveaway words don't catch me. *Can't,* short a. *Father,* long a. *Harper,* no aspiration on the p. If in doubt, stress the first syllable. It's a science, really. You don't get good at it if you are British or French and transplanted. (It's too useful to hang on to the open-mouthed vowels, the paper-thin T's, the serpentine sibilants.) You might rely on it if you are white South African, liberal and embarrassed, unless you lie well, also a science, and say convincingly that the accent is Australian. The caller, Ramesh, is no good at either science, it seems. But he may know a good student when he hears one.

It is not an unknown trick among some communities of new immigrants. You haul out the telephone book and look up the Smiths and Browns of your homeland — Patel, Singh, Subramanian — and call them. Often, it is not actually a trick at all. There are the callers who ask for money, and those who ask for assistance. I've even heard stories about family friends who have received telephone calls from perfect strangers who were homesick or lonely and plucked their names from the matrix of a New World telephone directory, just to chat.

There can be a camaraderie among those who share a language or a nation. In 1966, when my uncle came here, twenty-four and penniless but intellectually gifted and blessed with a brash, can-do individualism rare in the South Indian Brahmin, he shared his first apartment with a Sikh he met at the pizza place next door. A few months later, he sat at a community dinner and overheard the conversation, in Tamil, of the couple two rows ahead of him. He introduced himself, and inferred from the rosary-list of friends and relations they went through that he was a distant relative. (But then, in India, everybody is a distant relative.) They became friends. Once, he was tipped off about a job by a South Indian he had just met on a streetcar. At the job interview, the company's manager, a white Canadian who was pleased with his South Indian employees, asked if he spoke Tamil. Because he did, he was hired. I know all this and so cannot help but feel my connection to the elderly stranger on the subway, dressed in a salwar and Nehru cap, who offers me a piece of the orange he is eating. Or to the young man with the moustache and the brown polyester pants, who is walking up Toronto's Christie Street a few steps ahead of me. Or even, I confess in my weaker moments, to my repeat caller with his slight, young voice and his polite phone calls. They all give off Indian-ness, that quality that my family taught me at a very young age, and that I know by sight or sound.

I know from a different sense the longing and the loneliness that can come from being in a still-foreign country, and I can sense it in them. After all, I too know Pakistan from India from Sri Lanka, Gujarathi from Telugu from Malayali. I know the geography of movement — that flight across the Atlantic, twenty-six hours total, including the six-hour stopover

My Definition of Feminism

At various points in my life, I've defined feminism as a personal philosophy, a mathematical equation that explains why girls are better than boys, a social equation that explains why women are powerful or powerless, and a governing principle behind my choice of footwear. Feminism is still some of that for me, but it's often subtler and wrapped up in my personal identity, my world view, my social identity and my ideas about race, sexuality and politics.

in Frankfurt, where you window shop at the duty-free stores and tumble into sleep on airport seats. I know the longing for chikkoo and jackfruit and the *dhaka paratha,* delicate as filigree, that will never be known outside the small corridor of West Bengal and Bangladesh, and for aunts and uncles and grandfathers who are, in growing numbers, not just distant but gone. All since you left.

There can be an instant and blind camaraderie among those whose banner is their skin. Except if their other banner is gender. Then a "What part of India are you from?" on a subway platform easily segues into "Where is your house?" An innocent "Which way is Kipling Station?" quickly becomes "You are very beautiful." And a "Hi, how are you?" on the telephone suggests so much more. And so, sympathy thrown aside, I have fended off such "compliments" from scrawny, young men and from well-fed, middle-aged men. The encounters cut across class lines and state borders: Sri Lankan, Sikh, kurta-clad, suited and booted, any man may strike. I am approached more often when my hair is longer, but I get them skirt or jeans, lipstick or none.

Any man may strike. How paranoid it sounds. But the prospect is something all women endure, to varying degrees. And I get it from other men too — old Portuguese men outside coffee shops or young cats on the prowl in souped-up Hondas. But those encounters give me less to wrestle with. To roll my eyes or say something flip: that is the only question. It is different when it is one of your own. Then, the skin becomes a marker of another sort of power; loyalty, nostalgia, compassion, scorn and pride jostle for space. When I enter a subway car and see this breed of South Asian male on board, I am immediately reminded that I am both South Asian and female. I have always been Indian, and I have always been a woman. They are both identities I am proud to wear. Except when they are someone else's passport to freedom — the freedom to look me over, sidle up and flirt! Or to the silent compliment — that special, racially pure kind of leer you gather when you are both female and, as they say, ethnic. It's the gaze I remember from a gaggle of streetside Romeos in Delhi's crowded Janpath shopping district, or from the man in line behind me under the feverish heat of an Agra sun to see one of the seven wonders of the world who gropes me while he waits. (How striking I must be to compare so favourably with the Taj!) It has followed me all the way here. And here, as there, it tells me my place, where I belong.

I suppose that's what I want to tell the caller: You are making a mistake. That isn't where I belong. I'm a feminist, for Christ's sake. I've been one for more than twenty years. I grew up in the shadow of 1970s North American feminism. "Eve-teasing is a crime," proclaimed billboards across New Delhi, the arcane equivalent of sexual harassment laws, which still haven't quite made their way there. I have a vivid memory of racing around my grandparents' yard with my girl cousins, screaming at the boys, who had thrown some dismissive childhood insult in our direction. We were spouting something like this: "We are women's libbers. Don't dare talk to us like that, you pigs! Women's lib! Women's lib!" I was nine. I can be forgiven my confusion with the language. And my cousins and I did have all the "stridence" that sports commentators and neo-conservative columnists everywhere seem to associate with real, unshaven, bra-burning feminists.

Home, thankfully, was a small shelter from the constraints of both the old world and the new. None of us discovered these notions of "a woman's place," an achievement of parents, but also of aunts, uncles and grandparents. I suppose a prank caller could have broken through, but pranks are not much fun when you have to pay the few-rupees-a-minute charge to make the call.

Part of it was privilege, I admit, though it was the privilege of education, not wealth. No one in my family owned a house, but four of my five aunts had doctorates. And so at a time when many girls were expected to fall gracefully into the domestic world, I was encouraged (occasionally coerced) to read Jane Austen and George Eliot. At a time when many South Indian families were still putting a girl "out of doors" when she was on her period (during those "unclean" days, she would be confined to one room and barred from handling food, taking a bath — no wonder they were unclean days! — and even touching anyone else), my cousins and I were dressing down MCPs (a popular term for Male Chauvinist Pigs), younger and older, with stories about matriarchal societies in Kerala.

We were decidedly middle-class and not all that "modern" — obedience was the ultimate filial virtue, alcohol was sin, and sex, well, sex was something that went unnoticed except when you observed its fecund and wildly sensuous depictions on temple murals in South India, and marvelled at the artistic triumph. Still, while I had several friends whose first experience of their physicality was the shock of blood staring back at them in the bathroom, uninvited and unexplained, my mother, surprisingly, gave me the eggs-travelling-down-the-Fallopian-tubes routine.

But privilege was only part of it. I was also lucky enough to grow up in a place, for all the "backwardness" one hears about here, where girls were the top students in my science and math classes and there were no shapely dolls bemoaning arithmetic's insurmountable challenges. Lipstick and bras and boys were the stuff of Judy Blume books, and who read those? Indira Gandhi (for all her appalling political notions) was the prime minister for the first several years of my childhood. The idea of a woman as the head of anything never seemed that strange. Corollary: the idea of woman as object (never subject, never owning verbs) seemed preposterous. It's true that the brash, noisy filmic creations of Bollywood (and its lesser, regional counterparts) had no shortage of comely, feminine heroines bursting with sexual ripeness — literally, since on-screen kisses were disallowed and they had to resort to nuzzling peaches and caressing trees. But at least as far as I was concerned, that was film — trashy, low-brow, unreal. Every actor, man or woman, was also blessed with the voice of Mohammad Rafi or Lata Mangeshkar and they all gyrated equally around fountain and waterfall. It was, mostly, equal-opportunity objectification. In short, I never identified "femaleness" within the context, and constant threat, of the sexual gaze. That was an introduction I got later, after I came here.

You do not engage prank callers for long on the telephone. It tells you that on page 23 of the telephone book, the most basic training system. You hang up quickly, you don't act flustered and you never keep talking. This is not in the guidelines, but when you get a harassing call, you may also find yourself checking your windows. You will slant the blinds away from the street, cinch your curtains together, write the item "clothespins" on your mental shopping list. You don't do this the first time, of course, but if you have a regular harasser, your steady connection to creepdom, you don't take chances. You hang up the phone, you stand away from the glass. Refuse to be seen.

If the caller calls again, you hang up right away. Then if the phone rings again, you stop answering it. The ringer sends its signals off into the dead-letter voicemail box, you edge closer to total silence. Or you leave it off the hook. Disconnect the phone, disconnect yourself. The visible minority turns invisible. A friend tells me after the tenth or eleventh call that I should just get my number unlisted. I hate the thought. It is only practical but it bothers me. This isn't a stalker, there isn't any threat of violence; if there were, I'd vanish from view in a second. As it is, I'm just supposed to disappear off the urban map because a guy calls me all the time to ask how I am? How will old friends find me? How will people know I still live in this city or even exist? Why become invisible?

Invisibility can sometimes mean invincibility. I have tried my hand at that in various small ways in my persecution-complex days. I was in my twenties, reading about feminism and getting mad at the world. Catharine MacKinnon was on my reading list. I'd listen to my Walkman on the subway, wearing my sunglasses, feeling invisible, or making other people disappear by looking through them. When a friend said he bought the theory that all sex was a form of rape, I came to agree. I abandoned that primitive, fumbling women's libber within and traded power for social awareness. And I felt more helpless than I'd ever felt in my life.

I've since realized it's not that much fun to be invisible, or angry. Unfortunately, I like talking to strangers, I like the random conversation about *Lolita* and Richardson on the streetcar, and I like the tiny thrills of a smile or a nod from a beautiful boy across the aisle, at least when I can return it. So these days I have given up a little on my Naomi Wolf routine. (After all, even Naomi Wolf has given up on the Naomi Wolf routine, in favour of mawkish sexual memoir.) I am still a feminist, but I am no longer oppressed by every two-bit Lothario with a functional pair of eyes. A "hey baby" as I walk a downtown street doesn't feel like the entire patriarchy marching out and flattening me. A scantily clad, finely paid bimbo on a billboard isn't the Atlas of my gender, all but felled by the weight of her own sexualized, objectified image, and crying out for help from her billboard home. It's a good thing too: the Patriarchy is a big thing to be up against all on your own. It can become impossible to speak when you feel it's the whole System you're up against.

Mine isn't a perfect arrangement. If I have stopped feeling so defeated by my gender in recent years, I have sometimes achieved that at the expense of my ethnicity. I give myself permission to fake it. When a young lech from my country asks if I am from India, I say, simply: No. I am not. Nope, do not speak the language. I have never been there. My parents? No, not them either. It's absurd, of course. But if the spark of a connection ends up being a threat, you disconnect. It's an effective silencer for them, and, unfortunately, for me too.

Of course, my harassing caller makes it easy. I don't even have to lie: I am not Sri Lankan (though the language is the same and I do disown the tongue, pretend to not understand him). He is on the phone, so I test my power. I press star-69 to retrieve his phone number, write it on a Post-it and slap it on my computer screen, a weapon ready to be brandished at any moment. "What the hell is this?" I sputter once and hang up. He doesn't call back for weeks. I know I would defeat him if I just used the trump card — a racial slur. Listen, you Paki, get lost. I don't know who you think you're calling. (I practise it in my head with a *Dukes of Hazzard* voice.) I know it would work. I can't, of course, do it. Even in the gender versus ethnicity battle, that would be foul play.

So I'm not quite sure who's winning. But for now, I don't get my number unlisted. The calls have not grown in number, the message hasn't changed, so for now, I leave things the way they are. Perhaps my friend is right: I am letting things escalate and shouldn't be so foolhardy. And perhaps, if the caller had a different accent, I wouldn't be. If he called repeatedly to say: How are you? And are you from Morocco, Italy, Red River, Alberta? I might be more scared. As it is, some part of me understands. I have to. The calls, when they come, also seem to bother me less. He calls, I hang up, he calls, I hang up, he calls. I bring down my blinds over the dusk-lit cityscape and turn up the stereo.

My Top 10 Feminist Influences
(plus one, chronologically)

1. My mother and her five sisters who grew up in 1950s India and studied Hegel, female saints in South India and the Japanese economy. Also my grandmother, who has probably read five times as much as I can ever hope to read in my lifetime.
2. Jo from *Little Women,* George Eliot and Jane Austen.
3. Probably on some level, the pantheon of female Hindu deities and folk heroes (after all, Durga rides a tiger and Parvati created her son all by herself).
4. Kerala's matriarchal societies, which I heard about when I was young and thought were so cool.
5. Toni Morrison, Zora Neale Hurston, Jean Rhys who pointed me towards the interrelationships of feminism and race.
6. Camille Paglia, Katie Roiphe and gang, who made me so furious with their faux feminism that really cemented my own beliefs.
7. Punk rock girls (not womyn) like Kim Gordon of Sonic Youth.
8. Naomi Wolf, Andrea Dworkin, Catharine MacKinnon (for a time), Vandana Shiva and Dionne Brand.
9. Katha Pollitt, who writes with such a marvellous, acerbic sense of humour.
10. Hothead Paisan, crazed lesbian comic-book hero who is so fearless and insane and violent and crushes fratboy homophobic types in the streets.
11. Jeannette Winterson, whom I first encountered when a friend read me passages from *Oranges Are Not The Only Fruit,* over the phone, long-distance from Japan.

My Bio

SARMISHTA SUBRAMANIAN works for *Saturday Night Magazine.* She has also been an editor at *Chatelaine* and *This Magazine,* two entities not often spoken of in one sentence.

Part III

SCHOOLING FEMINISMS:
Big Brained Girls
Crack the Codes
with Chainsaws

— Alison Davis davisalison@hotmail.com

The following piece is excerpted from the zine "The Personal is Political"

THE PERSONAL IS POLITICAL

Emmy   Pantin

Do you remember being a kid and you were angry about something? Maybe you didn't get your way, or you were in pain. Remember you didn't have the words to articulate your anger, but it was still there, and you were swept away in rage, so you screamed and you screamed and you screamed till you thought you were going to explode? Remember your mother or whoever was looking after you at that moment would ask you to tell her or him or them what was wrong and you couldn't, you didn't have the words; it's not like you stubbed your toe; this was bigger than that? So you just screamed.

I remember being five years old and not being able to express to my mother what was going on when she left me alone to be looked after by my cousins and brothers. I had no access to words like "child abuse." I just screamed. And she would hold onto me and say "ok" and take me out for walks or to the movies. I would calm down but that rage never went away, nor did the terror that came with it. I remember being at school and screaming and screaming at other kids who called me names because I was an immigrant, left me out because I couldn't speak English, told me I smelled and that I was dirty because my skin was brown. I remember standing in the school yard screaming.

When I got older I had access to a bigger vocabulary, but I still couldn't articulate why I was so angry, and I would find myself in the depths of a rage and a terror I didn't fully understand, and I would scream, only when I screamed I would scream these words: "I just want to go home!" When I was ten or eleven I would weep and scream and I still didn't have the words to express what was happening to me, though I was already a theorist; I knew something was wrong, and I knew what I needed to do to fix it. I needed to go home, but there remained an overwhelming and confusing problem: I was already at home.

bell hooks talks about her childhood and how she felt like she didn't belong because she refused to accept beatings from her father as a natural consequence of undesirable behaviour. She refused to accept what she now calls "patriarchal norms" in her house and questioned her parents all the time about their choices and behaviour, and her mother would look at her as if she were from Mars. She found a sanctuary in theory and through theory she could understand what was happening to her and imagine a world where these things didn't have to happen[1].

[1] bell hooks, "Theory as Liberatory Practise."
p. 60-61

4

When I was three I left my home, the place I was born, the house I was born in for another country. I left because my mum was escaping both a repressive home life (my father was abusive) and a repressive public life (we were in Argentina during the Junta period, and my mum was afraid of becoming one of the disappeared). We went to Brazil and were homeless for two years. When I was five, we came to Canada and moved into a one bedroom apartment with my grandmother. I was told that we were home, but there has always been a part of me that has never really felt at home both in Canada or within my family.

I could only speak Portuguese, while the rest of my family spoke only English. My interactions with my family were mediated through my mother; I would whisper to her in Portuguese and she would respond either by helping me get what I needed or laughing at my jokes or whatever was appropriate. One of my cousins was so angry at this behaviour that she would punish me in private, when I was left in her care. She hated what she saw as my refusal to normalize, to communicate with her or anyone else, and I was terrified to try, for fear that my English would be laughed at or misunderstood. I spent a lot of my childhood feeling like I was being laughed at. I felt a terror and a rage which I was unable to articulate, and I expressed a lot of that through screaming.

Sinéad O'Connor, in an interview in Spin Magazine, said that she thought the root of the world's problems was child abuse. Child abuse takes the form that the Children's Aid Society calls child abuse, but is not limited to hitting, screaming and sexual assault. Child abuse is the attack of a child's self-esteem, their emotional well-being, their sense of themselves as an agent in the world able to make choices. Racism, sexism, homophobia, ableism, poverty, corporate globalization, war: these things are all child abuse and leave traumatic scars on the psychic field of a child's mind. bell hooks (I really like her) talks about being a kid and walking to her grandmother's house, and the terror of travelling through white neighbourhoods to get there.[2] Whiteness was a terror, racism is a terror imprinted in a child's mind. It's not something you ever forget.

2 bell hooks, "Representing Whiteness in the Black Imagination." p. 334.

What we're talking about here is the gaze, the frame, who has control of the discourse, what can be said and what can't be said. Foucault (I like him a lot too) talks about this thing called a Panopticon. A panopticon is a type of prison with cells that circle a tower in the middle. Guards are located in the tower and watch the prisoners and watch the prisoners at all times, but the prisoners can't see the guards. This produces a disturbing situation where, after a while, it's not even necessary to have guards in the tower at all, because prisoners start "watching" themselves. [3] The terror of being punished causes people to police themselves.

One of the most rigid experiences of policing I've even encountered in my life was inflicted by my self on my self. When I was about thirteen I was terrified that people would figure out that my biggest crush wasn't on Johnny Dep or John Cusack or the boy in my math class, but on my best friend who was a girl. I was so terrified of getting caught in the act of being a dyke, a queer, a freak, that I applied strict codes to my behaviour. I decided what things were "queer" and what things weren't. Not only did I force myself not to act in ways that were queer, but also to act in ways that were as far away from queer as I could get.

3 Michel Foucault, "From Michel Foucault Discipline andPunish." p. 85.

9

What I mean is, I went crazy heterosexual. I remember being at a Teen Dance when I was thirteen, and forcing myself to dance with a boy, weeping the whole way through. Althusser talks about how what he calls Ideological State Apparatuses (schools, churches, courtrooms, the media and in this case a teen dance) "hail" us as concrete individuals, and we respond in an appropriate way. "We are always already subjects."[4] The teen dance wanted me to behave in a specific way; I already knew how I was supposed to behave. I knew dancing with a girl would NOT be cool.

After the dance I felt violated and I screamed. I couldn't understand what was going on, and my friend kept telling me, "If you didn't want to dance with him you didn't have to. Why'd you do it if you didn't want to?" I knew why I did it, but I couldn't tell her. I just said, "I had to dance with him. I had to." I couldn't say no because I was supposed to want to say yes, and I was in danger twenty-four/seven of being discovered. I knew if was discovered I'd be punished. When I read about the panopticon, I knew exactly what those prisoners felt like.

4 Louis Althusser, "Louis Althusser from 'Ideology and Ideological State Apparatuses. (1970)." pg. 55.

10

My experience in the world is sexualized, racialized and gendered. All the ideas about what it means to have my skin colour, be a girl, and same sex desires are applied to me and hail me to understand myself in a certain way. Edward Said (another really smart person) talks about how the identity of "the Oriental" is constructed not only by the West, but how "the Oriental" constructs himself in response to the West 5. A lot of that is internalizing the notions of what it means to be different, an Other. Some of that is self-policing, and some is resistance. For a long time I defined myself as a lesbian woman of colour, in an attempt to resist and reject the label "Spic dyke." It's important to name ourselves, cause as Foucault says naming is power and whoever has control of discourse has power, but I've laid off calling myself a lesbian woman of colour, mostly because I'm still defining myself against what's in the center: the white male heterosexual, and I don't want to do that any more.

5 Edward W. Said, "Orientalism". p. 89.

11

LA QUERENCIA ★

It is too warm to see
breath curling out of hot wet nostrils
an animal pounding a hoof at the
packed dirt to say
                    I am wounded
                    I am wounded
The bullfighter reigns supreme in this contest
The bull, on the other hand, stands
with spears and flares and dust and stands
alive.
        This is what this means:
                LA QUERENCIA: this is the place
                                     this is the place where the bull
                                     stands wounded and gathers
                            his wits about him
On my way outta here
        I pass:
                so many concrete landscapes
                I offered my life to
                when I was feeling particularly down
and so many street corners I never kissed you on
and so many corners I did.

                I saw her on her porch
and ran into her on the street in front of
Le Chateau/The Gap/Club Monaco
I was gonna say I've been in this city 96 hours and I never stopped running
but what I really mean is my feet hit the ground running before I was even born
    ...beacoup a ete decide avant de votre naissance...
                    This is as much my mother's story as it is mine
Don't cry for me Argentina
The truth is....
The truth is this:
        I left because of my daddy
        I left because of the Junta
        I left because of Los Madres de La Plaza de Mayo
        I left because of my mother had other places to go
How do I get back to Argentina?
More to the point: what do I do when I am there?
LA QUERENCIA:
        the sweet spot in the ring
        the safe space
This is the place where I stand
This is the place where I attempt so many breathless tactics
It's too hot to see them

Everything everything in this city
is an echo.

by Emmy

My Definition of Feminism

In the dictionary, it might say something about the movement towards political, social and economic equality between men and women The gang of girls I work with just finished a zine on feminism, and they added things to the definition including beauty, power of choice, power to stand up for yourself. I think that the main thing for me is that feminism has always boiled down to choice. For everyone to have a chance to make choices, lots of things have to be addressed, and feminism has always been about making choices.

My Top 10 Feminist Influences

1. My best friend in high school, Martha MacDonald. She taught me everything a seventeen-year-old needed to know about feminism, including buying me my first copy of *Backlash* by Susan Faludi for my birthday.
2. My mom, because she's a grassroots activist hero.
3. bell hooks because she's the kind of writer and activist and thinker I'd like to be.
4. Sinéad O'Connor validated my right to be angry and to resist. I will always have an emotional response to her voice whenever I hear it.
5. Maggie and Hopey from *Love and Rockets*. I know this comic is drawn by a boy, but he created two of the coolest, punk rockinest chicana girls ever to grace the pages of a graphic novel. I really related to these girls as a teenager.
6. Riot Grrrl and DIY feminism. I love zines, Bikini Kill, Kathleen Hannah et al.
7. *Daddy* by Sylvia Plath. Again, a validation of my anger and a call to speak up.
8. My first summer job was working on a young women's magazine called *Venus*. When I was about twelve or thirteen years old, I helped to start the girls group that created *Venus* because a zealous youth worker named Kate grabbed me and said, "You wanna start a girls' group?" Thanks Kate!
9. *Ms. Magazine*, *Bitch Magazine* and all the excellent feminist journalists and activists in the world.
10. All the kick-ass girls I meet everyday.

My Bio

EMMY PANTIN enjoys writing, sewing and bouncing around her living room to Sonny and Cher records. She's living and working in Thunder Bay, Ontario, at a youth centre. She's doing anti-racist workshops and hangin' with the Rev girls making zines and DIY feminism.

BETTY FRIEDAN'S GRANDDAUGHTERS:

Cosmo, Ginger Spice & the Inheritance of Whiteness

Jennifer Harris

It is now almost forty years since the publication of Betty Friedan's *The Feminine Mystique*, the little book that spoke so compellingly to the North American white suburban housewife. It is, however, not fashionable to talk about *The Feminine Mystique* in young feminist circles today. We are too well aware of its shortcomings, its almost exclusive focus on the problems of middle- and upper-middle-class white women, and its blindness to women who did not fit into its neat analysis, for any number of factors the book overlooks, and it admittedly overlooked a lot. Similarly, it is also not fashionable in young feminist circles to talk about the granddaughters of Friedan's women — often still white, still suburban, still privileged, and mostly still heterosexual, but still women — unless it is to bemoan their perceived politics. Nevertheless, the women Friedan influenced, educated and in possession of the leisure time to analyze their own lives, helped galvanize the women's movement in the 1960s. We cannot afford to overlook their inheritors today. But just what kind of inheritance is it?

I find myself asking this question a lot recently. Not that I quite fit the Friedan profile: one grandmother was a farm widow, the other a divorcée with nine children to support. Moreover, my formative years were definitely not spent among the secure middle- and upper-middle-classes, though I later commuted across town to join their ranks and attend a "better" high school. While this "joining" was never quite successful — joining is, after all, dependent upon being accepted, and outsiders are never easily accepted — the experience certainly did give me the skills that I can use today to pass as someone from a secure middle-class background and acquire the related privileges. I am aware that my being white has a lot to do with this acceptance, but I am not sure that I would have been as aware of this had I not, for a period of my life, felt like an outsider who was quite literally from "the wrong side" of town. Nor do I think that I would have aligned myself with feminism so openly if I had not already felt alienated by class differences. I think it is more likely that I would have settled into the world of whiteness with little discomfort. (Instead, my work today is explicitly concerned with how categories of otherness function for certain turn-of-the-century women writers in their relation to a mythical "white" and male America.) It is this same whiteness that I would suggest Friedan's granddaughters have inherited as part of their feminist legacy.

After years of astute critiques of whiteness and power by African-American authors and critics, whiteness has finally received significant critical attention in North America, or at least in the academy.[1] This is in no small part due to the influence of authors like Toni Morrison, whose 1993 publication *Playing in the Dark: Whiteness and the Literary Imagination* called upon white critics to recognize the role of an unacknowledged Africanist presence in shaping constructions of whiteness in American literature and culture. Recent publications dedicated to whiteness include the anthologies *Whiteness: A Critical Reader; Off White: Readings on Race, Power and Society; Critical White Studies: Looking Behind the Mirror* and *White Trash: Race and Class in America.* There are also the works of Ruth Frankenberg, David Roediger, Noel, Richard Dyer and Theodore Allen, as well as several special issues of journals, most notably *Transition.*[2]

Nevertheless, whiteness remains largely undefined, unrecognized and amorphous for those most in possession of it. The work of sociologist Charles A. Gallagher demonstrates that the majority of educated young whites today perceive of themselves as racially neutral members of a colour-blind society. While identity politics has made whiteness a visual racial category, working- and middle-class whites do not see themselves as benefit-ing from their skin colour.[3] In fact, asking whites to define whiteness is like asking a fish to tell you the colour of water: people general-ly don't see what is taken for granted. Peggy McIntosh's 1988 article "White Privilege and Privilege: A Personal Account of Coming to See Correspondences through Work in Women's Studies" has been influential in its unpacking of what McIntosh describes as a "knapsack" of white privileges that are often invisi-ble to whites.[4] Likewise, in *Cultural Etiquette: A Guide for the Well-Intentioned,* Amoja Three Rivers directs attention to behav-iours that many whites may perceive as "neutral" but are in fact highly racially charged.[5] However, as Gallagher's research demon-strates, these publications and others like them have had little influence on how educated whites see themselves. This is as true for educated white women as it is for their male counterparts. Both are apt to see themselves as "human beings" first and foremost, before seeing themselves as white, gendered and classed.

> ## My Definition of Feminism
>
> In an ideal world, a responsible and accountable investigation of power, particularly women's relationships to it, in all kinds of contexts, and a commitment to expose or labour against inequitable power relations wherever possible.

This rhetoric of individualism disturbs me for all kinds of reasons. In North America, individualism has historically been a white privilege, for instance. The American political ethos, which so nobly enshrined the individual's right to "life, liberty, and the pursuit of happiness," did not extend those rights or the ability to vote on them to its full population.[6] Furthermore, the constitu-tion decreed that some individuals, being African Americans,

197

were in fact not individuals at all, but rather only 3/5ths human. Canada also wants to forget that it too supported the right of the individual to own human property and denied the vote to all sorts of "individuals," including women. Women are now "persons" (thank you so much, Judge Emily Murphy),[7] but being granted the legal rights of an "individual" does not mean that the door was opened all the way, or that it necessarily remained propped open for those who might follow. Finally, the way in which the mainstream has taken up "individualism," particularly as it relates to women and "women's liberation," concerns me.

Of course we all have our critiques of how the mainstream entertainment industries perpetuate dated and dangerous stereotypes and myths without addressing the critiques from outside the industry. It is probably impossible for most young feminists to watch an hour or two of "must-see TV" without at least one twinge of impatience. I am primarily interested in the select ways the mainstream media have chosen to incorporate aspects of feminist critiques, beginning with the 1960s, focusing on women's "articulation of the individual self" through the assertion of financial independence and that now almost clichéd phrase, "sexual liberation." The first concerns me because financial independence has become just another way to sell goods to women. Betty Friedan astutely pointed out in 1963 that "the really important role that women serve as housewives is to buy more things for the house,"[8] taking up the slack of terminated defence contracts after the Second World War. Friedan's granddaughters, however, are encouraged to articulate their individualism through their purchasing power. They must attest to their belonging to the American Dream (just as prevalent in Canada as south of the border) by buying more stuff.[9] But not just any stuff: stuff that will demonstrate that they belong and that they are free, sexually and financially. Is it any wonder that Martha Stewart now publicly trades her very practised whiteness on the New York Stock Exchange?

One only has to turn to the largest selling women's magazine in North America to see how important selling a particular kind of female identity to a particular target market is to our economy. With over 2.5 million subscribers, twenty-nine international editions and over $156 million in advertising revenue per year, *Cosmo,* like it or not, dominates the market. White, and sexy in its whiteness, it has its roots in the same period as *The Feminine Mystique* and an appeal to the same white middle-classes.[10] One year before Friedan published her self-advertised "controversial bestseller," Helen Gurley Brown published the now infamous *Sex and the Single Girl,* which would quickly lead to her editorial transformation of *Cosmopolitan* into the racy *Cosmo* of the 1970s. According to Dawn H. Currie in *Girl Talk: Adolescent Magazines and Their Readers,* Brown's *Cosmo* targets a generation of newly liberated heterosexual women and "promotes 'entrepreneurial femininity' as a developed skill that helps every woman get what she wants, in part through manipulation of her sexuality and physical appearance." As *The New York Times* quipped, *Cosmo* offers "half a feminist message" to women who wouldn't even have that otherwise.[11]

Known for its covers of cleavage, cleavage, and — if at all possible — more cleavage, the contemporary *Cosmo* encourages young women to have fun while being phenomenally dressed, and undressed. And while their readership is obviously not uniformly white and financially privileged, there is little acknowledgement in *Cosmo* of issues that might be specific to women who are not in this category, or to genuinely encourage consideration of women outside this category. This is not to say that contemporary young heterosexual women might not find this "reflection" of their ideal self as defined by sex, money and whiteness somewhat troublesome, but 2.5 million subscribers clearly find something redeeming in this magazine and others like it, not to mention "must-see TV." I'm not sure that it isn't precisely this vision of sex, money and whiteness that sells *Cosmo,* at least to those of Friedan's granddaughters who subscribe. After all, it is difficult to move beyond this popular definition of the female individual, precisely because it does not challenge in any substantial or meaningful way the power relations that govern North American society. And, after all, doesn't an "admit one" ticket always makes the recipient feel special?

Is it any surprise then, that in the late 1990s, there is a

199

sudden wave of nostalgia for all of those "innocuous" signifiers of male privilege? All of the sudden Playboy Bunnies are back, they're hot, and it's all the rage for young male Hollywood stars to be photographed at the Playboy Mansion with Hugh Hefner. Hef is hip, and it seems some men are never too young or old to be enthused about having one's face photographed sandwiched between the ample white breasts of women who have, I suspect, been invited to the party precisely because of their ample white breasts: boys are apparently still entitled to be boys until they die. (This probably explains the success of the restaurant chain "Hooters" in the U.S. and Canada.)[12] However, more interesting than the male nostalgia for Bunnies, are the recent documentaries and books produced by former Bunnies, directed towards women, and aired and discussed on women's cable networks. In them, women wax nostalgically and uncritically about the ways in which being a Bunny empowered them. They are, for the most part, white and financially successful women, and I suspect that is probably why they have received so much press. What tales would those unsuccessful Bunnies have to tell, or perhaps those rare Bunnies of colour?

We don't need this nostalgia, however, to inform us that the mainstream continues to feed its female consumers a "half feminism" no different than the type promoted by Brown in *Sex and the Single Girl,* and moreover that they listen. After all, we have Monica Lewinsky, whose behaviour in her affair with Bill Clinton was straight out of the section on conduct in adulterous affairs included in Brown's 1962 advice manual. However, the public appears to have "forgiven" Monica her indiscretion, despite their overwhelming disapproval of adultery in opinion polls. She has been championed as "everyone's daughter" (read: white middle-class America) and has been forgiven on this basis. Some might say this public acceptance of Lewinsky indicates that female sexual liberation is complete. Maybe for the white middle classes: I would challenge them to consider how the media coverage allotted Lewinsky would have differed had she been a young African-American woman, rather than a young white woman. One only has to look to the public representation of Professor Anita Hill to know how much better off Betty Friedan's granddaughters are than, say, Jesse Fauset's or W.E.B. DuBois's granddaughters.[13] *Cosmo* may have secured "public" sexual liberation for middle- and upper-class white women, but it hasn't done much for anyone else. Will *Cosmo Girl* have anything to offer to Professor Hill's daughters?

Yes, that's right. In August 1999 *Cosmo* launched a junior magazine, *Cosmo Girl,* targeting teenage girls whose buying power had been demonstrated once and for all by the popularity of the movie *Titanic.*[14] Boasting articles like "Turn your Crush Into Your Boyfriend" and a horoscope section that promises to deliver "Love and Life Tips," the magazine is exclusively about boys, fashion and makeup. One section includes boys discussing what they don't find attractive in girls, and another directs you to their Web site where you can rate a featured male. Like its parent magazine, it is resolutely white and middle-class, and perpetuates individual identity through clothing and boys. In the midst of the Spice-Girl phenomena this is not unusual. "Girl Power," co-opted from the Riot Grrrl movement, has come to mean for many young girls encountering it for the first time the celebration of "girl things": fun tied to conventional definitions of femininity that is often dependent upon consumption. In its mainstream permutations it cannot be confused with feminism: even the former Ginger Spice, Geri Halliwell, describes "feminism" as "a dirty word." However, less "serious" than feminism, Girl Power is playful and does not "threaten boys."[15] While *Cosmo Girl* is not explicitly anti-feminist, it does not offer young girls information about non-fashion issues specific to women. This lack of information remains consistent in "less salacious" girls' magazines like *Jump* and *MXG,* which, while offering more informative articles, still prominently feature boys and makeup. In fact, *MXG* only features clothes that are sold through its Web site, and despite its inclusion on magazine racks and its articles on activities like skydiving (or maybe because of them) it is ultimately a catalogue targeting affluent teen girls.

Whatever else the market is selling these young women, however, sex remains central.

This misguided centrality of sex in mainstream culture as the representative inheritance of feminism perhaps explains why there is a movement afoot among some of Friedan's granddaughters today. Led by those like Wendy Shalit, the young author of *A Return to Modesty: Discovering the Lost Virtue,* these young women aspire to a return to courtly love. Women, Shalit argues, should climb back on the pedestal, and stay there. Sexual reticence is "natural" for women: the sexual revolution was a mistake, and feminists are implicated. Sex is for marriage, and the predominance of sex in the mainstream media is to blame for eating disorders, depression, sexual harassment, stalking and rape. In short, women have no one to blame but themselves for their own unhappiness.[16]

If I had to name anyone in my generation most likely to be voted "a direct descendent of Friedan" by young feminists today, it is Shalit. Her women are the same women Friedan addressed in *The Feminine Mystique.* They are not women negatively affected by poverty, class or racism, and they are most certainly not lesbian, bisexual or transgendered women. The only factor that influences their lives is their sex, and in this it is impossible not to read these women as exclusively white middle- and upper-class. In advocating a return to male protection in return for respect and protection, Shalit advocates a false and romantic view of the past and courtly love. Certainly both of my grandmothers were courted, and their marriages were not ones that I would consider happy or respectful. Moreover, in claiming that the rise of acquaintance rape has a direct correlation to a decrease of modesty, Shalit overlooks the reality that no matter how modest African-American or Latina women might be in the United States, historically they have been characterized by many whites as sexually available — particularly African-American women under slavery — and therefore were often more vulnerable to rape by white men than many white women. Clearly, the respect Shalit aligns historically with modesty only applied to a certain privileged group of women. Or more pointedly, perhaps, has been imagined as belonging to a certain group of women, whether or not they actually possessed it was another matter. Nevertheless, many women find Shalit's view "liberating" and "refreshing"; *A Return to Modesty* is in its fifth printing at the time I am writing. Shalit has been heralded by many young women as both a leader in the "future of feminism" and as a woman who "finally" debunks feminism once and for all. This confused perception of what feminism actually might be suggests a definite lack of awareness of feminism itself and of the complexity and breadth of issues feminists of diverse backgrounds have brought into focus in North American society.

I feel that I have come full circle, from Friedan to Shalit, and have offered no real hope or insight as to where young white upper- and middle-class girls and women might be going in relation to feminism. Let me offer you another view: I think that there are very real challenges to ideas of whiteness circulating in our society. The most significant challenges to whiteness, of course, come from those whom it has historically excluded. It appears, at least from the recent flurry of publications, that their critiques, ongoing for centuries, have finally begun to "hit home." While whiteness remains a discursive and physical reality (though not a scientific one), it is not indestructible. That said, the destruction of whiteness or white privilege is not imminent unless those who profit from it the most are willing to participate in its dismantling. This includes those of Friedan's daughters, like Shalit, who must move beyond reading the "problems" of contemporary women, as well as the concerns of feminism and the freedom of women, in particularly narrow ways.

Certainly Friedan has granddaughters who have taken up this particular challenge. But how do we as young feminists respond to the reality that more North American women read *Cosmo,* than all pro-feminist magazines in North America combined? How do we counter the reality that those who responded so powerfully to Friedan, for the most part failing to recognize the limits of her analysis, have been succeeded by those who respond in similar ways to Shalit, suggesting that very little progress has been made after all? I have no answer, and it is not insignificant that I end this essay uncertainly, with a smidgen of hope, some dismay and not even convinced that this battle can be won. I am convinced, however, that there is much work to be done, and if anything, this

is the real inheritance of Friedan's granddaughters, should they
choose to accept it.

Notes

1. It would be impossible to include a complete list of these African-American
authors. For those seeking further references, however, I would definitely
include W.E.B. DuBois, *The Souls of Black Folk* (New York, NY:
Signet/Penguin Books, 1995), and James Baldwin, *The Price of the Ticket:
Collected Nonfiction* 1948-1985 (New York: St. Martin's Press, 1985), as well
as the works of Ralph Ellison, Toni Morrison and Dorothy West, bell hooks
and Patricia J. Williams. This is not to say that critiques from other quarters
have not also been influential. Works regularly read in Women's Studies
include Cherrie Moraga and Gloria Anzaldua, eds., *This Bridge Called My
Back: Writings by Radical Women of Color* (Watertown, MA: Persephone Press,
1981); *Making Face, Making Soul, Haciendo Caras: Creative and Critical
Perspectives by Feminists of Color* (San Francisco: Aunt Lute Books, 1990), and
Trinh T. Minh-ha, *Woman, Native, Other: Writing Postcoloniality and
Feminism* (Bloomington: Indiana University Press, 1989). Post-colonial
scholars are indebted to the work of Gayatri Chakravorty Spivak, *The Post-
Colonial Critic: Interviews, Strategies, Dialogues* (New York: Routledge, 1990);
Frantz Fanon, *The Wretched of the Earth* (New York: Grove Press, 1968);
Frantz Fanon, *Black Skins, White Masks* (New York: Grove Press, 1968), and
C.L.R. James, *Beyond a Boundary* (Durham, NC: Duke University Press,
1993).

2. Mike Hill, ed., *Whiteness: A Critical Reader* (New York: New York University
Press, 1997); Michelle Fine et al., *Off White: Readings on Race, Power and
Society* (New York: Routledge, 1997); Richard Delgado and Jean Stefanic,
eds., *Critical White Studies: Looking Behind the Mirror* (Philadelphia: Temple
University Press, 1997); and Matt Wray and Annalee Newlitz, eds., *White
Trash: Race and Class in America* (New York: Routledge, 1997). See also Ruth
Frankenberg, *White Women, Race Matters: The Social Construction of Whiteness*
(Minneapolis: University of Minnesota Press, 1993); David Roediger, *The
Wages of Whiteness: Race and the Making of the American Working Class* (New
York: Verso, 1991); David Roediger, *Towards the Abolition of Whiteness: Essays
on Race, Politics and Working Class History* (New York: Verso, 1994); Noel
Ignatiev, *How the Irish Became White* (New York: Routledge, 1995); Richard
Dyer, *White* (New York: Routledge, 1997); and Theodore Allen, *The
Invention of the White Race* (New York: Verso, 1994).

3. Charles A. Gallagher, "White Racial Formation: Into the Twenty-First
Century," in Delgado and Stefanic, eds., *Critical White Studies: Looking*

Behind the Mirror, 6–11.

4. Peggy McIntosh, "White Privilege and Male Privilege: A Personal Account of Coming to See Correspondences through Work in Women's Studies" (Wellesley, MA: Center for Research on Women, Wellesley College, 1988).

5. Amoja Three-Rivers, *Cultural Etiquette: A Guide for the Well-Intentioned* (Indian Valley, VA: Market Wimmin, 1990).

6. The first settlements by Europeans in the Americas established the precedent for the denial of individual rights to racial others by excluding First Nations peoples from all forms of civic life and government, and denying them the right of self-determination within the new nations that arose. This treatment of the racial other as being fundamentally "outside" America and American life resulted in widespread disenfranchisement of many ethnic groups and still resonates today. That African Americans were deemed 3/5ths human at all was a ploy by slave owners to gain more representation in the federal government, where the number of regional seats are figured by the population of the area.

7. Judge Emily Murphy was part of a group of Canadian women who challenged the Canadian government to recognize women as "persons" and therefore eligible to hold certain government posts. The women won their case in the Privy Council of England on October 18, 1929.

8. Betty Friedan, *The Feminist Mystique* (New York: Dell Pub. Co., 1963), 197.

9. This practice is obviously not confined to white women alone. It is part of the American machinery of consumption, which establishes who constitutes a "good American." Booker T. Washington, in *Up From Slavery* (Oxford: Oxford University Press, 1995), attempts to prove to his audience that African Americans are capable of becoming consumers and therefore capable — and deserving — of full participation in American society.

10. Which perhaps explains the large number of quite successful magazines directed at groups of women that *Cosmo* overlooks. I do not intend to elide their importance or the functions they serve, particularly in constructing counter images of femininity and women, whether organized around race, ethnicity, sexuality, age or politics. However, for the purposes of this essay, I am concerned with how white affluent heterosexual femininity is perpetuated as "normative" in particular ways and does not acknowledge the existence of counter voices.

11. Dawn H. Currie, *Girl Talk: Adolescent Magazines and Their Readers* (Toronto: University of Toronto Press, 1999), 31. See also Helen Gurley Brown, *Sex and the Single Girl* (n.p., 1962).

12. "Hooters" is an American restaurant chain whose uniformly buxom waitresses wear hot pants and tight 'n teeney tops.

13. Neither Jesse Fauset, an African-American fiction author of the 1920s, or W.E.B. DuBois, a major African American leader of the late-nineteenth and

early-twentieth century, had grandchildren, but I would posit Anita Hill as a "symbolic" granddaughter. For those interested in pursuing the treatment of Anita Hill in the popular press and other places, please see Toni Morrison, ed., *Race-ing Justice, En-gendering Power: Essays on Anita Hill, Clarence Thomas, and the Construction of Social Reality* (New York: Pantheon Books, 1992).

14. Again, it is not my intention to suggest that it was only white teen girls who made *Titanic* such a success. But the new awareness of female teen buyers treats them as almost uniformly white. Girls of colour often appear in advertising in a way that sells their race or ethnicity as an accessory, if it does not attempt to erase it. This has much in common with the way Canadian rhetorics of multiculturism function.

15. Anonymous, interview with author, London, Ontario, August 1999.

16. Wendy Shalit, *A Return to Modesty: Discovering the Lost Virtue* (New York: Free Press, 1999).

My Top 10 Feminist Influences

1. My Women's Studies classmates and colleagues
2. Patricia J. Williams
3. My girlfriends who never stop asking questions
4. Anita Hill
5. Toni Morrison
6. Daphne Marlatt
7. Audre Lorde
8. Adrienne Rich
9. The fourteen women who died in the Montreal Massacre
10. Judith Butler

My Bio

JENNIFER HARRIS is a PhD candidate at York University. She is the co-editor of *Blackness and the 49th Parallel*, a special issue of the *Canadian Review of American Studies*, an associate editor at the cultural studies journal *Alphabet City: Culture, Theory and Politics*, and a contributor to *Contemporary Novelists* (7th Edition). She has also published in *Atlantis, Fireweed* and *The Journal of the Association for Research on Mothering*.

THE SILENCING OF SEXUALITY

Cassandra Lord

There are many times I have felt silenced in talking about my sexuality, which is often the result of the negative responses I have received from friends, family, community, and also from society, when the term "lesbian" is mentioned. Depending on my location, it becomes even more distressing when I have to constantly negotiate my sexual identity with my race and class position. The silencing of black lesbian sexualities continues to exist outside as well as inside various black communities, and in many ways is influenced by race, class and gender stereotypes about black women's sexuality. These factors, along with social and cultural factors, contribute to this silencing.

In her essay "Black (W)holes and the Geometry of Black Female Sexuality," Evelynn Hammonds points out that "black women's sexuality is often described in metaphors of speechlessness, space, or vision, as a 'void' or empty space that is simultaneously ever visible (exposed) and invisible and where Black women's bodies are always already colonized."[1] Through the historical legacy of slavery, black women's bodies were exposed on auction blocks and viewed as commodities that could be bought and sold at the slave master's request. As a result, black women's bodies, even more than white women's, were constructed as sexual commodities, with no intrinsic non-commercial value. This distorted view continues to reinforce negative stereotypes about black women's sexuality. Black lesbians have shared in this history, with the added oppression of being forced into denying our sexual orientation. This denial has forced some of us to remain in hiding, not only from our families but also from ourselves.

The well-known "closet" often functions in ambiguous ways: it acts as a protective skin from society at large, but at the same time contributes to the multiple oppressions we face as black lesbians. We are sometimes forced into the "closet" by white lesbians, who focus on their sexual oppressions but fail to recognize how these oppressions, as well as how racism, operates in the lives of lesbians of colour. This is made evident by black lesbian theorist Ekua Omosupe in "Black/Lesbian/Bulldagger" when she writes that "the term 'lesbian' without racial specificity, focuses on and refers to white lesbian culture."[2] Can we even imagine the TV sitcom *Ellen* featuring a black lesbian?

Race also functions as a factor in the relationships we choose to form with other lesbians. I recall a telephone conversation with a friend to whom I had not spoken in months. When I proceeded to tell him I was dating a woman, the first words that came out of his mouth were "I hope she is not white." At that point in time, my sexuality seemed irrelevant; the main concern was, if I was seeing a woman, it might as well be a sister. In Terri Jewell's essay "Short Account of My Behavior," she describes her mother's response to a letter she wrote informing her that she was a lesbian. Her mother responds by saying, "You had to get a white woman. Going around hugging and kissing the enemy. White women get the best of the black men and now they are getting the best of black women."[3] If black lesbians choose to have relationships with white women, we are viewed as committing a double act of betrayal: becoming traitors to the black race and at the same time preventing its continuity.

As a black lesbian, I am very familiar with the term "double life," as this is how I have existed for most of my adult life. Leading two separate lives is a difficult thing, as you have to negotiate your sexuality based on whether you live at home or on your own. As a friend told me, "If you live at home it is even more difficult, telephone calls are censored, 'she' is replaced by 'he,' you also have to make sure at all times that your personal space is made lesbian free." Family and community gatherings are also the places where you are expected to leave the other part of you behind. On one occasion, before my family headed off to my aunt B's house for a celebration, I was warned by my mother to not bring up issues concerning feminism or lesbianism, as the family will not understand. Audre Lorde best describes the dilemma we feel as lesbians in *Sister Outsider:* "Being an open lesbian in the Black community is not easy, ... being closeted is even harder."[4]

The most difficult thing about coming out as lesbian is your parents' denial of your sexuality. My mother's denial of my lesbianism is exemplified by responses such as "don't worry you'll grow out of it; it's just another phase." I think that by ignoring this part of me, she is trying to find a way of accepting my lesbianism. She does not understand that I am almost thirty and I don't expect or want to grow out of this. Donna Allegra writes in "Lavender Sheep in the Fold," that her parents' denial of her sexuality was also coupled with the hope that she would also grow out of this phase. It was an experience akin to her vegatarianism: "After 10 years of my being a vegetarian, my mother had asked ... but wouldn't you like some meat dear? An after 20 years, my father says you still on that no meat-eating kick?"[5] The lack of acceptance of our sexual orientation by our families is influenced by how lesbianism is viewed in black communities. bell hooks speaks to this issue when she states, "Black communities may seem more homophobic than other communities because there is a tendency for individuals in black communities to verbally express in an outspoken way anti-gay sentiments."[6]

The creation of alternative communities helps black lesbians develop support and, at the same time, reinforce positive

> **My Definition of Feminism**
>
> Pushing the boundaries in order to challenge assumptions about race, class and gender, and understanding how these interlocking forms of oppression operate differently across cultures.

209

affirmations of sexual identity. The importance of such communities is stressed by Audre Lorde in *Zami: A New Spelling of My Name:* "We tried to create a community…[to] survive within a world we correctly perceived to be hostile to us."[7] In these communities, friendships as well as relationships were formed, and this acted as a wider social network for meeting new people.

Lesbian communities were also established across racial boundaries in the 1950s, which is described in the book *Boots of Leather, Slippers of Gold.* "Black and white lesbians," the authors write, "began to interact on a regular basis and to participate in a shared culture."[8] Although communities based on shared experiences continue to exist, there is also the need for subcommunities within these groups to be formed, as the larger community in which they are located may not be able to address certain concerns. In "Man Royals and Sodomites: Some Thoughts on the Invisibility of Afro-Caribbean Lesbians," Makeda Silvera writes: "The white lesbian organisations/groups have barely (some not at all) begun to deal with or acknowledge their own racism, prejudice, and biases."[9] I have experienced feeling marginalized in certain women's collectives, where I may be the only woman of colour within the group who is also lesbian. There is the problem that, when issues are raised about black women or black lesbians, I am placed in a position where I am looked upon as being the voice for all black women. As a result, it is sometimes easier to be part of a group of similar racial histories because you are able to speak for yourself.

The function of the "closet" and the reasons many black lesbians are afraid of coming out is an area where critical attention must be placed in order to understand how "silencing" functions within black communities. We will only be able to break this silence when we are able to speak freely about our experiences as black lesbians, wherever we are.

Notes

This essay was originally published in a different form in Tiphanie Gundle, ed., *Oshun's Light: Rebirth of Anansi* (Saint Bani Press, May 2000).

1. Evelynn M. Hammonds, "Black (W)holes and the Geometry of Black Female Sexuality," *Differences* 6, nos. 2/3 (Summer/Fall 1994), 132.

2. Ekau Omosupe, "Black/Lesbian/Bulldagger," *Differences* 3, no. 2 (Summer 1991), 108.

3. Terri Jewell, "A Short Account of My Behavior," in Lisa C. Moore, ed., *Does Your Mama Know? An Anthology of Black Lesbian Coming Out Stories* (Decatur, GA: Red Bone Press, 1997), 33.

4. Audre Lorde, *Sister Outsider* (Trumansburg, NY: Crossing Press, 1984), 99.

5. Donna Allegra, "Lavender Sheep in the Fold," in Moore, ed., *Does Your Mama Know?* 158.

6. bell hooks, *Talking Back: Thinking Feminist, Thinking Black* (Boston, MA: South End Press, 1989), 122.

7. Audre Lorde, *Zami: A New Spelling of My Name* (Watertown, MA: Persephone Press, 1982), 179.

8. Elizabeth Lapovsky Kennedy and Madeline D. Davis, *Boots of Leather, Slippers of Gold: The History of a Lesbian Community* (New York, NY: Penguin Books, 1993), 117.

9. Makeda Silvera, "Man Royals and Sodomites: Some Thoughts on the Invisibility of Afro-Caribbean Lesbian," in Moore, ed., *Does Your Mama Know?* 182.

10. Allegra, "Lavender Sheep in the Fold."

11. hooks, *Talking Back*, 122.

12. Lorde, *Zami*, 179.

13. Lapovsky Kennedy and Davis, *Boots of Leather*, 117.

14. Silver, "Man Royals and Sodomites," 182.

My Top 10 Feminists Influences

1. Susan Schelle (Visual Studies Professor U of T), for making me believe in myself.

2. Cynthia Wright (Women's Studies Professor U of T), for challenging me.

3. *Does Your Mama Know? An Anthology of Black Lesbian Coming Out Stories* by Lisa C. Moore
4. Audre Lorde
5. Angela Davis
6. bell hooks
7. Jewelle Gomez
8. Barbara Smith
9. Ekua Osmope
10. *High Art* (the film)

My Bio

CASSANDRA LORD aka kah-san-dra is a black/lesbian/feminist/visual artist whose work crosses borders and genres. She lives her politics and sees her creativity as a gift from the goddess that has saved her many times. She graduated from the University of Toronto with a BA in Visual Arts and Women's Studies and is a past member of the editorial collective of *Fireweed: A Feminist Quarterly*.

— Allison Jack *Can you see yrself: zine* allithena@hotmail.com

HER HOME/S.ca:
Feminist Post-ings
On-line

Carmela Murdocca

My first encounter with the literary and theoretical dimensions of what can now be considered to be early strands of post-colonial feminisms appeared in *This Bridge Called My Back: Writings by Radical Women of Color,* edited by Cherríe Moraga and Gloria Anzaldúa. By post-colonial feminisms, I mean a body of knowledge informed by ongoing debates within and at the crossroads of post-colonial theory, feminist theory and cultural studies. Groundbreaking at the time and groundbreaking now, *This Bridge* invokes the intersections of history, tradition, migration, exile, racism (and more particularly white feminist racism) and homophobia, all the while conscious of its contribution to a new trajectory of feminist thought. It is clear that more recent developments in feminism theorizing of the post-colonial have borrowed explicitly from this early publication by women of colour in the United States. In their introduction, the editors identify their six-part analysis:

1. How visibility/invisibility as women of color forms our radicalism;
2. The ways in which Third World women derive a feminist political theory specifically from our racial/cultural background and experience;
3. The destructive and demoralizing effects of racism in the women's movement;
4. The cultural, class and sexuality differences that divide women of color;
5. Third World women's writing as a tool for self-preservation and revolution; and
6. The ways and means of a Third World feminist future.[1]

Fragments of emerging post-colonial feminist thought also abound in Gloria Anzaldúa's *Borderlands: The New Mestiza = La Frontera* where la mestiza is perhaps the inevitable "post-colonial woman." Speaking candidly she writes: "I am a border woman. I grew up between two cultures, the Mexican (with a heavy Indian influence) and the Anglo (as a member of colonized people in their own territory). I have been straddling that tejas-Mexican border, and others, all my life. It's not a comfortable territory to live in, this place of contradictions. Hatred, anger and exploitation are the prominent features of this landscape."[2] Not only did *Borderlands/La Frontera* facilitate the inclusion of notions of hybridity into the ongoing debates about "difference" within feminist circles, it also negotiated the often elusive borders and tensions between theory and literary production, between autobiography and history and between "home" and "foreign" territory. As Ania Loomba has suggested, "postcolonial studies have been preoccupied with issues of hybridity, creolization, mestizaje, in-betweenness, diasporas and liminality, with the mobility and cross-overs of ideas identities generated by colonialism."[3]

Unparalleled in their scope, it is without question that *This Bridge* and *Borderlands/La Frontera* made possible the potential to envision the current strands and developments of post-colonial feminisms. As resources, they are indisputably connected to the development of feminist theory by women of colour, Third World feminism, Chicana

> My Definition of Feminism
>
> Feminism is an axis of transformation along the lines of race, class, gender and sexuality. It is above all an anti-racist and anti-imperial practice.

feminism, African-American feminism and anti-racist feminism.

Recently, while navigating my way into the on-line feminist and activist community, I found further contributions to developments in post-colonial feminist thought being made through the "Third-World-Women Web-Ring." The "Third-World-Women Web-Ring" functions as a virtual link as well as an attempt at building community on-line between sites on the Internet that poses a decidedly feminist and Third-Worldist agenda. Invoking the six-part mandate that was central to the development and production of *This Bridge,* "Third-World -Women Web-Ring" reiterates those early literary and theoretical aims:

> The main point of the third-world-women web-ring is to "connect" our sites and to try and make ourselves more visible. Sites must be owned and maintained by men and women who have connections, interests and sympathies with women of color and with women who are economically, socially and culturally underprivileged — whether or not they are geographically of the "third-world."[4]

Surfing through the Web-Ring, I began to ask questions: What new ways of formulating constructions of feminist postcolonial theory and activism exist on-line? What are young feminists saying about the intersections of post-coloniality and their on-line/off-line lives? What are they doing about it? What happens when the not so clearly defined borders of academic theory invade and inform the development of virtual communities? And more specifically, are these new productions of "theory" and resources crucial when thinking about applications of feminist theory to young feminists?

One way to answer these questions is to navigate your way through the post-colonial on-line feminist community and explore on-line feminist electronic zines and resources. One contribution to the ongoing development of feminist post-colonial thought is entitled *exoticize this!* by mimi nguyen. She refers to it as the "cyborg diaspora." "The notion of the 'cyborg diaspora' refer(s) to the formation of virtual imagined communities of diasporic postcolonials on-line."[5] I suppose it is fitting to say that my role here is that of the navigator, the consumer, the voyeur and always the interested. More specifically, I am not interested in the post-colonial woman and her various formations per se, in as much as I am interested in the way theories of post-coloniality, coupled with groovy academics and activists, make up and occupy post-colonial feminist space on-line. I am particularly interested in the reshaping of current trends of on-line post-colonial feminism. By all accounts, I am venturing into a classed space of privileged access. Speaking to this, Maria Fernandez has suggested that while we might exalt the Internet revolution as welcomed transnationalisms, it is just as important to "identify the imperial underpinnings of the electronic revolution in order to be able to contest the reenactment of time-tested imperial strategies in this new field."[6] As such, my exploration is a partial one.

As mimi nguyen suggests in her introduction to *exoticize this!*:

> The internet is never going to foment any kind of revolution — except maybe a commercial one (witness the number of businesses exploding on the web) — for reasons of access (it's limited to those with the capital to buy a computer, a modem, and other techno-gadgets), but y'know, when a girl's standing screaming into a hurricane, it's nice to have your friends next to you, shouting and fist-waving, too.[7]

Situated Sites or My Bookmarks

The *exoticize this!* site reflects the funky radicalism to be found on most electronic zines produced by young women on the Internet, but it does so in a way that challenges the construction of academic theory as it relates to young women whose lives intersect with the production of on-line feminism. The home page to *exoticize this!* is an image of an East Asian woman whose extended clenched fist occupies the majority of the (virtual) frame. We see her peering behind her clenched fist-as-focal-point while the caption reads "Exoticize my fist." It is without question that this "oppositional aesthetic" evokes Pratibha Parmar's (now historical) production of an oppositional poster campaign:

> Parmar attacked racism through a "guerilla" poster campaign designed to end "Asian bashing." The group gained visibility with a poster which depicted a young Asian woman warning: "If anyone calls me a Paki, I'll bash their heads in." Parmar's oppositional political aethetic was already obviously formed before she began to use the cinema as a forum for political action.[8]

Can we think about the Internet forming a new strategic forum for political action? From her original statement we are able to decipher nguyen's aims, anger and motivations:

> I should explain why I — an already burdened graduate student with multiple zines, articles, and other media projects in both development and production — felt inordinately compelled to pick up the gauntlet and tackle this Xenian task (yes, I am a rabid Xena fan): I got annoyed. That is, I got exceedingly irritated trying to find rad Asian/American women's work on the web and figured everybody else must be sick of it too. So this will always be under construction. Note that I am (unapologetically) feminist, poststructuralist, leftist, whatever, and this reflects my commentary, my links, my everything. This is a feminist site. This is an Asian American site. This is an Asian American feminist site. And, as far as I know, it's the only Asian American feminist resource site on the Internet.[9]

217

exoticize this! is a comprehensive resource that includes links and multiple pages on art, film, academics, authors, articles, politics and activists, bibliographies, zines, queer resources, allies, pop culture, grrrls and personal pages as well as the ever inclusive "miscellaneous" link. But how does e*xoticize this!* reshape the development of post-colonial feminist theory? It uses the six-part mandate from *This Bridge* and makes visible some alternative forms of radicalism developed specifically by women of colour. It points to the "destructive and demoralizing effects of racism in the women's movement" both on-line and off-line and ultimately utilizes "writing as a tool for self-preservation." On a simple but important level, *exoticize this!* exists and is produced outside the walls and confines of the academy. As an on-line zine, it is not a tangible text and as such relies upon input, construction, collaboration and cross-pollination as evidenced through nguyen's various links. In effect, these new developments in feminists' theorizing of the post-colonial are as much about the discursive work of theorist Gayatri Spivak as about grrrl culture and staple-bound zines.

My Links

The production of on-line feminist electronic zines and resources fits into a larger conceptual framework of both cultural and political significance related to the changing nature of the construction of feminist theory. More specifically, it is about feminist cultural production and social change. Such feminist projects can be posited in relation to ethnic, racial, regional and national locations where the construction of feminist on-line space has its own semiotics. This semiotic underlines intersections of colonialism, racism and heterosexism. These places, therefore, can be articulated as places/spaces of resource in as much as they are places of departure from the realm of more traditional academic feminist theorizing on post-coloniality. They are spaces of active theory and virtual theory. These are places of community, albeit a classed community of access.

mimi nguyen's writes about the process of making of her on-line electronic zine *exotcize this!* as her attempt to create a "virtu-al" community for Asian-American feminists and build coalitions and networks with asian feminists abroad. Without question, *exoticize this!* is about negotiating borders. It is about negotiating the transient borders between creativity and politics, virtual space and "real" politically active space as well as between co-optation and collaboration with the very corporate forces we seek to chal-lenge. It is above all, a (virtual) site of contradiction. It leaves me to wonder whether this relatively new phenomena of feminist electronic resources is transnational feminism par excellence or yet another hegemonic imbroglio to be battled by future feminist academics.

Notes

1. Cherríe Moraga and Gloria Anzaldúa, eds., *This Bridge Called My Back: Writings By Radical Women of Color* (Watertown, MA: Persephone Press, 1981), xxiv.

2. Gloria Anzaldúa, *Borderlands: The New Mestiza = La Frontera* (San Francisco: Aunt Lute Books, 1987), i.

3. Ania Loomba, *Colonialism/Postcolonialism* (New York: Routledge, 1998), 173.

4. Radhika Gajjala, "Third-World-Women Web-Ring Mandate." *Third-World-Women Web-Ring.* <http://www.pitt.edu/~gajjala/tww.html>. December 2000.

5. Radhika Gajjala, "Cyborg-Diaspora: Observations from the Cyberfield," in Kris Knauer, ed., *On the Move: The Net, The Street and The Community* (London: The Write-On-Line Publishing Company, 2000). See

<http://www.write-on-line.co.uk/Frames/works.htm>.

6. N. Fernandaez, "Digital Imperialism," *Fuse* 21, no. 4 (1998), 38.

7. mimi nguyen, "filmic interventions." *exoticize this!* <http://members.aol.com/Critchicks/index2.html>. December 2000.

8. Gwendolyn A. Foster, *Women Filmmakers of the African and Asian Diaspora: Decolonizing the Gaze, Locating Subjectivity* (Illinois: Southern Illinois University Press, 1997), 74.

9. mimi nguyen, "welcome to exoticize this!" *exoticize this!* <http://members.aol.com/Critchicks/index2.html>. December 2000.

My Top 10 Feminist Influences

(or almost)

1. Women's Studies
2. Simone de Beauvoir
3. Mom
4. Wench Radio
5. Chandra Mohanty
6. *Woman, Native, Other,* Trinh T. Minh-ha
7. *Fireweed*
8. bell hooks
9. Ella Shohat

My Bio

CARMELA MURDOCCA is a graduate student in the Sociology and Equity Studies in Education/Collaborative Women's Studies Programme at the Ontario Institute for Studies in Education of the University of Toronto. She is a collective member of *Fireweed: A Feminist Quarterly.*

— Allyson Mitchell

THE WRITING'S ON THE WALL:
Feminist and Lesbian Graffiti as Cultural Production

Allyson Mitchell

eminist graffiti comes out of subcultures that are created by lesbian-feminist-punk rock-riot grrrl-youth-alternative cultural politics. DIY is the link that connects these subcultures — the Do It Yourself politic that urges people to create their own culture and not rely on the mainstream to do it for them. Making a zine about how to report a rape, organizing a women's self-defence collective, creating a homemade sticker campaign,[1] gathering a group to teach women how to use a sound board and writing a message of girl-on-girl love in a washroom stall are all forms of cultural production.

Feminist graffiti is made up of political slogans and icons like women's symbols. If it "defaces" a wall or surface via marker, spray-paint, pen, lipstick, scratched-away paint or sticker paper, I'm calling it graffiti. If it speaks of girl-on-girl love, lust, attraction, power, curiosity, break-ups or affection, I'm calling it feminist. Lesbians are intrinsically linked to and inseparable from feminism as a political choice and lifestyle. Graffiti represents lesbian and feminist voices and is an outlet for their self-expression and individual empowerment and political commentary.

As Jeff Ferrel argues, graffiti is a forbidden pleasure for the marginalized.[2] Feminist graffiti is a necessary "emergency storytelling" for those women who are marginalized by mainstream politics and culture. The marginalized also include lesbians, youth and girls. Society does not look to these groups as examples when it sets rules about who deserves to succeed, and often these groups are misrepresented in the media. Although most academic studies and news reports about youths tend to focus on boys, when young women *are* represented they are posed as dangerous, angry and out of control.[3] The demonization and intentional invisibility of these social categories means that girls, feminists, lesbians and youth are not considered when the rules are made about who gets hired for jobs, who gets access to housing, who gets their taxes subsidized, who gets legitimate space carved out in a megacity and who has access to information about the rules, laws and ideologies that affect them.[4] Thus girls remain marginalized in many ways by the mainstream and have an increased potential to drop out or be expelled from high school, or end up poor, homeless and disenfranchised. For feminists, graffiti is a way to speak out against these categorizations and break the hegemonic hold of sexist gender role promotion, which restricts the ways in which we live. Myths are exploded when girls pick up spray cans, carry sidewalk markers with them and start their own political sticker campaigns.

According to Ferrel, graffiti can break the hegemonic hold of corporations and governments over the urban environment and situations of daily life. By leaving a mark using non-legitimate means, graffiti resists the authority of those who control private

— Allyson Mitchell

property, of corporations and of laws — it makes visible the existence of the invisible on the very bricks and mortar owned by those in power. The subversive politics of graffiti writing demystifys who "owns" the city and reconfigures who "belongs" in a neighbourhood. It gives the marginalized the means to articulate their own stories and to answer back to a culture that too often erases their existence.

Because it is not "legitimate," graffiti is a successful means of resistance. This notion of illegitimacy reinforces the marginalization of the politics and the message. Graffiti is a successful means of resistance because writing on the wall *interrupts* what governments, bill boards and laws are saying. This interruption may not change laws and policies but it does change the experiences of individuals, sparks dialogue between different groups of people, helps to change attitudes and makes it less easy for us to accept the hegemonic corporate message. When it interrupts the physical city (the buildings, roads, signs and so on) and the ideological city (belief systems, laws and other rules of social interactions), feminist graffiti becomes a form of anarchy.

The physical anarchism of graffiti messes up the dominant/corporate/hegemonic landscape. Spraying messages on walls or scratching symbols on bathroom stalls destroys the smooth uninterrupted surface and colour. Ideological anarchism can mess up the landscape too if that landscape of systems and laws denies lesbian or feminist existence. "Messing up" becomes an ideological strategy. It says: "Listen to me because I'm going to mess up your business." The size and colour of graffiti on walls stands out so vividly because it doesn't belong there,[5] and this makes it even more powerful. This kind of action is at the heart of political strategies emerging from punk rock, anarchist, riot grrrl, lesbian and other less easily identified scenes.[6] It is through actions like graffiti writing that girls have made connections between musical subcultures and explicitly feminist politics. The messages sprayed on walls undermine the government and media restriction on their lives.

I found this kind of political action in a neighbourhood in Toronto called Kensington Market. While Kensington Market is in a definite "downtown" location, it holds a distinct character of its own as do many neighbourhoods in Toronto (population of almost five million). Kensington is the size of one city block, contained within four main streets, and is approximatley 500 square metres. I first started noticing graffiti in Kensington Market when I lived there between September 1994 and June 1996. I would see occasional women's symbols and phrases like "queers for choice," with all the round letters curled into women's symbols. After I first noticed the graffiti, I would watch to see how long it remained on the walls before it was removed. I looked for new markings with growing interest and began to make connections between how the territory in my neighbourhood was marked by this graffiti and the apparently political women who frequented and lived in the area. Occasionally, I would see women walking down the street arm-in-arm, women with suspiciously short hair and androgynous looks. When out and about in the area, I'd see lots of women who could be read as "feminist." I made the link between public displays of queer affection and dress and the physical space we made "feminist" by our presence and visibility. The graffiti sprayed on the walls in the area acted as neighbourhood sign posts.

While I was living there, I decided to do a presentation about the Market's lesbian graffiti for an undergraduate course. I photographed advertisements that I felt promoted heterosexuality and juxtaposed them with the photographs of queer graffiti to show

how the graffiti interrupted a heterosexual landscape. I was trying to recreate for the class how the graffiti had clued me in to who lived in my area and how, whenever I went out for groceries or to meet a friend for coffee, it made me feel that I was not the lone dyke of the neighbourhood. After this project, I continued documenting the graffiti. I looked for it aggressively — in alleyways and in the washrooms of restaurants and bars around the area. I rode my bike through the back streets looking for more and more of it, and I continued to find it.[7] I took my camera along and photographed the graffiti I found, which ranged from slogans like "pussy power" to double women's symbols to homemade posters that renounced dieting. A lot of it I found on outside walls, scrawled on storefronts. Often, feminist graffiti was competing with other more traditional "tag" graffiti. The graffiti I found in bars and restaurants was often written with marker or lipstick. Here I found more of a continuing dialogue with questions like "I think I'm gay, what should I do?" and answers like "Go for it!" and "Try kissing girls, it's nice."

The politics and demographics of Kensington Market have contributed to the growth of a feminist and lesbian community within its boundaries. In the 1960s, the first version of the Toronto Women's Bookstore began in a collective space shared with a lesbian-owned-and-operated printing press on Kensington Avenue.[8] The first all-women homeless shelter is still located on the border of the Market. Bars in the neighbourhood hold feminist/lesbian nights, such as Ciao Edie and the now defunct Shag and Sisters, a bar that catered to women of colour. There are still queer nights in anarchist spaces like Who's Emma? Other feminist organizations and businesses like *Fireweed: A Feminist Quarterly* and the sex-positive stores Come As You Are and Good For Her are located close to the Market, as well as services for women such as Sistering and the St. Stephen's Community Centre.

This feminist subculture has made Kensington Market a relatively obvious, if not accepted, space for alternative female expression. However, through my experiences living in and around Kensington Market, the attitude and feeling of the area is more along the lines of "If you're tough enough to take it, you're tough enough to stay." Taking it means bearing the cockroaches, overcrowding, unstable safety at night, no parking and question-able "woman friendliness." Kensington Market is chick-positive for those chicks who can snarl back at it as hard as they are being snarled at. The space that has been carved out for women in the area has been hard fought for and while lesbians and feminists still have a presence, there are many diverse subcultures that make up the community and that make use of its public spaces to convey their messages. Influences of punk, hardcore, feminist, lesbian and riot grrrl cultures, all of which are interlinked in their prac-tices and politics, are present. The anarchist-riot grrrl-punk-les-bian-feminist graffiti does not represent the feminist community as a whole; it is a subculture within a subculture that can extend our understanding of what a feminist is and how feminists repre-sent themselves.

Girls who write graffiti in Kensington Market are members of a subculture, because by spraying or scratching a feminist message on a wall, they are decidedly going against the ideals, values and beliefs of the mainstream culture, both in the method and the message of their communication. Susan Ruddick discusses youth subcultures and how the success of their forms of resistance depends on how their acts of resistance are framed.[9] Should I frame feminist graffiti in a larger struggle for lesbian visibility, or in women's class-gender struggles, or the counter cultural-anti-capitalist struggles for an alternative lifestyle? Or is the graffiti an act of resistance by individual lesbians and feminists to win space for themselves? In Kensington Market, both types of resistance are happening at once. Individual liberation and feminist communi-ty-building are dependent upon each other. Clearly, one relies on the other. A community, in this case a feminist, subcultural and anti-corporate community, is necessary as a forum where women can express themselves and build a support network. Feminists are in dialogue through graffiti, a kind of call and answer system where one message is erased only to be replaced with another.

Lesbian and feminist graffiti in Toronto has been used as a political tool for a long time. It's been used to expose the injustices of legislation and to hold politicians accountable for

— Allyson Mitchell

their oppressive policies. Women's Cultural Building, a group with a mandate to promote women's art (and credited by some for forging links between feminist and gay issues in the Toronto art scene), took their message to the street in 1985 with a campaign protesting rape and lack of action and attention to it. They sprayed "Disarm Rapists" over 500 times with a stencil on side-walks around the city.

In 1988, during a heat wave in the city, a group of roving graffiti bandits sprayed "dykes in heat" and "lezzie heat wave" all over the city. This campaign was particularly effective through its positioning of the graffiti — on construction sites and banks. The construction site is a macho, nearly all-male space where men hoot at women. Banks reproduce stereotypical gender regulations in a myriad of ways from unfair policies concerning women and loans to strict regulations on what employees can wear. What did it mean that the coffee was delivered to the construction site in a truck that had "lezzie heat wave" on the side of it? Or that "dykes in heat" adorned the wall of a bank in the financial district? It meant that those ideological spaces were rudely interrupted and a message for and by lesbians became a part of the everyday land-scape, however temporarily. There are numerous other examples of others acting individually, such as the graffiti produced around the city prior to the G7 economic summit in Toronto in 1989, about half of which appeared to be lesbian oriented or specifically dyke. The more we see lesbian and feminist messages the more

227

difficult it becomes to read the urban landscape simply through a straight and narrow lens because lesbianism and feminism become normalized and a part of our everyday visual vocabulary.

In time, the graffiti message is erased. It is seen as polluting the integrity of a "clean" downtown building and is often chemically burned off. The message needs to be suppressed because it is seen as dangerous. The need of property owners to erase graffiti is an acknowledgement that graffiti carries a political message of queer and feminist visibility. Those who erase graffiti are also committing a political act by subverting the graffiti's message.

Reclaiming Public Space

The struggle for sexual and gender identity has moved into a public space. As academic work in Women's Studies and Cultural Studies has opened up identities of race, class and gender for debate and discussion, so has work in fields such as geography opened up categories of place and space. Feminist geography embellishes the politics of identity by creating theoretical space for women to claim where they are, not just who they are; it has created the politics of place.[10]

Graffiti for the feminists, lesbians and girls of Kensington Market isn't just about who they are, but where they are. Ruddick claims that it is the city that allows for this sort of identity exploration because "certain spaces and neighborhoods by virtue of their transitional, indeterminate nature, their lack of fixity of meaning, become more fruitful ground for the production of new identities than others."[11] Kensington Market is a perfect place for lesbian and feminist graffiti and a perfect space for exploring identity. For example, when a message is sprayed on a wall in the Market and people identify with it, the Market becomes a space that forges a sense of community as well as a sense of participation in a larger movement. Joan Scott claims that this critical mass is what creates social movements and feelings of group politics: "Making the movement visible breaks the silence about it, challenges prevailing notions, and opens new possibilities for everyone."[12]

Understanding the importance of marking space and territory

— Allyson Mitchell

helps us move graffiti (and other cultural productions that feminists, lesbians and girls create) from base acts of misdirected angst and rebellion to integral acts of community voice and individual existence. I began graffiti writing in elementary school. I was looking for a feminist voice, a means to express my astonishment about unfair divisions between girls and boys. As I continued to write graffiti through high school and university, I started noticing lesbian graffiti and this prompted me to proclaim and explore my sexuality by writing it on bathroom stalls. These relatively safe spaces helped me shift my identity from heterosexual to lesbian, at first anonymously then publicly. In retrospect, I can see that lesbian graffiti has been an important part of my own coming out process. I have only in the past six years started making legitimate cultural productions such as films and writing. However, looking back I can see that I have always been a cultural producer, as a graffiti writer, a sticker-lady and an all round craft-maker. It has been difficult to see myself as someone who has the means to produce her own culture. This is partly because of my own insecurities around identifying as an artist and partly because of the atmosphere in some "legitimate" art scenes that create a jealously guarded entitlement of who is and can be a cultural producer.

But I have come to terms with issues of legitimacy and can proudly claim my position as a cultural producer. It is an empowering position. Do It Yourself politics have given me the inspiration to make my own culture rather than feel defeated because stories that are relevant to my life will never be told in newspapers, produced by Hollywood or sold in music mega stores. I found the means to create my own culture and I've found a community to swap it with. We all make culture, we can all make art — taking control of how this happens takes the power away from the cultural production monopolies like Disney and puts it into our own hands.

I want to legitimate the illegitimate. In the graffiti I've found in Kensington Market, feminists, lesbians and girls have taken ownership of their own cultural production and through their art are claiming responsibility for the meanings of gender and sexuality by writing their messages on walls for all to see. I encourage everybody to pick up a marker, a piece of chalk or use a tube of lipstick and leave your mark on the spaces you move through in your everyday life.

Notes

1. Sticker campaigns are actions where an individual or group makes a batch of stickers that target an ad campaign or social injustice. For example, I did my own sticker action called "I love fags." I placed the stickers on decidedly heterosexist or homophobic billboards and inside washroom stalls of heterosexual bars.

2. Jeff Ferrell, *Crimes of Style: Urban Graffiti and the Politics of Criminality* (New York: Garland Publishing, 1993), 190.

3. Tracy Skelton, Gill Valentine, and Deborah Chamberlain, "Introduction," in Tracy Skelton and Gill Valentine, eds., *Cool Places: Geographies of Youth Cultures* (New York: Routledge, 1998).

4. Chris Milne, "The Rights of Kids," *This Morning,* CBC Radio, April 8, 1998.

5. In this case what "belongs" in the city landscape is decided by land and building owners, who often have graffiti quickly removed from the surfaces of "their" property.

6. I am using the term scene here as a means to incorporate all that makes up a "scene" (generally referred to as musical scenes). I want to include all that comes out of particular scenes or political movements without giving music the priority or higher status of subcultural expression and creation. For example, scenes such as riot grrrl or hardcore or punk include cultural productions other than music such as film, video, zines, writing, performances, comics, stickers. All of these cultural productions are influenced by the individuals and politics within such scenes. When I refer to the Kensington Market "scene," I'm referring to a DIY scene as opposed to a specifically punk or hardcore or riot grrrl scene. DIY politics is a better fit because it recognizes the urgency to tell stories and claim territory without the assistance of anyone else.

7. These thoughts about the graffiti I found are drawn from "Graffiti Girls and Queer Community Building," the Major Research Paper I wrote for my master's degree in Women's Studies.

8. Joy Wilson, co-founder of the Toronto Women's Bookstore, interviews with author, Toronto, 22 August and 29 October 1995.

9. Susan Ruddick, "Modernism and Resistance: How 'Homeless" Youth Subcultures Make a Difference," in Skelton and Valentine, eds., *Cool Places,* 343-360.

10. Liz Bondi, "Locating Identity Politics," in M. Keith and S. Pile, eds., *Place and the Politics of Identity* (London: Routledge, 1993).

11. Ruddick, "Modernism and Resistance," 344.

12. Joan Scott, "Experience," in Judith Butler and Joan Scott, eds., *Feminists Theorize the Political* (New York: Routledge, 1992), 23.

My Top 10 Feminist Influences

1. Music: Karen Carpenter, Olivia Newton John, ani difranco, Dolly Parton, Princess Superstar
2. Authors: Judy Blume and Beverly Cleary
3. Events: The Michigan Womyn's Music Festival
4. Cultural Production: Girls who write and read zines, shoot film and make stickers
5. Phenomenon: Lesbians
6. Personal: All my fat friends
7. Family: My mom, sister and dad
8. Profs and Theorists: Adrienne Rich, Angela McRobbie, Linda Peake, Nancy Mandell, Susan Ehrlich, bell hooks
9. Mentors: Lynne Fernie, Jane Farrow, Ann Cvetkovitch, Gretchen Phillips, Roy Mitchell
10. Arts and Crafts: Margaret Keane, Alexis Vaughn, Rebecca Levy, Fiona Smyth

My Bio
See Editors' Bios

A FEW NOTES ON PEDAGOGICAL UNSETTLEMENT

Sharon   Rosenberg

Theory is then a living conversation, but historically and with time, bodies may become inhabited and in-flexible resisting *the new.*

> — Jacqueline Zita, *Body Talk: Philosophical Reflections on Sex and Gender*

Can — do — teachers make a difference in power, knowledge and desire, not only by what they teach, but by *how* they *address* students?

> — Elizabeth Ellsworth, *Teaching Positions: Difference, Pedagogy and the Power of Address*

I taught my first undergraduate course in the summer of 1991, when I was just turning twenty-seven and was close in age to many of the students in the room. Then I thought of myself as young and feminist, an identity pairing that fit easily on my skin. Having stepped recently into my middle thirties, I no longer think of myself in the category "young" (although I may be read differently, such is the conditional meaning of these markers). But I am also not "not-young," particularly if the phrase young feminism refers less to age categories and more to

233

the practice and substance of the feminism. For, while I have a profound indebtedness to those feminisms that came before me, that shone lights of critique into the shadowed corners of what girls and women had come to expect as normal life, such indebtedness does not hold me in this time and place. Instead, I have been most caught by those feminisms that are "young" in the sense of new, contemporary, not-the-dominant (in the academy at least) — feminisms refracted through post-structuralism, queer theorizing, cultural studies, post-colonialism, re-figurings of psychoanalysis.

While each of these theories cross different territories, what they have in common is a deep skepticism towards the founda-tions of the academic knowledge production and pedagogical practice. This skeptical stance unsettles the categories of repre-sentation and legitimation through which academic teaching and learning have been largely orchestrated, so that what has been long taken for granted is now not so secure. In (through, between, out of) these young feminisms, there is a flooding of questions; the self-evident nature of truth, the subject, reality, progress, reason, hierarchy, disciplines deteriorate under the force of asking: What is not made evident when these bound-ed categories of knowledge are taken as just the way things are? How are they held in place by a scaffold of isms — racism, sexism, heterosexism, classism, ableism, anti-semitism, colonialism? Might the world be different if it was known, taught, learned differently?

If teaching and learning feminist theory is conceived sim-ply as a matter of content, then the disturbances and troubles put into motion by these questions are easily contained. I want to argue, however, that the concomitant pedagogical challenges are not so readily addressed. Deeply informed by and commit-ted to these young feminisms, I (must) occupy a fragile pedagogical space as a Women's Studies professor. I am faced by any number of interminable questions. Most obviously, how to teach feminisms as (the making of) a discipline and, simulta-neously, as an unsettlement of the very terms of of the disciplines that have been laid through "second-wave" theorizing and politics? How to teach feminisms historically, without re-inscribing privileged women as the makers of change or gender as the primary marker of difference and oppression? How to value, pedagogically, "women's experience," when the categories "women" and "experience" fail in the encounter with post-modern critiques?

I am not alone in deliberating on these questions (nor are they particularly "new"). However, I suggest it is in how such questions become meaningful

My Definition of Feminism

Conceptual-practices produced by and resistant to local and global orchestrations of power through which "women" are constituted (the specificities of which cannot be determined in advance).

in the doing of feminist theory that marks this moment as one of young feminism in the academy. What most marks the specificity of these practices of feminist theorizing and politics, to my mind, is a postmodern approach to and use of pedagogies. "The difference" is less perhaps in what is taught than in how knowledge, teaching and learning are conceived.

Let me illustrate this by recalling an upper-level under-graduate course in feminist theory that I recently taught. In the development of this course, I sought to create a sustained engagement not only with feminism-postmodernism but also *from within* feminist unsettlements of the very categories of knowledge, politics, identity and history that organized its content. For example, taking up a skeptical stance to notions of knowledge as chronological accumulation, I shaped the course not as a sequence across time but as an arrangement within the space and place of a classroom. Thus, I designed a series of what I called "conceptual knots," or tense yet productive conceptual problematics, that are brought to the fore when feminism and postmodernism are in relation. These knots were represented by the headings of "knowledge / pedagogy," "identities / embodiments," "politics / ethics" and "history / memory." What I wanted to signal through the figure of "the knot" was an understanding of knowledge production and conceptual work as tangled, messy and difficult.

Over the span of four weeks in each knot, I endeavoured to juxtapose texts that brought to the fore a series of tensions between the two terms joined and separated by "the slash" — that is, for example, history *slash* memory. The deeper we worked into the knots, the clearer it became that the knots themselves were not discrete but made in and of and from the same theoretical cloth. Over the course, we were reworking knots within knots, tugging on ideas that we had encountered previously in a different material or with a sharper yank. In my approach to such moments, I endeavoured to put into practice postmodern ideas of knowledge not as canonical and timeless, but as provisional, partial and situated. At the end of the four weeks spent on each knot, I scheduled a fifth segment entitled "reading across / thinking through." No additional readings were scheduled for these last weeks. Instead, in line with the postmodern orientation of the course as an engagement with troubling and troublesome knowledges — and, anticipating that some students may indeed feel knotted up by the ideas they were working through — I designed these weeks as a space and place for students to focus on their grapplings with the previous four weeks of readings and discussions.

While I do not offer this pedagogical structure as "the answer" to the questions with which I opened this short essay (far from it!), I do offer it as one plausible model for those of us interested in creating and representing feminisms and knowledges differently. In the end, perhaps what I found to be most productive was the pedagogical practice of borrowing from one theory, clasping it in the hand of another, so they can nudge for conceptual attention to and against the normative (in feminism, Women's Studies and elsewhere). Such practice requires a doubled attentiveness: one conceptual foot tentatively reaching for the next curve of the ground, as the other traces how "we" came to be "here." It is in this doubled, difficult attentiveness to a past–present relation that the terms "young" and "feminism" come into significance for me. For, if I am hopeful of anything, it is how such unsettling of pedagogy and theory can arouse delight in ideas, chip away at dominant thought and keep us flexible in this living conversation on how we may be otherwise than we are.

My Top 10 Feminist Influences

1. Jacquelyn Zita
2. Hothead Paisan
3. Dionne Brand
4. Lorie Rotenberg
5. Kiss'n Tell
6. Dorothy Allison
7. Trinh T. Minh-ha
8. Shawna Dempsey and Lori Millan
9. Beth Brant
10. Jo Spence

My Bio

SHARON ROSENBERG currently teaches in the School of Women's Studies at York University, where "young" and "feminism" come together in many vibrant ways! She is a co-editor of *Between Hope and Despair: Pedagogy and the Rememberance of Historical Trauma* and regularly publishes on questions of trauma, public memory, cultural practice and contemporary feminism. For their engagements in the conversation of teaching feminist theory that informs her writing here, she gives thanks to Susan Heald, Marlene Kadar, Tanya Lewis, Susanne Luhmann and Diane Naugler. She is grateful also to the students in her fourth-year feminist theory course, with whom some of these ideas have been taking form, and to the editors for their editorial suggestions on this text.

— Sarah Evans *in morningclouds#14 zine* sjevans@is2.dal.ca

SLEEPING WITH THE ENEMY AND LIKING IT:
Confessions of a
Bisexual Feminist

R u b y   R o w a n

I occasionally visit enemy territory. As is the case in most wars, the enemy is not an individual or a group of individuals defined by their sameness to each other and differences to us. The enemy is an institution; our bodies, our souls and our minds are the sites of warfare. My citizenship is multiple and resists definitions, but my membership requires that I pack myself into a uniform of identity.

Among other things, my passport reads "Feminist." The word sits beside a smiling photo of me. When it was taken, the photographer immortalized a moment in time, a slice of me and a fragment of identity. I was not born a feminist but, rather, I immigrated. I have come to own feminism, and it has come to own me. My feminist citizenship dictates where I am safe and protected, and determines my enemies. These enemies have many faces. One of them is the institution of heterosexuality.

Bisexuality is most commonly understood as the intersection between homosexuality and heterosexuality, rather than a type of sexuality unto itself. This perception is symptomatic of the dichotomous framework from which it comes, and ignores the multiple complexities of bisexuality and its potential to challenge that very framework. The need to describe bisexual relationships as either heterosexual or homosexual limits our understanding of them. Applying the word "heterosexual" to opposite-sex-bisexual relationships assumes that this type of relationship perpetuates the institutions of heterosexuality. This assumption is a major factor in a tendency for queer or feminist communities to be heterophobic, to fear and judge sexual relationships between men and women.

In many ways, patriarchy (compulsory heterosexuality is integral to the existence of patriarchy) is the archenemy of feminism. Likewise, heterosexuality is the archenemy of homosexuality. The sociocultural perception of heterosexuality as normal implies that homosexuality is deviant or abnormal. Given these structures, lesbianism has been mythically equated with feminism and deemed anti-patriarchal. Heterosexual relationships have been mythically homogenized and deemed anti-feminist. This mythologizing occurs in a mythical world that, for the sake of simplicity, reduces multiple feminisms to one. Where do bisexual relationships intersect with these myths, and more specifically, what are the effects of these myths on the bisexual feminist?

Heterophobia has specific significance to those of us who

are not heterosexual but who engage in relationships which appear to be heterosexual. The politicized bisexual woman (being both queer and feminist) has in all likelihood absorbed, as if by osmosis, the legacy of heterophobia. She will come in contact with it at her local women's centre. It will be rampant at feminist marches and in Women's Studies classrooms. She will encounter it in dyke bars and at potlucks. It will be expressed in insidious ways, and she may even partake in its expression.

I have ingested it; I hate myself for wanting men. I am a politicized, bisexual feminist, and I am heterophobic. I have learned to hate and fear a part of myself because of its symbolic relationship to my feminist agenda.

The acquisition of my first dildo occurred almost a year and a half after I came out as a lesbian. As I welcomed the plastic pink phallus into my life, I marked the completion of my journey from bisexual to lesbian to bisexual again. It took me an embarrassing amount of time to recognize the links between my fear of men and the internalized heterophobia which was preventing me from coming to terms with my sexuality. My dildo is a good place to start unravelling my bisexuality because, although it is only made of plastic, to me it strongly conjures the institution of heterosexuality.

I have had to deconstruct the meaning of this plastic penis in order to accept it, just as I have had to deconstruct the meaning of heterosexuality in order to accept myself. Dildos are like penises: based on, modelled from, but expanded upon, embellished even. You buy them; they come in a rainbow of colours, sizes, shapes. They are like penises, but they are not penises. I could, after all, still have my fill of dick and remain officially lesbian. But my desire doesn't seem to differentiate between boy dick and toy dick. This has caused many a sexual identity crisis over the years, not just for me but for the community who's opinions I so care about.

Contending with internalized heterophobia is not entirely unlike internalized homophobia in lesbians and gay men. Ironically, where bisexuals are presumed to have access to heterosexual privilege, we are in fact contending with both externalized and internalized homophobia and heterophobia, all at the same time.

Heterophobia is the very root of biphobia in the queer community. Heterophobia in the queer community has been as challenging for me to supersede as homophobia in mainstream culture. In queer contexts I enjoy something I call homosexual privilege. I have located myself within a feminist and queer social setting. My social contexts tend to be

My Definition of Feminism

A way of seeing and acting which I have grown into. A part of me which can no longer exist outside of, or separate from, any other part of me. A framework/vocabulary for understanding intricate systems of oppression, especially the oppression of women.

lesbian feminist. This means that in a dyke bar for example, I am assumed to be a lesbian; my bisexuality is invisible unless I make it known. Unfortunately, I value this privilege because, as a result of internalized heterophobia, I have come to experience lesbianism as a more valid kind of sexuality. It is a privilege to be assumed to be a lesbian in queer contexts because it means that I can claim a much needed solidarity which will not necessarily be extended to me as a bisexual. At one point, painfully closeting my bisexuality and identifying as a lesbian seemed the only way to gain membership to a queer community. While in the closet, it is no wonder that I became more heterophobic than ever. This reaction illustrated how I had come to fear and hate an integral part of my sexual self.

Still, the queer community is not heterophobic simply out of the necessity to define "the other." It is true that all wars are waged against the constructed other and, in the case of homosexuality, heterosexuality plays that role. However, I would like to suggest that heterosexiality is also the other to feminism and so, when feminist community and queer community overlap, negative attitudes towards heterosexuality are intensified.

Heterophobia and homophobia are perpetuated in much the same way. Their manifestations can be blatant or insidious, but the most foul type of phobia is the unconscious one. This kind of hatred tends to seep out from the source into the world around, poisoning those who come into contact with it. I don't mean to say that all feminist discourse is inherently heterophobic. Rather, some feminist thought is, and I have experienced this heterophobia first hand. Heterophobic talk is pervasive enough that it is common among non-queer feminists and non-feminist queers — who do not require feminist discourse to justify heterophobia. Heterosexuality has, as I have said, been constructed as the other to homosexuality, and hence does not require feminism to further vindicate heterophobia. Straight feminists are likely to find themselves asking, Can I reconcile my heterosexual relationships with my feminist framework?

Feminist and queer overlap for me. Both my feminism and queerness have resisted my bisexuality because it implies the acceptance of heterosexuality. As a result, I have had to alter my feminism, my queer politics and my understanding of heterosexuality in order to create a space within my political framework for an integrated identity. I have employed my bisexual experiences with men and my own feminist thought to this end. My homosexual experiences work in conjunction with a keen knowledge of gender role socialization to provide me with a unique approach to heterosexuality. Furthermore, I have also seen how homosexual relationships do not entirely escape the heterosexual archetype. By this, I am not referring to the butch/femme model. However, sometimes it seems as if our models for sexual or romantic relationships are heterosexual, and homosexual relations often reflect this. These experiences have made me radically aware of the effects of gender role socialization on my behaviour in relationships. My objective is to engage with women and men in relationships that are not defined in any way by the institution of heterosexuality. Recognizing that all of my relationships with men are not necessarily heterosexual gives me the freedom to incorporate

242

them with ease into my bisexual feminist identity. Suddenly, it is possible for me to have heterosexual relationships, which are not anti-feminist by definition. Now I have the tools with which to combat internalized heterophobia.

The process of coming out as bisexual involved a transitional time when I felt I had no other choice but to identify as lesbian. This period of time was necessitated by internalized heterophobia. I was more afraid of rejection from the queer community because of my desire for men than rejection from the straight community because of my desire for women. My sexuality is subversive, and affirmation from others in my community is integral to my emotional well-being in a culture which despises sexual deviance. Many of us are radically aware of the necessity to combat homophobia, but the struggle to free ourselves from heterophobia involves a very different strategy.

Bisexuality is a potential political tool that could be used to deconstruct dichotomized relationships between such binary opposites as male/female, homosexual/heterosexual and homophobia/heterophobia. I am living proof that these constructions only exist outside of ourselves. In partnership with mainstream culture, we have written a fiction that serves solely to broaden the gap between who we actually are and who our politics require us to be.

My passport reads many things. As I grow, the list gets longer and the pages fill with stamps signifying all of the places which I have visited. But why do I need a passport at all? If I held my passport next to yours we would quickly see that there are many places where our identities overlap; we have shared citizenship. What is the purpose of all of these borders? Why is border crossing made so difficult? Our shared citizenship is proof that these borders are constructions that impede our efforts to locate community in a world of difference.

My Top 10 Feminist Influences

1. University
2. Rape
3. Fear
4. Rage
5. My mom
6. The nagging feeling that something was wrong
7. Music
8. Persistent childhood desires to be on the boys' team
9. The girl I fell in love with in high school
10. My grandmothers

My Bio

RUBY ROWAN is a rough 'n tumble guitar slingin' city slicker, now defunct vegan cattle rancher. Now a lesbian, forever changing her mind.

CHOCOLATE BUNNIES FROM HELL:
My Easter in the Czech Republic

Sabine Hikel

I can't say I wasn't warned. I had read about the Czech Republic's Easter Monday ritual well before I ever arrived in the country. *"At Easter,"* one guide book informed me, *"the age-old sexist ritual of whipping girls' calves with braided birch twigs tied together with ribbons is still practised. To prevent such a fate, the girls are supposed to offer the boys a coloured Easter egg and pour a bucket of cold water over them. What may once have been an innocent bucolic frolic has now become another excuse for Czech men to harass any woman who dares to venture onto the street during the period."*[1]

Despite the warning, I didn't think much about it; after all, this tradition was not going to deter me from seeing the country I had wanted to visit for several years. Indeed, after graduating from university, I left Winnipeg and arrived in Jihlava, a small town southeast of Prague. I moved in with a Czech woman, Lenka, and her daughter, and started my job teaching English. Living in a town of 53,000 people took a lot of getting used to, but I had a lot of help from my friends, both Czech and otherwise.

Then, in March, I began to notice Easter-related paraphernalia in the shops around town, including the dreaded *mrskacky*

— the whips made from braided twigs I had read about. They ranged from stiff little *svicka* that were just over a foot long to monster-sized three-foot ones that drooped over. There were other things to enhance Easter fun, too. Postcards depicting men whipping women, or women turning the tables and beating men suddenly made their appearance in paper shops and tobacconists. There was even a special Easter beer put on the market, whose labels showed a cartoonish drunk man, whip in hand. I started getting nervous when I realized that the Czechs seemed to take this tradition seriously, and that maybe, as a woman, I was going to be on the receiving end of it. So I asked some of my Czech friends about it.

They told me that on Easter Monday, all the men in town — and their sons, if they have any — gather in groups and go out very early in the morning to visit the homes of their female friends. When a woman opens her door, the men come in and start hitting the women's tushes with their whips. For the sake of fun, the women should shriek a bit, and let the men chase them around the house. As the men whip the woman, they recite a verse, which translates to something like, "give me your hen's eggs so you will have fertility all year." This is, after all, a remnant of a pagan fertility ritual, begun centuries before, and surviving through communism. Afterwards, the men are offered a shot of alcohol, and if there are boy children with them, they get chocolate. The women also tie a brightly coloured ribbon on the end of the men's whips (a sort of symbol of the conquest, as it were), and after an exchange of pleasantries, the men leave and go on to their next female friend. This happens all morning on Easter Monday, and is supposed to stop at noon. By noon, however, most men in town are thoroughly pickled, which makes it a little unsafe for women to go outside because the drunker, ruder ones might take a swipe. Women do have one defence, however. Tradition dictates that any time after noon, women can throw water on men.

Upon hearing of these details from my Czech friends, I asked two Canadian friends, Candice and Simon, about the tradition. They had lived in Jihlava for a couple of years, and were more familiar — and more blasé — about many facets of the culture that I was still unused to. Did this bizarre whipping ritual really happen in our town?

"Oh, yes," they confirmed. "Everyone really gets into it."

"Maybe I can escape to Prague," I reasoned. "They can't possibly do this in Prague."

Candice and Simon only laughed. Evidently, there was no way out. The realization that I was going to be whipped was fully dawning on me.

> ### My Definition of Feminism
>
> A theory and practice that continuously struggles to articulate an analysis of gender in relation to the state, culture, family and society, in an attempt to transform those relations.

"But this is like sanctioned violence against women in their homes!" I exclaimed.

"It's their culture," Candice answered.

Thus I beheld my feminist quandary. Did I have any right, as a Canadian, to judge Czech culture? But before I could even deal with my imperialist tendencies, I had to worry about the fate of my ass. How could I protect myself from being whipped? My friend Leona had invited me to her apartment, where we could simply not answer the door. But I was afraid to walk to her place that morning, worried that even at 7:00 a.m., there might be a man drunk enough to try to whip me. So I stayed at my apartment with Lenka, my Czech landlady, and her daughter.

The night before, Lenka fastidiously cleaned her apartment and dyed Easter eggs. Easter Monday morning, she prepared ham sandwiches and laid out a dish of chocolates. She told me that most Czech women go to great lengths to clean their homes and make everything presentable in preparation for Easter Monday "celebrations." Well, I thought to myself, if the women make such an effort to prepare their homes for this tradition, perhaps it wouldn't be so bad after all.

Still, I wanted to be on the safe side, and stupid me thought that I would be able to avoid the whip entirely if I just stayed holed up in my room. Not a chance — it seemed that the men who visited our apartment took their whipping duties very seriously and did not let the Canadian girl go unscathed. The first person who knocked on my bedroom door was a student of mine named Líbor, with his four-year-old son in tow. In a daze, I obliged tradition, and turned my back to Líbor. I was surprised that he only tapped me lightly with his whip. I remained standing there as I allowed his four-year-old son to similarly tap my ass with his whip, shyly, quietly reciting, "*hody, hody, hody, dobrou vody ...*" What I remember most about it was that when I turned back to Líbor, it was he who was blushing.

While I was grateful to Líbor and his son's gentleness, it had lulled me into thinking this whipping business was not going to be that bad. I was terribly mistaken. A steady flow of men — a few were my friends, but most were Lenka's — came into my bedroom to whip me, and most of them delighted in using a fierce touch. I was certainly not pretending when I shrieked and tried to get away from them. The most bizarre moment occurred just after one of Lenka's friends (a total stranger to me) whipped me quite vigorously. When he finally stopped, I turned to face him, grimacing. He smiled broadly, and heartily wished me a "*hesky velikonoce*" — happy Easter — like he had just done me a favour. Lenka and I moaned and rubbed our asses after each visitor departed. My ass started stinging and getting really red, and were those welts I was feeling? By the end of the morning, when the gentlemen callers ceased their onslaught, I tallied up about a dozen men who had whipped me on the butt.

Here I was, just a white gal from Winnipeg, wanting to learn about a different culture, and definitely finding out the hard way. My feminist knickers, beneath which was my burning butt, were definitely in a knot. All of my feminist alarm bells were going off and suddenly I became Andrea Dworkin: this *is* sanctioned violence against women in the home! This is gendered terrorism that teaches boys and men that hitting women is acceptable! It reinforces heterosexism! The whip is a phallus and the whipping is simulated rape! I felt like I was somehow letting my feminist sisters down by letting these men hit me with their switches. I should be fighting back, I thought, or at least bellowing out a fine treatise on the error of the Czech ways.

But was the guidebook right? Was this ritual just "another excuse for Czech men to harass any woman" they so chose? I wasn't so sure, partly because my feminist training had also instilled in me the dangers of judging other cultures. But part of me genuinely felt that this was simply a harmless tradition that was played out in the Czech spirit of fun and humour. In my classroom, most of my female students said they thought the tradition was funny and that it didn't bother them much. I also knew, however, that many of the women who made that claim also made a point of not going outside, locking their doors or even disengaging the doorbell to avoid being disturbed all Easter Monday morning. Away from the classroom, a few of my female friends confessed that they were less than fond of the ritual. My friend Irena said that she hated the tradition and so did her boyfriend, because he hated having to get so incredibly drunk so early in the morning and acting so macho. The two of them would sit in their apartment together and refuse to open the door to whoever rang.

While I did not think that the tradition was actually simulated rape (once I talked myself down from being Andrea Dworkin), it was clear that there was something distinctly sexual about the practice. After all, its origin was as a fertility ritual. The tradition as it exists now is like a game between people acting out an exaggerated masculinity and femininity. The man plays at being a he-man, who wields a big stick, chases after a woman and conquers her. Instead of the man putting a notch in his proverbial belt, the woman ties a ribbon on the end of his whip to indicate his conquest. When I thought of it this way, the tradition seemed to me silly and harmless. But I knew that the silly yet sexual nature of the "game" might also translate into adult men behaving like a boy in the schoolyard, who shows a girl he likes her by pulling her hair. For example, one of my students, a sixteen-year-old beauty named Michaela, would go to her cottage in the countryside with her parents in order to avoid the stream of teenage boys that would no doubt be lining up at her door. I suspected that for high-school students like Michaela, the prettier and more popular you were, the more likely it was for boys to want to express their attraction through this particular form of "teasing."

In a way, the ritual did seem ideally suited for children, not grown adults. I was highly amused by Lenicka, the five-year-old girl I lived with, because she really enjoyed the Easter Monday festivities. She liked screaming and running around the apartment and having so many visitors over. It was fun for her to give out goodies to other kids and to play with the ribbons tied on the ends of the *mrskacky.* I wondered how long it would take for her to start disliking the day, if she ever would.

I didn't come away from the day with any of these issues resolved in my mind. While my first instinct was to call the whole thing misogynist, I knew that I might not be in a position to make that judgement. My Czech friends, meanwhile, thought the tizzy I was getting into was quite laughable. While I was initially suspicious when they said they weren't particularly bothered by the tradition, I began to realize that for them, it was precisely that: a tradition. It was not an expression of present-day male-female relations, or an expression of their own everyday lives. It was a tradition that could even be fun for them. While the tradition had lost its original pagan meaning, it still had significance as a national practice.

Just when I got over that, though, I heard about May 1st, the day when Czechs celebrate "the burning of the witches" ...

Notes

1. Rob Humphreys, *Prague: The Rough Guide* (Rough Guides: London, 1992), 38.

My Top 10 Feminist Influences

1. My mom
2. My cool, kick-ass, girlfriends
3. My amazing feminist profs
4. Filmmakers Shawna Dempsey & Lorri Milan
5. Women's Health Clinic in Winnipeg
6. Liz Phair
7. My sister
8. Judy Blume
9. *Bust Magazine*
10. *Bridget Jones's Diary*

My Bio

SABINE HIKEL is a graduate student in political science at York University. She has a fondness for public transportation and enjoys eating bite-sized snacks. One day, she will happily return to her home base of Winnipeg.

— Laura Fisher *Other Ramona Zine* whylaura@popstar.com

INNOCENCE UPSTAGED

Miriam Johnson

I stood on stage, my bass in my hand, music in my soul and pride in my mind. Pride because this was my first show and so far in life I had made it as not just another girl. I was about nine years old when I developed a fear of what I was, what I am. I'm afraid of falling into a pattern of nothingness in which my saviour becomes at first the makeup that hides my facial features and then the makeup that hides my soul. Somehow being in a music scene where there is a growing number of girls and women (but still not that many) always makes me feel like I've done my bit and therefore escaped the previous fate. I am a musician.

Then from somewhere in the back of the room, behind the lights and below the smoke, someone in the crowd whistled at me. The mood was shattered. I felt like Mattel might as well have come out with "Rock and Roll Barbie" so I could be her, sitting in my fluorescent pink box with boobs too big to see my feet and a painted-on smile. I left that night with thoughts that, believe it or not, had never really entered my mind before. Sure I'd thought about sexism, and recognized it when it was there, but for the most part it wasn't something I personally was familiar with. In a child's mind, if something does not exist in their world, then it does not exist at all.

Somehow in the entrancing bubble of the suburban lifestyle, we become blind. We close our eyes to the world trusting that whatever needs to have been said and fought for was done by those before us. But more remains to be said and fought for. Injustice, torture and pain still exist. They wait for those who were not born into sheltered lives.

Growing older, I realize Gloria Steinem only skimmed the surface of the waters into which we must all dive. As we swim within that ocean we will begin to understand that feminism is as much an ever-evolving word as is citizen. The women before us had different battles to fight and have handed down their words to rest upon our shoulders. We no longer need to campaign for suffrage or the right to work. The struggle has changed as the prevalence of sexual abuse becomes more apparent, as we learn more about equality and how it can fit with society's progress.

Feminism to me is fully embracing your identity as a woman. It is being proud of who you are, what you are. Being aware of the role your gender plays in society, and being willing to stand strong and fight for your team. We've come a long way in the last fifty, even twenty-five, years, but cast your eyes over some issues again and you will see that there is still a long way to go.

In the seconds that it took you to read that paragraph, there is someone being sexually abused or raped. She may be ten, she may be fifteen, she may be thirty-five. It may be a stranger that forces himself upon her, or, almost worse, it may be someone she once called a friend. It's scary. Scary that there are things in the world you can't escape, shadowy things that gnaw at your heels and tear at your soul. And they're always there. Feeding on the unprotected like death feeds on war.

> **My Definition of Feminism**
>
> **Feminism is being aware of the role women play in society, and being willing to stand up and speak out about what role that should be.**

It makes me mad that, as women, we cannot walk alone at night. It makes me mad that there are those who can only picture rough hands on their neck as they try to fall asleep, or as they try to go about their normal lives. How can they, when they have been so mistreated? Most of all, I think it scares me how real the issue is and how, at fifteen, so many of my friends are survivors of rape. It feels like I've been plucked off a tree named innocence and thrown into a thorny garden bed that is reality.

It shouldn't be this way for young people. People can be bitter and cynical in their old age, but somehow it seems that youth should not be the tangle of sorrows experience can bring. If only there was a way to prolong innocence, or to ensure that everyone's first and last sexual experience is by choice.

Maybe it doesn't matter if the process of age and elimination of innocence can't be stopped. What matters is that there are people like you, people who read books like this, who will listen to young women who have been raped, harassed, whistled at during their proudest moments. People who can bring hope to the child whose life as a woman won't be as wonderful as she deserves it to be.

My Top 10 Feminist Influences

1. Katy Erlich, the teacher who proved to me you can have both a career and a family instead of having to choose between one or the other.

2. My sister, whose strength of mind and social awareness has hopefully rubbed off on me.

3. My mother, who inspires me to be conscious of my decisions and not settle for a lesser life than that which I dream of.

4. My grandmother, who chose marriage over everything else and still regrets it.

5. All the women I've ever seen on stage, because I leave the event thinking, That could be me. That WILL be me!

6. All the women in bands, because music is unfortunately a male-dominated industry, and I'm proud of the few who dare to pick up a guitar and play for people.

7. Stephanie Hinton, who wrote *The Outsiders* at sixteen years of age but could not sign more than her initials for fear that her book would not be published because of her sex.

8. Joni Mitchell. This is one I can't explain for I'm not sure what it is about her; I think it's the way she seems to embody a certain feminine power.

9. Queen Elizabeth I. This is a woman I respect a lot, because she was so determined in her life, regardless of the people who didn't believe in her, and contributed greatly to the ways of her times.

10. All the women who have fought for something. There are too many to name and every single one of them touches my soul when I hear of their relentless struggles through hell on earth, battling for equality and equal say. It is to these women we owe our identity.

My Bio

MIRIAM JOHNSON is fifteen years old and lives in small-town Ontario. She is in a band and works in a music store.

TALKIN' 'BOUT WHOSE GENERATION?!

Candis Steenbergen

I was born in 1972. Over the course of the last decade, that date has bestowed upon me an almost instant identity: cohorts based on population data; a supposed apathy towards inequality, injustice, politics, economics and culture; overeducation; underemployment; an inclination to navel-gaze; and a bleak outlook on the future. I was also born female. The result of that genetic lottery expanded my prescribed selfhood even more. I am a beneficiary of a still-rigid sexual code, successor of the women's movement; a daughter of the Sexual Revolution; a "modern woman." At some time between my birth and right now, I had my feminist "click." Since that moment, I have watched — largely in amazement — my identity augment even more. At twenty-seven, if popular rhetoric is to be believed, I am already an elder member of the new feminism. Power-feminism. Career feminism. "Do-me" feminism. Lipstick feminism. Babe feminism. Dissident feminism. Capitalist feminism. Consumer feminism. Postmodern feminism. Millennium feminism. According to mainstream media over the last few years, these tags, and variations on them, define members of my feminist cohort.[1] These labels characterize the "new faces" of feminism and, in effect, popularly identify "the next generation" of the women's movement.

Sweeping generalizations based on demographic affiliation are nothing new. The number of babies born from 1946 to 1964 in North America has held the interest of futurists, historians and journalists alike, and the aging, influence and affluence of the "baby boom" continues to receive public attention.[2] The "Woodstock generation," the "revolutionaries," the "radical" counterculture of the 1960s successfully transformed popular culture and rapidly became the focus group of virtually every institution: from government and education, to advertising and television programming. Due, in part, to the enormity of the baby boom's size and also to the tumultuous political environment (manifested both at home and abroad), the decade of the 1960s has come to be known as one of the great mythological eras of modern times. In retrospect, the baby boom grew to fulfill "a special historical destiny," and the social, cultural and economic experiences of an entire group of North Americans were branded into history.[3]

By the early 1990s, the generation born after the baby boom — mine —received its very own label: Generation X. Douglas Coupland's best seller, *Generation X: Tales for an Accelerated Culture* (published in 1991), launched a media catch phrase that swiftly and effectively classified an entire group of people born in the late 1960s and early 1970s.[4] Remarkably different from their predecessors in size and (apparently) values, the generation entering adulthood in the midst of an economic recession and a neoconservative environment seemed to be plagued by contradiction, and mainstream media scrambled to define them. Speculation and analysis of the new generation abounded, and popular understanding of the successors of the baby boom was illustrated through the application of even more dubious tags: the Baby Busters, the Lost Generation, the 13th Generation, Generation Redux, twentynothings, Generation Why?, Generation After (after the 1960s, after it all happened), Generation Ecch!, The Recycled Generation, and the like.

Nine years and an equal number of publications later, Coupland's epithet has endured the media bombardment of features and editorials concerning the plight of an entire generation destined to be little more than apathetic slackers; a group of people with "no identity, standing for nothing, and going for nothing."[5] While media fascination with the "Baby Boom vs. Generation X" phenomenon has long since evaporated into little more than a marketing tool for financial investors, the generational descant surrounding feminism and the women's movement seems to be picking up speed. Announcing the arrival of a young, independent, confident, sexually free and aggressive generation of women into the public sphere, popular discourse has exalted the victory of women's liberation and, consequently, professed the imminent death of feminism. At first gloss, it appears as though North America, at the turn of the new century, has entered a "post-feminist" era.[6]

In the summer of 1998, the cover of *TIME Magazine* featured black and white photos of the antiquated faces (and, in effect, perspectives) of Susan B. Anthony, Betty Friedan and Gloria Steinem next to the fresh, full-colour visage of the fictional prime-time television character Ally McBeal. Under McBeal lay the question "Is Feminism Dead?" The cover story by Ginia Bellafante announced that a new generation of "enlightened" women has emerged, actively promoting a new version of "female empowerment":

> ... feminism at the very end of the century seems to be an intellectual undertaking in which the complicated, often mundane issues of modern life get little attention and the narcissistic ramblings of a few new media-anointed spokeswomen get far too much ...What a comedown for the movement ... But if feminism of the 60s and 70s was steeped in research and obsessed with social change, feminism today is wed to the culture of celebrity and self-obsession.[7]

Ginia Bellafante argued that the next generation of feminists is concerned with little more than individual gain, the consumption of material goods and the exertion of their own "enlightened" power and concluded that the insurgence of young self-absorbed women has contributed to the "flightiness" of feminism at the millennium. Critics argued that *TIME* failed to look at the larger picture and that Bellafante consciously selected very particular written materials as "proof" of the current apolitical, post-feminist climate. According to Marcia Ann Gillespie, editor of *Ms. Magazine,* the failure to mention the activism and written work of young feminists was intentional, and that the lack of interviews with "any of the many women of that generation who are doing righteous work" was another indication of the media's misunderstanding and misrepresentation of the women's movement itself.[8]

Heterosexual, white, able-bodied, well-educated, financially successful, aggressive and overtly sexual women have received an enormous amount of print space and air time for their assertions that women in the 1990s have "made it."[9] Emerging in mass-market books, works of fiction, in glossy magazines and on television, such women (even the fictitious ones) have been touted as the heirs of the sexual revolution and, more often

My Definition of Feminism

To me, feminism means so many things. It is the theoretical framework I unknowingly adopted in an undergraduate politics class remarkably low on other women; it is the still-evolving history that continues to teach me about the intersections of sexuality, age, race, class and ability; it is my language, my politics and the cause of some of the most heated discussions I've ever had. It is the internal wince reacting in situations where it's probably best to keep my mouth shut; a pejorative tag stuck to my forehead; an often contradictory, complicated and downright frustrating paradigm; a fluid and flexible (and often context-specific) praxis that encompasses the bizarre multiplicity of things I've felt, seen, learned, purchased, listened to, wrote, read and still hope to experience.

than not, the new faces of feminism.[10] Post-feminist texts present the women's movement as the mastermind behind stringent sexual and moral codes, as the promoter of a villain-versus-victim mythology, and as antiquated protectors of "political correctness." Feminists (on the whole) are portrayed as anti-men, anti-sex and obsessed with notions of women as hapless victims. The post-feminist herself, however, is the antithesis of the second-wave stereotype: she is "successful and independent, and less likely to espouse 'dangerous' feminist ideals."[11]

By way of particularly (and often personally) nasty criticisms of feminism and its proponents and the clever manipulation of celebrity, power and the authority to speak publicly (bestowed by mainstream media), post-feminism has chic, inoffensive, commercial qualities. It is an easily absorbed, painless product for the public to consume.[12] As bell hooks has commented, "like any other 'hot' marketable topic, feminism has become an issue that can be opportunistically pimped by feminists and non-feminists alike."[13] Post-feminist ideology has been, to date, analytically weak but, surprisingly, rhetorically persuasive. Based on the presumption that equal opportunities for all women are a reality, their texts celebrate the successes of certain women in previously male-dominated realms. In doing so, post-feminists render the oppression of marginalized women even more invisible and undermine the ongoing history of the women's movement as a whole. As Maglin and Perry have noted, "while their individual messages vary … the overall effect of their work is to suggest that because some women have prospered, the systematic inequalities facing all women have vanished into history."[14]

In the spring of 1999, Germaine Greer, one of western feminism's more noted spokespersons, published *The Whole Woman*, the book she had said she would never write. Presenting a harsh critique of the current state of the women's movement, Greer thrashed contemporary feminists and feminisms:

> The future is female, we are told. Feminism has served its purpose and should now eff off. Feminism was long hair, dungarees and dangling earrings; postfeminism was business suits, big hair and lipstick; post-post-feminism was ostentatious sluttishness and disorderly behaviour. We all agree that women should have equal pay for equal work, be equal before the law, do no more housework than men do, spend no more time with children than men do — or do we?[15]

Greer devoted a small portion of her text to young women's misguided (non)participation in the women's movement. In less than ten pages, the feminist icon added her perception of the latest generation of young women to a list of what she called "false starts and blind alleys" in feminism's history. Greer erroneously correlated Riot Grrrl activism in the 1990s and the Girl Power of the Spice Girls and discarded both as mediocre facsimiles (corrupted by corporate media) of 1970s-style rockers Vivienne Westwood and Chrissie Hynde. Independent pro-feminist zines were mentioned with nostalgia, and Greer stated that the "fossilized remains of the feminist fanzines" can only be found buried deep (or in an appropriated commercial form) in the pages of glossy fashion magazines and on television. Young women's activity in cyberspace was limited to one Internet site: Australia's "Geekgirl." Essentially, Greer negated the struggles of young feminists with her own mainstream feminist privilege: the power to dictate feminist membership, the control over deciphering "good" feminism and "bad" feminism, and the ability to captivate a popular audience. Consequently, young feminist attempts at activism were dismissed as a "cultural phenomenon" amounting to little more than the recycled work of "kinderwhores."[16]

Similar, more subtle sentiments can be found in Canada as well. In October of 1999, prominent feminist journalist and social commentator Michele Landsberg wrote an article on a progressive young woman who was earnestly involved in the eradication of child labour in Nepal. Landsberg characterized this woman and her colleagues as "liv[ing] outside the anxious clatter of consumer culture," and contrasted them with youths who more often capture the attention of the mainstream media: youths who party at "all-night raves," those with "tongue-piercing," and users of "illicit drugs." With a sweeping generalization of an entire generation in her opening line, Landsberg discounted the work of young feminist activists who have been vigorously engaged in complex critiques of popular culture and consumerism. Because they do not fit the description of "clear-eyed, bright activist youths," women who work outside the realm of a prescribed definition of "feminist activism" remain invisible.[17]

Both Greer and Landsberg expressed (explicitly and implicitly) their frustration with the seemingly unsympathetic and apolitical generation of women following in their wake. The "parent generation," which Greer labels herself and her contemporaries, has not (as yet) recognized that a younger, activist and unmistakably feminist generation of women has emerged in recent years. To many, they exist solely as spotlight-hungry post-feminists. To others, they simply do not exist at all. Greer asserts that women at the millennium are in crisis and expresses her distress over the prevalence of apathy in contemporary feminism. She declares that "it's time to get angry again."[18] But young feminists *are* angry. And vocal. And active. The problem, as many self-described third-wave feminists would attest, is that no one has been listening.[19]

It is plain to see why post-feminists have received more mainstream visibility and public attention than the diverse struggles and accomplishments of third-wave feminists. Glamourous, media-friendly icons are more fitting illustrations for items reporting the women's movement's "cat-fights," and declarations of feminism's decline make far better copy than accurate representations of burgeoning activism among young women. Although it is easy and trendy (and very tempting) to blame the media for the mass promulgation of post-feminism, a more realistic assessment of the current circumstances would also recognize that pop culture reflects (with a heavily distorted lens) the ever-changing ideological climate of its host. A new generation of young feminists has emerged in recent years — and the tension that often marks relationships between generations is alive and well — but the true "generation gap" in the contemporary women's movement has eluded both mainstream and feminist commentators to date.

The intergenerational hostility within the ranks of the women's movement at the current time is indeed grounded in the successes of feminism itself. I certainly grew up in an environment remarkably different than my feminist foremothers. In many ways, I am a "daughter of feminism": mine is the first generation of women able to benefit directly from the accomplishments of the contemporary women's movement (to put this into perspective: I was born exactly eleven months after the birth of *Ms.*

Magazine). Access to and participation in previously male-dominated realms and a broad spectrum of legal rights were facets of my growth that I've taken for granted, not battles that I have fought. I enrolled in courses in established (but impoverished) Women's Studies departments, learned the theories and the histories, and actively sought to fit a feminist framework into my work in other disciplines and in my everyday world. In many ways, feminism is my birthright, and I do feel a sense of entitlement as a result. However, my reality has also been shaped by a multitude of other concerns; some new, others persistent: HIV/AIDS, date rape drugs, neo-conservatism, advancements in information and communication technology, increased commercialism, post-feminism, racism, homophobia, poverty and the spread of pop culture influences. The world has changed immensely in the last quarter-century, and young feminists like myself have inherited a complex social environment, an increasingly complicated women's movement and an unfinished sexual revolution.

The third wave is still very much in the process of emerging, but it is nevertheless an active, if amorphous, group. After all, third wavers are writing zines, publishing on-line ezines, contributing to magazines of the mainstream and alternative varieties, geurilla stickering, postering, graffiti writing, boycotting, critiquing both mass media generally and popular culture specifically, negotiating and re-negotiating relationships, contemplating the contradictions of sexuality, challenging paradigms, questioning dogma and resisting, resisting, resisting in their own innumerable private and public ways. While there are few organizational structures surrounding them as a "wave" (outside of the National Action Committee's Young Women's Caucus or the Third Wave Foundation in the US), there is a shared concern for the agency, rights and status of women at this transitional moment in history. In many ways, they are an ideological generation.

But that doesn't make the third wave any less legitimate or any more apathetic; it simply translates into the development of a movement that looks markedly different than what has come before. A movement that is resisting both in reaction to and in conjunction with the confused and confusing world in which we currently live. But common threads can still be found in the feminist work of younger women. Their written work to date has indicated an ardent interest in sexuality, body politics and pop culture. An ever-increasing number of young scholars, writers, artists, activists and critics of the mass media have attempted to link the allure of (and their participation in) the hyper-sexualized culture of consumerism and consumption with their identities as women, sexual beings and feminists. Jennifer Drake writes:

> Third Wave women talk a lot about pleasure. This could be because we're young or because we're such well-trained consumers or because we're into some kind of playful postmodern aesthetic or because we watched too much TV growing up, but I can't dismiss this, for it's such a hunger and a joy in Third Wave texts ... clearly, the pleasure-seeking impulse makes its unruly way through the personal and political play with sex/uality, but it also consistently informs Third Wave claims to feminism itself.[20]

That focus, I would argue, has contributed to their invisibility as legitimate members of the women's movement. Reviewing and critiquing the shortcomings of the so-called "Sexual Revolution" of the 1960s has only been part of that analysis; another has been to respond to and attempt to counter the post-feminist persona, and yet another has been to demystify the power of the popular media. Although representations of sexually confident, seemingly "empowered" women hold considerable allure, third wavers would agree that "a sexualized society does not guarantee sexual pleasure for individuals."[21] As such, the realities of women's lived experiences must be acknowledged:

> Consumption does not simply represent "the power of hegemonic forces in the definition of women's role as consumer," but rather "is a site of negotiated meanings, of resistance and of appropriation as well as of subjection and exploitation." Along with this concern with consumption, there is the related attempt to analyze gender in the context of other dimensions of power such as class and race, thereby building upon the foundations laid by socialist feminism.[22]

That negotiation process, between the alluring, pre-packaged, advertised and purchased version of femininity and the difficulties of translating it into a lived reality in our current cultural climate, is paramount to the future of feminism. To many third wavers, those pursuits have revolved around continual self-analysis and personal negotiation, an attempt to reconcile a desire to create their own version of "femininity" and their fear of betraying their allegiance to feminism and the struggle for female empowerment.[23]

While "some second-wave feminist angst has fixed itself on what 'younger feminists' are doing (or not doing) to and with the achievements of the 1970s and 1980s," the third wave is struggling with the task of defining feminism for themselves.[24] That has necessitated not only the deconstruction of stereotypes, traditional assumptions and strategies, but also the active redefinition and renaming of women's disparate conditions in the process of expanding the meaning of feminism to include and bring together diverse perspectives. Many young women have attempted to incorporate differences, tackle inconsistencies of thought and modes of activism, and confront the seemingly irreconcilable paradoxes of what constitutes feminism today. Having their ideas recognized, validated or legitimized, however, has been an even tougher challenge. Fenella Porter explains how this has affected her as a daughter:

> This is clearly because their experience and the way in which they see their identity as women does not fit into the linear structure of the women's movement as it has been defined by our mothers. Nor does it fit into the definition of "feminism" as it has been defined and lived by our mothers. Feminism, if it is to include the experience of all women, needs to be much more diverse and complicated — uncontrollable even.[25]

Charges by the second wave that younger women are "reinventing the wheel" and comments suggesting that there is "nothing new" about young feminist approaches have become almost commonplace.[26] Although the "mainstreaming" of feminist thought and the "professionalization" of feminist organizations affirms the

265

accomplishments of the movement as a whole, authority structures within its ranks have been created that must be acknowledged.[27] As self-described third waver Devoney Looser asserts, "younger feminists are not counterfeits in the face of the older and more genuine article. We are not the badly manufactured copies of second-wave originals."[28] We are only doing our feminism the way we have learned: by questioning, critiquing and challenging what we know.

Young feminists exist as a new wave within the ongoing history of the women's movement; a generation addressing, in various ways, the complexities of young women's everyday experiences and the personal and structural relations affecting them. Their comments and criticisms are intended to improve the status of women and to move feminism forward, not to slander the movement or its proponents. Nonetheless, solidarity (in any form) with their predecessors has been difficult to attain. As Rebecca Walker notes, third wavers "have a very different vantage point on the world than that of our foremothers. We shy away from or modify the label in an attempt to articulate our differences while simultaneously avoiding confrontation."[29] But perhaps confrontation is precisely what is needed. One of the distinguishing features of feminism has been the synergy of the personal and the political, the connection between women's personal experience and the political context within which it is organized.[30] Members of the early women's liberation movement took pride in "listening to each woman's experience and respecting her decisions."[31] Dialogue — open, mutually-respectful discussions conducted with strong, shared objectives between and among the waves — stands as one possibility of bridging feminism's generation gap. As Imelda Whelehan suggests, "the legacy of radical feminist politics provides, perhaps, the strongest potential for both defense and counter-attack."[32]

Threats to contemporary feminism have been aggressive and insidious, and the public demonstration of a strong women's movement, one which supports the interests of women of all sexual orientations, ages, colours, ethnicities, abilities, education, and economic backgrounds, has become an important and immediate endeavour. The decade preceding the millennium has experienced persistent calls for a re-evaluation of the last thirty years of feminism. At present, as Vicki Coppock, Deena Haydon and Ingrid Richter have noted, "feminism is learning to reconstitute itself as a social force that takes account of women's differences rooted in experiential identities."[33] The time has come, strategically, for feminists to re-examine both the accomplishments and setbacks that have occurred over time. That will require in-depth investigations of the challenges facing contemporary feminism: those of privilege, participation and control.

The generation known as the baby boom assumed epic proportions largely, in retrospect, through the oversimplification of events by the mainstream media and grandiose accounts of "the decade of the sixties" by members of the cohort.[34] The "Baby Boom v. Gen X" war has, in actuality, been waged by a limited number of people. Anecdotal descriptions of "the way it was" and historical accounts of the "Swingin' Sixties" have generally been created, perpetuated and maintained by those with a voice: frequently white, well-educated, heterosexual, middle-class scholars and media. Generation X, a smaller and infinitely less influential generation in terms of broad structural change, has been besieged with simple descriptions and unjust comparisons to their large predecessor. Some members of the younger generation like Kiké Roach, have responded swiftly to such condemnations:

> People of my age have been branded "Generation X" and accused of apathy and indifference. But our realities, anxieties, and accomplishments cannot be summarized or symbolized by a letter in the alphabet. Activism is not unique to any generation. It is not the property of the sixties, although there are a lot of important lessons to be drawn from that time. Progressive young people do exist, and there is still reason for us to organize.[35]

And others remain silent and invisible, resisting, organizing, waiting for time to pass and for new histories to be written. Until thorough re-evaluations of our current moment in time occur, narratives on post-feminism, the decline of feminism and the apolitical tendencies of my generation will undoubtedly remain "truths" within the pages of history texts and people's minds. I suspect that the real story has not yet been told, and that we will see, years from now, the beginnings of a strong, unprecedented, revolutionary movement rooted in the "untraditional" mobilizing and activism happening at the turn of the twenty-first century. Never thought I'd say this, but I can't wait to get older.

Notes

1. Rose L. Glickman, *Daughters of Feminists* (NY: St. Martin's Press, 1993) xiii, identifies "young feminists" as women between the ages of eighteen and thirty-five. Leslie Heywood and Jennifer Drake in *Third Wave Agendas* (Minneapolis: University of Minnesota Press, 1997) make a similar estimation.

2. Doug Owram, *Born at the Right Time* (Toronto: University of Toronto Press, 1995), xiii. Owram admits that the dates are somewhat arbitrary and that "in cultural terms the baby boom was born sometime between the late war and about 1955 or 1956" (xiv). John Kettle, *The Big Generation* (Toronto: McClelland and Steward Ltd., 1980), 19–20, maintains that the boom consisted of 6,715,000 people born between mid-1951 and 1966, and dismisses birth rates from before and after that time frame as "not all that startling."

3. Owram, *Born at the Right Time,* 309.

4. Douglas Coupland, *Generation X* (NY: St. Martin's Press, 1991). Coupland coined the term "Generation X" for his own cohort in the 1990s, but he borrowed the title from Billy Idol's punk band Generation X, who co-opted it from Charles Hamblett and Jane Deverson, who originally penned it to describe the emerging young generation of the 1960s in the text, *Generation X* (London: Tandem Books, 1964). Hence the tag "the recycled generation."

5. A. Cash, as quoted in Peter Yannopoulous and Alex Gray, "Generation X: Literature Review and Hypothesis," *Aruba* (December 1995), 4.

6. Janet Boles and Diane Hoeveler, *From the Goddess to the Glass Ceiling* (London: Madison Books, 1996), 235, define post-feminism as a term used in the US to describe the supposed disintegration of the women's movement and the death of feminism following the defeat of the Equal Rights Amendment (ERA) in the 1980s. Post-feminists assert that gender equality has been achieved, and that "feminism has become an anachronism, irrelevant to and even reviled by women, especially within the younger generation." According to Susan Bordo, *Unbearable Weight* (Berkeley: University of California Press, 1993), 241, the term post-feminist was originally used in 1919 by a Greenwich Village female literary group to describe the glamourous "new woman" of the 1920s.

7. Ginia Bellafante, "Feminism: It's All About Me!" *TIME* 29 June 1998, 48–56.

8. Marcia Ann Gillespie, "Equal Time," *Ms.* (September/October 1998), 1. See also Roberta Hamilton, *Gendering the Vertical Mosaic* (Toronto: Copp Clark Ltd., 1996), 43, who notes that mass media proclamations of feminism's demise are not unique to the current period. In 1977, *Weekend Magazine* announced the death of feminism in a feature article entitled "Beyond Sisterhood," and "a large wreath of the sort that is placed on tombstones graced the magazine cover."

9. Imelda Whelehan, *Modern Feminist Thought* (NY: New York University Press, 1995), 105.

10. See particularly Katie Roiphe, *The Morning After* (Boston: Little, Brown and Co, 1993), and Christina Hoff Sommers, *Who Stole Feminism?* (NY: Simon and Schuster, 1994). For Canadian examples, see Donna Laframboise, *The Princess at the Window* (Toronto: Penguin Books, 1996) and Kate Fillion, *Lip Service* (Toronto: HarperCollins, 1995). For an example of post-feminist fiction" see Lily James, *The Great Taste of Straight People* (Normal: Black Ice Books, 1997). For how the mainstream media portrays "new feminism," see, for example, Stephanie Nolen, "Girls Just Wanna Have Fun," *The Globe and Mail,* 13 February 1999; Ian Nathanson, "Speaking of Women," *The Ottawa Sun,* 2 March 1999; and Valerie Gibson, "Women's Success Scares off Men," *The Toronto Sun,* 2 March 1999.

11. Whelehan, *Modern Feminist Thought,* 240.

12. Dawn Currie, *GirlTalk* (Toronto: University of Toronto Press, 1999), 138, effectively illustrates how post-feminism has been pre-packaged and sold by the media. An anti-perspirant ad features a woman sitting between two men in business suits at a shoeshine stand, getting a polish. The slogan reads: "She's nobody's baby. She's nobody's fool. She knows what she wants. She just stays cool. Soft&Dri." The scene, albeit contrived, is intended to depict reality: "The product is hard-working and so is the woman. She is success-

ful. The product is soft, and so is the woman — that is, feminine, as indicated by the pink jacket. The woman is distinctively modern; she has successfully gained entry to a traditionally male domain. She uses the product, so it is distinctly modern." The ad implies that the magazine reader could enjoy what feminists want and have made possible, "without the feminist rejection of patriarchal heterosexuality" (139).

13. bell hooks, "Dissident Heat," in Nan Bauer Maglin and Donna Perry, eds., *Bad Girls/Good Girls: Women, Sex and Power in the Nineties* (New Brunswick, NJ: Rutgers University Press, 1996), 58. hooks also expresses concern over the lack of knowledge of feminist praxis and the ignorance of race and class in the work of post-feminists, asserting that the writing is "self-indulgent, opportunistic, [and] … shows no concern for promoting and advancing the feminist movement."

14. Bauer Maglin and Perry, eds., "Introduction," *Bad Girls/Good Girls,* xiv.

15. Germaine Greer, *The Whole Woman* (London: Bantam-Dell-Doubleday, 1999), 4.

16. Ibid., 310, 314, 315.

17. Michele Landsberg, "A Teenager for a Generation to Look Up To," *The Toronto Star,* 17 October 1999, A2.

18. Greer, *The Whole Woman,* 3.

19. See for instance, Boa d'Ruelle, "The Longest Days The Most Ignored The Cupboards Too High The Adults Too Narrow," *Revolution Girl Style,* Special Issue of *Fireweed* (Fall/Winter 1997), 120–122.

20. Jennifer Drake, "A Review: Third Wave Feminisms," *Feminist Studies* (Spring 1997), 106.

21. Mariana Valverde, *Sex, Power and Pleasure* (Toronto: The Women's Press, 1985), 35.

22. Dominic Strinati, *An Introduction to Theories of Popular Culture* (NY: Routledge, 1995), 218.

23. Questions surrounding women's bodies have, of course, always been at the core of feminist analyses, but I would argue that the current approaches arise from a different lens than previous investigations. See, for example, Baukje Miedema, Janet Stoppard, and Vivienne Anderson, eds., *Women's Bodies / Women's Lives: Health, Well-Being and Body Image* (Toronto: Sumach Press, 2000). The negotiation process has informed other third-wave texts as well. Leslie Heywood's "Bodymakers" in *Third Wave Agendas* (Minneapolis: University of Minnesota Press, 1997) outlines the author's vision of female bodybuilding as an act of resistance; Trina Robbins and Carla Sinclair's *From Girls to Grrrls* (San Francisco: Chronicle Books, 1999) presents zines as highly personal feminist manifestos. As well, young feminist anthologies like

Rebecca Walker's *To Be Real* (NY: Doubleday, 1995) indicate a return to the personal, experiential and anecdotal as political.

24. Devoney Looser, "GenX Feminists? Youthism, Careerism, and the Third Wave," in Ann Kaplan and Devoney Looser, eds., *Generations* (Minneapolis: University of Minnesota Press, 1997), 31–32.

25. Marilyn Porter and Fenella Porter, "Making New Feminisms: A Conversation Between a Feminist Mother and Daughter," *Feminist Voices,* no. 6 (Ottawa: CRIAW, 1999), 18.

26. Comments explicitly made by Greer, *The Whole Woman,* 312.

27. Porter and Porter, "Making New Feminisms," 24–25.

28. Looser, "Gen X Feminists?" 44.

29. Rebecca Walker, *To Be Real,* xxxii-xxxiv.

30. Geraldine Finn, ed., "Introduction," *Limited Edition* (Halifax: Fernwood Publishing, 1993), 12.

31. Joanna Dean, "Mothers Are Women," in Finn ed., *Limited Edition,* 31.

32. Whelehan, *Modern Feminist Thought,* 241.

33. Vicki Coppock, Deena Haydon, and Ingrid Richter, *The Illusions of "Post-Feminism": New Women, Old Myths* (London: Taylor and Francis, 1995), 185.

34. Owram, *Born At The Right Time,* 217. Owram admits "not all baby-boomers were students at university, much less students on a picket line. Moreover, many of the best-known radical leaders of the decade were pre-boomers" (160). Michael Medved, "The Wilting Myth of Flower Power," *The Ottawa Citizen,* 12 March 1998, A17, concurred, arguing that despite accounts of the legendary decade of Flower Power, "those defiant attitudes never involved all young people or even most of the famous Baby Boom generation." See also Dionne Brand's "Bathurst" in *Bread Out of Stone* (Toronto: Coach House Press, 1995).

35. Judy Rebick and Kiké Roach, *Politically Speaking* (Vancouver: Douglas and McIntyre, 1996), 10–11.

My Top 10 Feminist Influences

1. The three women in the world that I couldn't respect and love more: my mom, Lynne, who can do everything and has the gift of listening and actually hearing; my sister (and current roommate) Heidi, who is my confidante and co-critic of everything from advertising campaigns to B-movies to late-night snacks; and my gramma, with whom I've argued until I was blue in the face, who knits the best socks, and who gives the warmest hugs in the world. The four best friends a girl could ask for.

2. Simone de Beauvoir, Leslie Heywood and Jennifer Drake, Angela McRobbie, Linda Hutcheon, bell hooks, Susan Bordo, Lynn Crosbie, Mariana Valverde, the Brontë sisters.

3. Lynne Segal, Gary Kinsman, Dorothy Smith, Dionne Brand, Sherry Ortner and Karl Marx.

4. Archie comics, particularly the Betty & Veronica Double Digests.

5. A graduate Women's Studies class held by Katherine Arnup at Carleton University where I met a roomful of feminists who disagreed on virtually everything but got along fabulously.

6. Wonder Woman, The Bionic Woman, Kate Jackson on *Charlie's Angels,* the X-Men's Storm, Nancy Drew and her sleuth chums.

7. Aretha Franklin, Luscious Jackson, Lesley Gore, Bikini Kill/Kathleen Hanna/Julie Ruin/LeTigre, PJ Harvey, ani, Prince, Sleater Kinney, Janis Joplin, Cibo Matto, Patsy Cline

8. Tori Amos, Billy Holiday, Ella Fitzgerald, Nina Simone, Dusty Springfield (at different points in my life).

9. The industry that is Britney Spears.

10. Being a teaching assistant and doing workshops with young women, an experience that always makes me want to question, critique and resist.

My Bio

CANDIS STEENBERGEN is a perpetual student currently wearing the letters off of her keyboard towards a doctorate in Interdisciplinary Studies in Society and Culture at Concordia University. Interested in the spaces where feminisms lurk, she is researching the interplay between, and influences of, feminism, sexuality and pop culture on the complicated and often paradoxical politics of women of her "generation."

PART IV

FUN FEMINIST
ACTIVITIES:
Activism Exposed

Warning: For best results don't buy *girl power*.

Grow your own!

— Carly Stasko *Uncool Zine* carly@intrinsik.net

—Carly Stasko *Uncool Zine* carly@intrinsik.net

ACTION GRRRLS IN THE DREAM MACHINE

Carly Stasko

At age sixteen I made my first zine. I did it because it seemed fun, different and a little mischievous. It wasn't as if I had sat down and said, "Hmmm, seems like the representation of women in media is doing a real number on my self-confidence. I know! I'll recontextualize those images and affirm my personal world view in a zine!" That level of deconstruction would have to wait for later. At the time, making the zine was about play and experimentation. It felt good to subvert the idealized images in my *Seventeen* magazines, and I was curious about my own capabilities.

Media is a powerful tool, and the Do It Yourself philosophy of zine culture inspired me to engage my media environment instead of simply reacting to it. The zine gave me a voice within the cacophony of mediated messages and images. The confidence that I developed as a result of my zine encouraged me to experiment with other mediums and to reach out further within my environment. Now at age twenty-two I am still making my own media, but I am also encouraging other young people to do so as well. I do workshops in high schools and at community events promoting media literacy, critical thinking and creative expression. Involving young people in media production gives them the skills to express their own personal narratives in the same mediums they regularly consume. This is an essential skill since it promotes self-confidence as well as media literacy.

Insomnia In The Dream Machine

Today, many of us are exposed to more disconnected images and stories than in any previous era. Every day people can participate (as observers) in events both real and fictional, which have little or no connection to their "real" lives. With no way to connect or contextualize these messages and images, it is easy to experience a form of "information indigestion." Consider the disjunctive experience of channel surfing. Click, the television is on and you are confronted with images of starving children in Africa. Click, the next channel displays an audience of excited North Americans shouting out prices on *The Price is Right.* Click, a lab-coated scientist pours some strange blue liquid from a test tube onto a feminine napkin. Click, tearful children surrounded by rubble cling to each other while a newscaster reports on the events of an earthquake. Click, a frustrated middle-aged woman squeezes the cellulite on her thighs in front of a full-length mirror. Click, the television is off and now you must try to contend with all the disconnected images and emotions you have just witnessed. How do you fit into these different stories? How do they relate to each other and to you?

In her book *Where the Girls Are,* Susan Douglas deconstructs her experiences of growing up female with the mass media.[1] Douglas argues that the mixed messages of the mass media have engendered a form of identity crisis among today's women. She de-scribes herself and many of her peers as "cultural schizophrenics." As a baby boomer, she experienced the first wave of marketing tailored for young women. Today, more than ever, young girls at ages as young as four and five are exposed to sophisticated marketing campaigns designed specifically for their demographic. Billions of dollars are spent to successfully market products to women, but how many resources are directed towards providing them with the skills they need to navigate this onslaught of messages? Douglas argues that today's women are made up of "many shattered pieces" that "don't yet fit together into a coherent whole." Without the skills to analyze and discriminate among the contradictory female identities of mass media, women are destined to flip-flop between feminism and femininity as though they were two separate channels.

My Definition of Feminism

Feminism is an ever-changing way of seeing women, power and the possibilities for positive change in the world. The goal of feminism is more a direction than a destination. That direction leads towards a place and a time where women are enabled to live and share their lives in the best and most free manner possible. Feminism is sustained by continued dialogue, action, analysis, growth and community. Like an ecosystem, the diversity of the feminist movement is a symbol of its strength. Feminism moves beyond the binary opposition of oppression and dominance towards a playing field of equality where both men and women can evolve beyond restrictive social structures, stereotypes and social scripting.

277

Media-Play

Finding a voice within this media sphere is about developing a coherent identity. It means engaging with the images and messages that surround us, instead of simply reacting to them. This engagement allows us to explore relationships between the divergent identities we encounter daily. How is this accomplished? Consider how young children contend with a daily onslaught of new and seemingly disconnected experiences and observations. What do they do? It's simple, they play. Play is an intrinsically motivated activity through which children engage with their environment and hence gain a better understanding of it. Similarly, playing with media can help us to better understand our relationship to the mediated world. There is a Chinese proverb which goes as follows:

Tell me and I may forget.
Show me and I may remember.
Involve me and I may understand.

As a teenager people *told* me that I shouldn't compare myself with the idealized images in the media, but I tended to forget this when I looked critically in the mirror or flipped through the pages of a glossy magazine. Mass media *showed* me brands, idealized realities and disjointed images, and while I remembered these images I often had a hard time contending with them. Making my own zine *involved* me in the process of media production and after that I could never watch television or experience advertising in the same way. From that point on, every ad and every image was potential material for my collages and satire. In a sense, mass media became my toy and there was no turning back. Instead of being played by powerful images, I could play with them. Instead of constantly consuming spin, I could churn out my own.

This is not to suggest that I was completely unaffected by mass media. To do so would involve shutting myself off and hiding in a cave. What it does mean, is that through media-play I came closer to achieving a sense of balance between the inside world and the outside world, between my story and all of the other stories I encountered daily. When I first began to play with culture, I was not so confident. It took me a while before I began to share my collages with the outside world in the form of a zine. For this reason, like many other girls, one of my first mediums for self-expression was my bedroom. I pieced together posters, postcards and torn pictures from magazines into collages, which eventually covered almost every surface in my room. While many of the collages that I made for my zines served to ridicule popular culture, the walls of my bedroom became the display area for those which I embraced.

Down The Rabbit Hole

As I became more confident and more engaged in communicating with images, my work expanded beyond the walls of my room. My interest in self-publishing really kicked off at age twelve when I met my first photocopy machine. In elementary school there was a strange aura of magic that surrounded it. I would invent situations in which I was allowed to use it for class projects or presentations, and I was intrigued by the way in which it could take my drawings or collages and make them seem somehow more official and professional. During the summer I would go to my dad's office and play with the photocopy machine for hours, creating posters and personalized stationery. The photocopy machine became a toy that seemed to lend a certain authority to my creations.

In high school I started to work on a zine called "Quit Gawking" with some friends. It was so exciting to see our work all put together. Not only did working on the zine provide us with a venue for self-expression, but it opened us up to new communities and subcultures. I remember being blown away when I attended my first zine festival. I had never really seen any other zines before, let alone met other zinesters. Most people swapped one of their zines for one of ours and by the end of the day we had our own library of independent publications. Our community seemed to be ever expanding and it was a very empowering feeling. Once, while leaving a pile of zines in my favourite café, I was invited to attend a meeting for a new group called the Media Collective. Curiosity drove me to attend and the meeting rocked my planet. The room was an odd collection of "culture jammers" and social activists who liked to play with culture and media. I was quickly introduced to new mediums for self-expression, which ventured beyond the zine format.

I started making stickers that were like miniature zine pages and I would post them all over the neighbourhoods I hung out in. I also started to carry around a big black marker so that I could "improve" offending advertisements. It was like I was jamming with my environment the same way a musician jams with music. Instead of using scissors and paste to rearrange the imagery of advertising, I had to work with what was already there. By writing down new "improved" slogans or blocking out some words in the original text, I could recontextualize the intended meaning of the advertisement. I especially liked to write "feed me" beside anorexic models on bus-shelter ads, but I took a great deal of joy in the spontaneity of inventing an unrehearsed "jam." This made me feel like I was engaging with the advertising directly, which was the exact opposite of what a good little consumer should do. It felt especially good when I would come across my stickers or marker handiwork days later. I felt like I was advertising my right to dialogue, a dialogue that I felt was lacking in my culture. With other members of the collective I started to throw events, perform street theatre and pull off media stunts.

The more I became involved in the creation of media, the more I began to understand the politics of communication. I became very politically passionate and the collective was helping me to explore new ways of expressing my perspective. Through a fluke, a member of AML (The Association for Media Literacy) saw us on a documentary about cigarette and alcohol advertising and sponsorship. They invited us to start doing media literacy workshops in different high schools across Toronto. We would start off the workshop by sharing some stories along with pictures, video or print media that illustrated the work we did. Our hands-on Do It Yourself philosophy resonated within the classes and inspired dynamic group discussions. We had stumbled across another very powerful medium: the classroom. Because we were guests, we didn't have to be teachers or authority visitors, we were simply storytellers. We talked about the media that surrounded us, how it made us feel and how we engaged it. Most classes seemed thirsty for this kind of dialogue and I realized that this was a truly powerful form of direct action.

The next fall I started university and one of my seminar courses required that I do volunteer work at an art organization. I arranged to "facilitate" a class on street art and social change at SEED Alternative School. My class consisted of ten brilliant teenage girls. Together we made a zine and explored issues in media literacy. I watched many of them go through empowering changes over the year, and it was through watching their developments that I was inspired to look back and consider the role of independent media within my own life. This whirlwind of experiences left me excited, curious and inspired about the possibilities that lie ahead.

In talking with friends, zine-makers, culture jammers and students in different classrooms around Toronto, a certain trend kept re-emerging: people tend to feel powerless until they begin to play. Playing with media allows us to engage with it and hence develop a better understanding of it. Since so much of our daily lives are mediated, and so many of our tastes and values are shaped by media, I believe that this kind of play is essential in the development of critical and empowered thinking.

Girl Power

My yoga teacher always comments about how there should be a full credit course on "Confidence" offered in all schools. I agree 100 percent. The problem is that confidence means power, and, in today's global economy, empowerment is a commodity that people are meant to consume and purchase, not develop and create for themselves. Just think about how many empires would crumble if we all woke up tomorrow and felt good about ourselves? In her revealing book *No Fat Chicks,* Terry Poulton explores the connection between the unhealthy body image of most North American women and the billion dollar industries that stand to profit from them. She dubs this phenomenon the "billion dollar brainwash" and draws clear connections between mass insecurities and the economies and empires that they sustain.[2] Self-confidence is an economic and political issue that is too often dismissed. Talk of self-confidence is often stereotyped as being too warm and mushy for serious debate, and yet the hard and cold realities of the insecurity industry enforce power dynamics that deserve serious attention.

Stepping outside of these power structures, questioning the source of our own insecurities and creating our own opportunities and avenues for the development of personal empowerment are all very subversive and rewarding activities. In other words, "Confidence 101" is a course that we must all develop within the contexts of our own lives. This activity involves more than looking in the mirror and saying "I'm good enough, I'm smart enough and gosh darn it people like me!" It requires a critical analysis of our cultural environment and the roles that we play within it. Aside from analyzing culture, we must also take action. As consumers of empowerment, our autonomy is only expressed through the act of choosing. By creating new choices for ourselves and expanding opportunities for empowerment outside of the consumer sphere, we can be activists in the best sense of the word. Sarah Dyer, creator of the *Action Girl* comic book, puts it simply when she says:

> Remember — ACTION IS EVERYTHING! Our society, even when it's trying to be "alternative" usually just promotes a consumerist mentality. Buying things isn't evil, but if that's all you do, your life is pretty pointless. Be an ACTION GIRL (or boy)! ... go out and do something with that positive energy![3]

Dyer didn't feel that "Action Girls" were properly represented within her media landscape, so she expanded their terrain and created a safe and fun space for them in her comic book. Instead of being dissatisfied with the limitations of her media sphere, she took creative action and expanded the realm of possibilities.

 Developing a personalized sense of media literacy can help us navigate the spin and hype that abounds within today's dream machine. In "Language, Gender and Power," Susan Gal argues that "the strongest form of power may well be the ability to define social reality, to impose visions of the world."[4] The imagined limits of a mediated and consumer-obsessed society must be questioned and explored. The kind of "symbolic dominance" that Gal discusses, takes its form in our own perceived limitations and powerlessness. Engaging these perceptions head-on can allow us to expand the possibilities for identity and action. One of the first questions I ask at the start of a media literacy workshops is "Do you feel you can effect change?" While the initial response is bleak, further discussion about our relationships to media and power expands the classes' perceived possibilities for change and action. This is inspirational and empowering for all involved.

Wonderland

Alice didn't explore the rabbit hole because she thought it would be an empowering experience, she did it because she was bored and curious. Play is an ideal remedy for boredom, curiosity and low self-confidence. The problem is, the older we get the more we distinguish "work" from "play." In fact, leisure consumerism seems to be the dominant form of adult play in our culture. Young girls (and boys!) need to have opportunities and encouragement to chase their white rabbits through their own forms of play and exploration. As media technology becomes more and more pervasive in our culture, these toys too must be available to the playful spirits of developing minds. Stereotypes, symbolic domination and media intimidation can be abolished from the inside out through creative play. Encouraging this kind of thinking and action is my white rabbit and my form of feminist activism.

Notes

1. Susan J. Douglas, *Where The Girls Are: Growing Up Female With the Mass Media* (New York: Times Books, 1994).
2. Terry Poulton, *No Fat Chicks: How Big Business Profits Making Women Hate Their Bodies—How To Fight Back* (Secaucus, NJ: Carol Publishing Group, 1997).

3. Sarah Dyer, "Action Girl Comic," in Trina Robbins, ed., *From Girls to Grrrlz A History of Comics from Teens to Zines* (San Francisco: Chronicle Books, 1999), 120.

4. Susan Gal, "Language, Gender and Power," in Kira Hall and Mary Bucholtz, eds., *Gender Articulated: Language and the Socially Constructed Self* (New York: Routledge, 1995).

My Top 10 Feminist Influences

1. *The Second Sex,* Simone De Beauvoir

2. *Gender Articulated: Language and the Socially Constructed Self,* edited by Kira Hall and Mary Bucholtz

3. *Where the Girls Are: Growing Up Female with the Mass Media,* Susan Douglas

4. *The Woman in the Body,* Emily Martin

5. *Revolution Girl Style,* Special Edition of *Fireweed,* edited by Zoe Neumann and Kelly O'Brien

6. *Jo's Girls: Tomboy Tales of High Adventure, True Grit and Real Life,* edited by Christian McEwen

7. *From Girls to Grrrlz: A History of Wimmin's Comics from Teens to Zines,* Trina Robbins

8. *Language and Woman's Place,* Robin Lakoff

9. *Bust Magazine*

10. *The Ecology of Imagination in Childhood,* Edith Cobb

My Bio

CARLY STASKO is a self-proclaimed "Imagitator" who agitates imagination for the sake of positive cultural change. At sixteen she began to publish her own zine called "Uncool," which poked fun at consumer culture and deconstructed mass media. This led to her involvement as a founding member of the Media Collective, a loose-knit network of culture jammers, hacktivists, artists and pranksters. Carly speaks at conferences and facilitates classroom workshops on issues of cultural literacy and media activism. Her favourite pastimes are "Reclaim the Streets" parties, guerilla theatre, self-publishing, bicycle parades, free schooling, art factories, community organizing, and trying new things. With a brand-spanking-new specialist degree in semiotics from the University of Toronto, who knows what she'll do next. Check her out at www.intrinsik.net.

Unite & Fight

— Jessica D. *Because We Matter Zine* womyn_riot@femail.com

BURNING FOR A REVOLUTION

J u l i e   D e v a n e y

"I was struck like a match, I had no option but to burn."
— *The Piano Man's Daughter,* Timothy Findley

The fire that moves us is deep inside and all around. It is fuelled by indignation at injustice, and by the confidence that we are not alone. Activism is neither a choice nor a sacrifice for me ... it's survival. I wanted to write this piece to explain why I fight. I'll start with today's battles in the hazy humidity of Toronto in July of 1999. As I write there is a group of North York women fighting for their safety. They work at a battered women's shelter where the employer wants to reduce the number of workers on the overnight shift from two to one. The women who work at the shelter are on strike for their own safety and the safety of the abused women who flee dangerous and often life-threatening situations. On the same day that I joined their picket line, the news media was flooded with the story of One Brave Cop who was shot in the face while courageously pursuing a criminal. "The biggest manhunt in Toronto's history" was then launched to find the man responsible. Where are these cops when women's safety is on the line? Certainly not outside of the Cabbagetown Women's Clinic where anti-choice bigots, who sometimes pose as medical professionals offering "counselling," harass women going in to their appointments. Certainly not out finding the terrorists who kill women's doctors. Actually, not anywhere but protecting the interests of those rich and powerful enough to warrant it.

Yup. The same folks who just raised my tuition.

The very corporate criminals who found their way onto Hospital Restructuring Boards and decided that Toronto's St. Michael's Hospital should take over the Wellesley Hospital. Oh, was that the Catholic hospital taking over the hospital that served the gay and lesbian community and performed one thousand abortions a year? Hmm, bad planning or ulterior motive? Oh yes, the same gentlemen (usually) who made their millions working their way up from the mailroom floor to the corner office (whatever!), where they rake in their millions or billions of $profits$ from the sweat of women and men who live under the constant threat of wage cuts and layoffs.

So what's to be done?

I take my lead from the thousands of militant men and women walking picket lines across Canada every day. If I have any pride in being Canadian, it would have to be because we are the strike capital of the world! Apathetic, eh?

And how are we fighting the bigots in front of the abortion clinics? We start by standing outside the clinic every day, relegating the anti-choicers to leafleting uselessly down the street. We poster the neighbourhood with the picture of the ring leader to warn women. All but a few of the businesses on the street have now put signs in their windows. Our postering not only warns women who haven't seen him but also gives confidence to those women he harasses on the street. Intimidate the sexists, reclaim the space! And oh, is that St. Michael's Hospital that has now been forced to disseminate birth control? Hee hee hee.

I'll happily take my lead from the medical residents at U of T who were informed that they were to pay tuition to work in hospitals, a mere day after the university bragged of its million-dollar endowment. The residents refused to pay and held mass rallies downtown and on the campus. The fee was revoked.

> ## My Definition of Feminism
>
> Women's liberation has to be an active theory, a theory that is based on women's struggle at the same time as it inspires women to fight for change. It has to challenge the basis of an extremely oppressive system and therefore also has to be based on solidarity between anyone who wants to fight.

The list goes on and on. It's true that we don't always win. But with every fight we gain the knowledge, experience and confidence to beat them next time, and one day beat them for good.

And so I burn with the fuel of living my twenty years under the inequities of this greedy system, with the fire of all the fighting young women out there, because that's what it'll take to burn it down.

There ain't gonna be a revolution without us, girls.

287

My Top 10 Influences
(in no particular order)

1. Alexandra Kollontai
2. Rosa Luxemburg
3. Clara Zetkin
4. Lindsey German
5. Carolyn Egan
6. Cherie MacDonald
7. Michelle Robidoux
8. Maya Angelou
9. Frida Kahlo
10. Toni Morrison

My Bio

JULIE DEVANEY is a dedicated activist and a not-so-dedicated student at York University. An active member of the International Socialists, she fights for women's rights alongside a movement for broader social change.

—Jessica D. *Because We Matter Zine* womyn_riot@femail.com

DESPERATELY SEEKING SISTERHOOD

Cara Banks

I've been a feminist for as long as I can remember, with a strong sense of justice even as a wee girl. My mom recalls that when I was four or five years old, I was already pointing out the gendered division of labour at home. I couldn't understand why it was always *her* who did the dishes, both when she cooked *and* when my dad did. I dreamed of a wedding where I would wear brazen red velvet, and an engagement where I would do the proposing. By seventh grade, I was having angry discussions with my friends about our male teacher's tendency to massage the girls' shoulders during class. The *injustice* of it all — boys just didn't suffer the same humiliation.

High school was ripe for my burgeoning feminist analysis — it was four years of girls competing rather viciously for the borderline-abusive sexual attention of boys. Of course the infamous virgin/slut dichotomy was out in full force; either way, you couldn't win the respect of the boys, the teachers or yourself. The saddest part for me, though, was that there was little solidarity among the girls. I yearned for sisterhood.

Thankfully, I grew up in a politically minded household where my mom had a subscription to *Ms.* and my dad campaigned for good lefty candidates. Political discussions were commonplace at home, and my curiosity about the workings of the world was indulged by the adults in my life. My parents and their friends cultivated in me a critical mind and a feminist perspective.

In university, I did an honour's degree in political science and was the first University of Regina student to also do a second major in Women's Studies. But I was always an outsider in the Political Science Department because I insisted on talking about feminist political theory. Not a single woman taught in the department during my entire time at the U of R — no role models, no sisters.

I thought I was in heaven when I arrived at York University to do a master's degree in Women's Studies. What a relief! I found a community of women, some of whom had felt just as alone in their feminism as I had. I met women who shared many of my experiences, and I spent much time with them plotting how to change the world through our personal relationships, academics and politics.

I was also lucky enough to land a summer student position at the Saskatchewan Federation of Labour (SFL), which slid into a continued part-time position. I learned quickly that in Saskatchewan, too, I need not fight my feminist battles alone. The SFL, the umbrella organization for unions in Saskatchewan, taught me that there are practical and potentially radical channels that are ready and waiting for feminist and class activism.

The face of the labour movement in Saskatchewan is, to a

large degree, female. For a young woman just getting involved in her union, there were lots of feminist role models — many of whom I had met, worked with and interviewed for my thesis on feminist activism in unions in the 1970s and 1980s.

Of course, a woman leading a union or leading a movement doesn't guarantee a feminist approach. We all know too well that women can make fine tyrants. But we're lucky in Saskatchewan, we're a small and feisty population. We have a great history of political activism — the CCF (the precursor to the NDP)

My Definition of Feminism

Feminism is: 1. the struggle for the political, socio-economic, psychological, emotional and spiritual liberation of all women; 2. the attempt to radically transform all human relationships that have formed under patriarchy, including those among women, among men and women, and among humans and the earth; 3. on a personal level, accepting contradiction, i.e., living in a constant state of analysis, conflict and doubt, but with healthy doses of joy, strength and sisterhood.

and the Waffle Party — and a populist feel to our politics overall. Women and men have been coming together to fight for social justice throughout Saskatchewan's labour history, and being active in the labour movement means I'm a part of something much larger than myself.

In the 1960s and 1970s, Saskatchewan saw an explosion of feminist activism in unions and the community. Out of this activism came feminist leaders who are thriving today; leaders who, in turn, draw more young women into union and feminist movements. Barbara Byers, president of the SFL, my boss and my mentor, is a great example. Barb took me under her wing early in my employment and made sure that I met the leaders in the labour movement and that I was involved in challenging and interesting projects at work.

This positive precedent of involving young women continues today and there are many strong, active and inspirational women to look up to. The most recent example of inspirational women are the members of the Saskatchewan Union of Nurses (SUN). In April 1999, 8,400 nurses, the vast majority of whom are women, walked off the job. Not even Premier Romanow's last-minute attempt to swoop in and placate the nurses would be enough to halt the strike — these women and men were exhausted after years of dangerous workloads and forced overtime. When Romanow decided he wouldn't let the nurses walk out in the middle of an argument and legislated them back to work, the nurses refused to go back and stayed on illegal strike for eleven days.

No one predicted the nurses were capable of such militancy, such stamina, such *balls*. General membership meetings during the strike consisted of 4,000 nurses cramming into the Saskatchewan Centre, where they yelled, chanted, sang and rallied. The strength of the women when they came together sent shivers up my spine. These nurses were a solid example of sisterhood and solidarity in action. Of course, they would never have felt that level of solidarity without the groundwork of SUN's leadership, President Rosalee Longmoore and Chief Negotiator Beverly Crossman, both strong feminists.

And it is not only in times of crisis that the labour movement excites me. Take the Prairie School for Union Women — a four-day educational retreat for female union members, which was founded in Saskatchewan in 1997. Every March in the Fort Qu'appelle Valley, women get together for the most visibly feminist thing happening in these parts on an annual (and growing) basis.

The Prairie School is all about sisterhood. It's organized by a steering committee of female volunteers from several unions, myself included. The goal is to create a safe but energizing environment for all women who come to the School. We were the first ever union conference in Saskatchewan to provide free childcare so mothers need not despair. We also offer scholarships for equity-seeking women, including young women, lesbians, women of colour, Aboriginal women and women with disabilities.

Some of our most popular courses focus on women organizing, like Shopfloor Militancy; Women and the Clerical

Revolution; and Negotiating Family-Friendly Workplaces. A lot of women are like me, they feel like they've been struggling alone, many of them are just tired. For them we offer courses like Women and Self-Esteem; Women and Ageing; and Self-Defence for Women. We are always trying to build equality among women, a crucial element to sisterhood, so we offer Aboriginal Women and Unions, Time for a Change (a course about homophobia), Challenging Racism, and Young Women and Unions.

I've been lucky enough to facilitate three courses at the PSUW: the one about young women, the History of Women and Unions and, most recently, Big Macs, Running Shoes and Solidarity, a course about corporate rule. I love these courses because they include learning from feminist radicals of the past, mobilizing and educating future women activists and struggling against the consumer capitalist hell we all live in.

The goal of PSUW is to mobilize grassroots women workers from all walks of life. By the end of the week, 200 women leave the School full of new knowledge, energy and the most incredible feeling of solidarity. Five days with no men in a learning, activist, feminist environment is a beautiful thing.

I have another soul-feeding yearly event I must mention, as if further evidence is required about the vibrancy of Saskatchewan's labour ladies. It's the SFL's Summer Camp, which has existed since 1988. It is run by volunteer trade unionists (camp counsellors like myself) and is offered for youth age thirteen to sixteen. It may not be an *explicitly* feminist event, but it challenges young people to think about equality and justice.

Camp is probably one of the most profoundly exciting and moving experiences of my twenty-seven-year-old life. We all start out the week a little shy, and even unsure about what the camp is about. One of the most rewarding parts is seeing young people gradually come out of their shells over the course of the week as they realize that camp is an environment where everyone accepts them, so different from the world we generally inhabit. The abundance of tears and hugs at the end of the week is a testament to the camp being a safe place for kids who clearly don't always feel as safe at home or at school.

293

This isn't to say that creating this environment isn't a challenge. It can be tough to reach both boys and girls in their early teens. By thirteen, a lot of the girls have already gleaned from society and family that they should giggle a lot and act like they're stupid. Boys, developing a little later than girls, are usually somewhat easier to reach, if they haven't just discovered girls that week! Many of us remember how awful high school can be for kids who don't "fit in" and how the repercussions of this can carry on throughout a person's life. So counsellors have developed an educational session on sexism, homophobia, racism, classism, ageism and all the "isms" that divide us. While discussions and role-plays are sometimes difficult or emotional when we talk about "isms," I am astounded every year by the honesty and creativity that young people bring to these issues.

We also try to teach the power of working collectively. Every year the campers negotiate a collective agreement with the counsellors to set the rules for the camp. Hot issues for the campers include moving back the official sleep time, bargaining for more time on the beach and more time for recreation. Counsellors hold out for stricter rules about talking while others are speaking to the group, earlier bed times and commitments to keeping the camp environment clean. Negotiating can get really wild, with fifty-five kids and twenty or so adults battling it out. Ultimately, campers get a real feeling of power because they help make camp what it is.

The last few years we have also had a session on the mainstream media, its corporate concentration and its anti-union bias. Most kids, and adults like myself, have little or no education in high schools about unions or the history of the labour movement. Other workshops over the years have focused on the environment, violence against women and occupational health and safety. Oh, and we also have fun, blowing off steam with co-operative fun and games that build self-esteem, even for perpetual klutzes like myself. Campers tell us they feel free to try things they never would elsewhere, which to me is a great accomplishment.

Sometimes we take for granted that the next generation is apathetic or unreachable; SFL camp has shown me that young people care very much about their futures, about justice and equality and will fight for it if given the chance. As long as the labour movement in Saskatchewan offers such experiences as the Prairie School for Union Women and SFL Summer Camp, and keeps producing such inspiring female role models like the nurses and our union leaders, I can truly say that I have found a home for my feminism. Not only do I learn from the energy and knowledge of experienced women activists, but I also have opportunities to pass on this expertise and inspiration to up-and-coming activists.

I am part of a true sisterhood.

My Top 10 Feminist Influences

1. My mom
2. My best women friends, in all their inspiring, intelligent and funny incarnations
3. Tracy Chapman and ani difranco
4. Hélène Cixous, "The Laugh of the Medusa"
5. Everything written by bell hooks, plus seven years of Political Science and Women's Studies at university
6. Three years waitressing at a pool hall
7. Five years working for the labour movement
8. *Femininity and Domination: Studies in the Phenomenology of Oppression,* Sandra Lee Bartky
9. *Succulent Wild Woman,* Sark
10. *The Whole Woman,* Germaine Greer

My Bio

CARA BANKS works for the labour movement in Regina, Saskatchewan. She is proud to be a prairie activist and an educator.

KEEP ON KEEPIN' ON:
Me, My Period and
the Stars Above

L a u r a   E d m o n s t o n e

One of my earliest recollections of my own menstruation stems from my first trip to the drugstore to buy my own disposable maxi pads. Instead of feeling like I had finally achieved grown-up status, I felt ashamed about my menstruation and intensely annoyed with my mother for lacking the foresight to buy extra pads. How could she forget that I had my period? And did she really expect me to walk into that store and buy my own menstrual products? Did she not understand that if I bought maxi pads then everyone in Thunder Bay would know that I had my period?

As I grew older and got to know the girls in my high-school gym class, my menstruation became something that I could complain about out loud in the change room. We would share the dramatic stories of painful cramping and achy backs, and we knew well enough to give a friend an extra tampon or pad in a time of need because one day it would be one of us who would be desperate. Despite my newfound openness with my female friends, I would have been mortified if the boys found out that I had my period!

It wasn't until university that I really felt comfortable talking about menstruation. Up until that time I had participated in many conversations about the woes of being a woman, but I hadn't thought that there was anything more to menstruation than what I'd learned from my mom, from school and from teen magazines. Disposable tampons and pads were presented as the overwhelming ideal for women, and alternatives were not suggested. What was wrong with what everyone else was doing? Tampons and pads were a fact of life. I had resigned myself to living with "the curse," and I had relaxed a bit about people knowing that I had my period, but I still felt like my period was something interfering with my life; like it would be far easier for myself and other people if I didn't menstruate at all. Using disposable products allowed me to hide my shameful monthly state from everyone, provided I didn't exhibit any of the socially unacceptable symptoms of pre-menstrual syndrome!

Then I met Kelly. Kelly was an open book when it came to matters of her body and she lost no time in embarrassing me out of my own shyness. Kelly did not speak guardedly about her menstruation, or anything else for that matter. Through our talks I learned about a gadget called "the Keeper," a re-useable menstrual cup available to women in specialty stores or through mail order. The Keeper was described as a small cup made from natural gum rubber that could be inserted into the vagina to collect menstrual flow. One of the purported positive uses of this cup was that it could be used again and again for years and that it eliminated messing and fussing with disposable products. Folded in half and inserted into the vagina much like a tampon, the Keeper only needed to be changed once or twice a day, depending on the flow of each individual woman, and it could be placed in its own tiny cloth bag for storage between each menstrual cycle. I was skeptical, but I decided to try using the Keeper largely as a result of Kelly's rave reviews.

The idea of the Keeper appealed to me foremost because it eliminated the vast waste associated with disposable products, and it was much cheaper over time; I would not have to spend money on a box of pads every month and never again would I freak out because I didn't have a tampon handy! With easy access to information at my university, I was being exposed to articles and reviews that suggested that the chemicals used in disposable tampons and pads were not only bad for the environment but also potentially harmful to my body. These notions gave me the necessary motivation to go against all that I had been taught and to try something new.

My first experiences with the Keeper were horrible! I couldn't believe that other women actually managed to insert this thing that was the size and shape of a tuba mouthpiece! I had to fold the Keeper in half and then hold it gingerly between two fingers as I inserted it into my vagina. I would get it half way inside and then "phwoomph!" it would bounce aggressively back into its own shape. After numerous attempts at consciously trying to relax my pelvic muscles, which was about as easy as trying to wiggle my ears, I would give up in frustration, grab a pad and decide to try it again next month. When Kelly asked me how things were going with the Keeper, I would brush her off and suggest that everything was okay, but that it wasn't exactly as comfortable as I thought it would be. When two months had passed, I was beginning to think that there was something wrong with my body because I couldn't get the cup to co-operate, and I was very embarrassed because Kelly and her friends were all successful with it. I was so frustrated!

Sheer stubbornness was what kept me trying the Keeper until I succeeded. When I finally became comfortable with inserting the cup and changing it, I started to promote it to friends much like Kelly had with me. (Apparently natural rubber brings out the salesperson in users.) The response from other women was varied, but many were very positive and eager to try it. I discovered that I loved talking to women about their personal experiences with menstruation! I might as well have been back in the girls change room, but for one crucial difference — I was thrilled to talk to men about their questions and concerns too. Both men and women were curious about the menstrual experiences of others, but the subject was rarely discussed because it was socially taboo; people were uncomfortable talking about menstruation because it was considered a private matter for women only. Men were not supposed to be interested in or knowledgeable about women's periods.

My Definition of Feminism

My definition of feminism is ever-changing and growing, starting out small and growing to incorporate all of life. To me, feminism is a journey of recognizing oppression and acting positively to eliminate it.

My discussions with others were what prompted me to write my honours thesis on the Keeper. In order to graduate from the Outdoor Recreation, Parks and Tourism degree program at Lakehead University, I was required to complete a research proposal, to carry out that research and to then report on my findings. I realized that many women in the outdoor program at Lakehead had recently started to use the Keeper and I was curious as to what they thought about it, especially when they were on wilderness trips. Did it work for them? Would they recommend it to others? Why did they start using it in the first place? How did they dispose of the menstrual waste? Did they tell people on their trips that they used the Keeper, and how did those people react? I wanted to gain some sense of the Keeper as an alternative to disposable products in a wilderness environment, and I wanted to know if other women thought it was the answer to many of their complaints about menstruation while on a trip. Much of my curiosity stemmed from the fact that although I persisted with using the Keeper, I was never completely satisfied with it in terms of comfort and cleanliness in a wilderness or an urban environment. Did other women persist with the Keeper because they thought it was a good idea, or did it really work for them?

My own background in feminist theory was minimal, but, combined with the personal nature of my proposed study, it drew me towards a feminist approach in my work. I decided that I wanted women to feel comfortable enough with me to ignore the social barriers around menstruation and to be as honest as possible about their experiences using the Keeper. I felt that a high level of comfort between myself and the women in my study was necessary to promote answers to the questions I wanted to ask. Making people aware of my study and the results was also a very important goal of mine. My personal perspective on the social construction of shame surrounding menstruation motivated me to change the situation. My findings motivated me even more.

The women in my study predominantly indicated that they chose to use the Keeper because it offered them a positive environmental alternative to disposable products. They continued to use it despite concerns about cleanliness, Toxic Shock Syndrome and personal comfort because they felt that they were making the best environmental choice. These women also indicated that there remains a social construction of shame surrounding menstruation in both men and women, but that once people open up to the idea of discussing menstruation, many myths are shattered and attitudes are changed. The Keeper allowed them to become more connected to the natural process of menstruation within themselves, and it provoked in them an enthusiasm to share their experiences with others.

The responses of these women prompted me to further examine my own views about menstruation and how my perspective had changed since the years of the high-school change room. I now recognize that menstruation is a natural process, and, though I complain often about my period, I am honoured to be a part of that natural cycle. Even though I am not completely satisfied with the Keeper, I continue to use it because it offers me what I feel is the best solution to my concerns about the environmental impact of disposable products and my concerns for the safety of my body. I am no longer ashamed to talk about menstruation to others; I've even been known to disrupt the easy going nature of a party by discussing the merits and drawbacks of using the Keeper with some keenly interested party-goers! Something I've learned through all this chatter about periods and pads is that men and women alike are genuinely interested in talking about menstruation. It is my hope that through discussion young and not-so-young women will learn that they don't have to feel shame and men will learn that "the curse" is nothing to fear.

My Top 10 Feminist Influences
(or almost)

1. My mom and family
2. Liz Girard
3. Tobin Day
4. Rick Snowdon
5. Kelly Collins and Nathan Caswell
6. Writers Aritha Van Herk, Barbara Kingsolver and Starhawk

My Bio

LAURA EDMONSTONE has spent a terrific amount of time playing and learning outside. She has lived in Thunder Bay for most of her life, hanging out with wonderful people, going to school and working for a variety of causes. She has a deep interest in the impact that people have on the earth, as well as the relationships people have with the natural world. Laura plans to be a teacher and to travel whenever possible!

GIRLS NEED EZINES:
Young Feminists
Get On-line

Krista Scott-Dixon

It's a few weeks before Christmas, and a toy catalogue has appeared in my mailbox. I glance through it. Something catches my eye. It's pastel-coloured and girly, vaguely ovoid with sleek yet gravidly organic contours and covered in big retro flowers. It's the Barbie PC for girls, and it comes with a variety of appropriately feminine software (no chess games or logic puzzles here; rather, girls can indulge in Sticker Designer and Riding Club). As if a large, weird bug has just landed in front of me, I am both horrified and fascinated. This, apparently, is how the mass market continues to view the relationship between girls and computers. Girls and women, apparently, have a "problem" with technology, and while it's possible for them to have fun with it, their involvement with technology remains trivial.

However, girl geeks, contrary to the ideas of the folks at Mattel, have a long history. Ada Lovelace, after whom the computer language Ada is named, wrote "programs" for Charles Babbage's Analytical Engine in the 1840s. Women were the first "computers" — low-paid mathematic drones who painstakingly worked out complicated ballistics tables and performed cryptography tasks for the Allied Forces during the Second World War.

However, for most of the twentieth century, girls who dug technology were reduced to tinkering with wires in their basements, trying to break through the glass ceiling in technical firms and being portrayed in the mass media as dowdy bespectacled spinsters. It wasn't until the era of the personal computer that girl geeks could formulate a collective voice on a large scale. Systers, a technical mailing list for women in computing, was started in 1987 (http://www.systers.org/); and Webgrrls, a forum for women in new media and technology, got rolling in 1995 and now boasts chapters worldwide (http://www.webgrrls.com).

One of the most interesting feminist developments of the Internet age is ezines, or on-line zines. The roots of ezines are in-print zines (from "magazines," later "fanzines"), which began as self-produced publications, cheaply photocopied and circulated within a small group of like-minded individuals, generally sub-cultured youth involved in the punk music scene. They were about everything, anything and nothing at all. Constructed with a clear postmodern pop cultural consciousness and drawing heavily on so-called girl culture, zine creators appropriated from every source with cheerful irreverence. Zines were also a site of feminist activism, wherein women responded to, critiqued and envisioned alternatives to the often sexist and misogynist commercial media. The Do It Yourself (DIY) movement was a rich source of feminist activity and enthusiasm.

The ezine is very much the print zine's on-line congruent. Ezines are self-published and share the spirit of the witty tourism of girl culture. Since ezines and the majority of other sites on the Web are self-published, they provide a forum in which their creators can express themselves freely with little mediation between them and their audience through a publisher. The perceived immediacy of the electronic medium (plus our ability to interact with it on the microlevel through, for instance, sending e-mail to creators) augments the illusion of direct contact between creator and reader. Like print zines, ezines can act as a form of feminist political activism. However, the fact that ezines operate within a traditionally male-dominated sphere, that of cyberspace, means that they also exist as a form of resistance.

First, if I assume as my starting point that on-line culture has largely been created by and for men and, furthermore, by men in a certain privileged setting within the universities and military-industrial complex, the sheer act of female foray into cyberspace can be seen as resistance. The very fact, for example, that women are educating themselves and each other about how to use the technology. Webgrrls, for instance, shows that many women recognize the links between control of technology and control of resources. However, merely existing in a hostile environment is not entirely sufficient to constitute any kind of comprehensive resistance. Simply mounting a Web site or managing to send e-mail does not present a significant concrete challenge.

Second, even if cyberspace is not entirely hostile to women, the creation of an on-line voice can be seen as a form of resistance. Not everything a woman puts on-line is resistance in this sense, but many publishers of ezines find the connection between voice and activism to be important. This is not to suggest that "the female voice" on its own is privy to a unique viewpoint (though, of course, that could be debated), or to insist it even exists at all. What I mean to say here is that for many women the symbolic act of speaking and writing, particularly in an aware and critical way, is linked to an entrance into political space. One woman writes in the ezine *FaT GiRL*: "Give me a microphone. Hear what I say. Get ready, this world is going to rock apart."[1] Girls' ezines may or may not have an explicitly feminist viewpoint, but they generally manifest an awareness that they are providing an important resource and point of connection for women. Many ezine creators see their product serving as an opening for debate on feminist issues in a unique way: if a reader disagrees with the creator she can e-mail her directly and engage in discussion, and often ezine creators, such as the author of *Girlrights,* use forums like real-time chat to facilitate on-line discourse.[2] In addition, many creators express the feeling that ezines exist as a kind of outlet for their frustrations and political discourse. Sometimes ezine pieces involve sheer personal purging, like *Disgruntled Housewife's* "Dick List," a catalogue of affronts by men,[3] or the now defunct on-line *bitch dyke whore's* visceral account of a rape and its aftermath.

Sometimes "rants" lead to more complex political actions or community-building, such as *Brillo*'s call to arms around anti-feminist Web sites (see http://www.virago-net.com/brillo/).

This brings me to the third and most sophisticated form of resistance. Many women's ezines actively promote feminist issues, as well as serving as a network and a resource for women. Beyond simply gaining voice, women are now using this voice actively as a political tool. The voice has moved from *being* on-line to *acting* on-line. The author of the ezine *geekgirl* (http://www.geekgirl.com/au/) writes: "*geekgirl* [sic] is both liberating by example and also disseminates necessary information regarding networking, skill sharing and training. Readers have become designers of their own destiny, and know that helpful information can be gleaned in each and every issue." One of the concerns of many women's ezines, among other feminist issues, is promoting women's access to technology. Not only have they constructed their own site as a voice of resistance, they actively seek to aid other women in doing likewise.

My Definition of Feminism

A belief in the equality of men and women, a celebration of women's diversity and difference and a conscious commitment to the practice of making positive change.

Ezines often engage in some kind of reclamation of discursive or electronic space. While not all ezines function as Riot Grrrl-inspired publications (such as *Girlrights* or *Riot Grrrl* itself), most are nevertheless informed to some degree by the Riot Grrrl reclamation of "girl culture." This kind of girl culture is not a sentimental sort of femininity but rather a recollection of some of the messier parts of girlhood, parts which used to be too shameful to mention. Riot Grrrl culture not only reclaimed the word "girl" but also the words "slut," "dyke" and "cunt." This aggressive reclamation now forms part of the underlying culture of ezines. Since ezines are self-produced, they allow creators to control how they speak, write and inhabit discursive space. Ezine creators have power over their words (unmediated by editors or the desires

305

of a commercial market), and many present a conscious awareness of this fact in their acts of reclamation. Their work engages a post-modern ironic invocation of cultural forms that they presume the reader/viewer will understand. For example, the ezine *Brillo* uses title fonts derived from tampon boxes and tacky Valentine candies; *Disgruntled Housewife* incorporates pictures and topics from post-war "happy housewife" propaganda; *Riot Grrrl* uses cartoons of go-go girls with beehived hair.

Following as they do in the footsteps of their DIY predecessors, ezine creators like the comparative ease of dissemination that the Net affords. Lisa Jervis of the now-defunct on-line version of *Bitch* writes: "I realized that I really wanted to write feminist essays on pop culture and I also realized that most of them would never see print unless I published them myself."[4] Print zines generally have limited runs and mostly cater to urbanites in the city of publication who are hip enough to know where to find them. Ezines, in contrast, can be seen by anyone with a computer. I myself stumbled into the world of ezines quite by accident, and I suspect that thousands of other users discovered ezines in much the same manner. While ezines have restricted accessibility in the sense of requiring education and availability of technology, they also have expanded accessibility in that they can be made or seen by anyone who makes it on-line.

Though ezines have numerous positive attributes, they should not be regarded uncritically. The most obvious question is whether ezines are really a form of feminist activism or simply a narcissistic catharsis for the self-indulgent writer(s). Is there "true" public interaction occurring in a chat room sponsored by an ezine creator? I think to frame the question in this "either-or" way obscures the basic premise of cyberspace, which is inherently contradictory. The paradox of technology in general, and cyberspace in particular, is that it is *both* oppressive *and* liberatory; it is an organism that contains the seeds of its own subversion. Within the ambivalent possibilities of technology, ezines can represent a variety of things, both positive and negative.

Another significant criticism is whether, as Melanie Stewart Millar asks in *Cracking the Gender Code*, "organizing in cyberspace result[s] in social change in the real world."[5] If ezines represent a form of feminist activism, as I have proposed, what kinds of concrete results should feminists expect to see from them? Once again the "either-or" paradigm is problematic. The demarcation separating cyberspace from the "real world" is not entirely clear. How can we measure the intangible quality of a feminist consciousness manifesting itself on-line? When does networking on-line around a feminist project become "real"? Cyberspace requires us to rethink our definitions of concrete activism.

The significance of ezines for feminist resistance lies mainly, but not exclusively, in the possibility for networking, connection and community. Nerd girls with disparate concerns and identities can still mobilize together on-line around political initiatives. In practical application, women who connect over modem lines are engaged less with discovering individuals who share their physical identity configuration — after all, they may never see those to whom they are speaking — and more with forming relationships based on shared personal/political inclinations.

Ezines function most successfully as positive and visionary on-line forums for women. While they certainly engage in critical discourse and spare no pains to openly interrogate many problems still evident in the on-line medium, ezines nevertheless represent the fact that women are gaining knowledge about how to manipulate technology, and are making that knowledge evident for other women to see.

As Barbie herself can be both a symbol of oppression and infinite possibility, so too can cyberspace. Feminists are perfectly welcome to use a pink fuzzy computer or a steel-and-copper-wire self-creation held together by duct tape, as long they are getting on-line and getting active. Ezines provide a way for girls and women to explore female-created cyberculture and its sometimes conflicting philosophies, directives and sense of community.[6]

Notes

1. JoNelle, "Give Me A Microphone." *FaT GiRL*.
<http://www.fatso.com/fatgirl/>.
2. "Rachel." *Girlrights*. <http://www.mmotion.com/girlrights.html>.
3. Nikol Lohr. *Disgruntled Housewife*.
<http://www.disgruntledhousewife.com/>.
4. Lisa Jervis, personal communication with the author.
5. Melanie Stewart Millar, *Cracking the Gender Code: Who Rules the Wired World?* (Toronto: Second Story Press, 1998; now available from Sumach Press, Toronto), 170.
6. In keeping with the spirit of feminist scholarship and cyberculture, I have created a Web page devoted to links and reviews of the ezines. It can be found at <http://www.stumptuous.com/zine.html>.

My Top 10 Feminist Influences
(or almost)

1. bell hooks, who cuts through the crap

2. Donna Haraway, who makes language dance

3. Naomi Wolf, who spoke to my sixteen-year-old self

4. Annie Sprinkle, who showed me the power of sluts and goddesses

5. Hothead Paisan, who indulges my shameful homicidal fantasies

6. Sojourner Truth, whose deceptively simple words keep me honest

7. Xena, who kicks ass

8. Aliza Sherman, aka Cybergrrl, who encourages other girl geeks

9. Hildegard of Bingen, who envisioned

My Bio

KRISTA SCOTT-DIXON is currently working on her PhD in Women's Studies at York University. Her dissertation topic is the women's technology organization Digital Eve. At her real job, she teaches, writes and talks about tiresome academic things. She has developed and presented various workshops and lectures on media literacy, women's technology work, gender equity and anti-oppression activism. In her secret other life as Mistress Krista, she runs a swell Web site on women's weight training. She encourages people to eat their vitamins, get sweaty and move some heavy things around on a regular basis.

FROM NATTY DREADS TO GREY PONYTAILS:
The Revolution is Multigenerational

Joan Grant Cummings

From the moment we are delivered into the world with the words "It's a girl!" our lives assume a certain complexity. We are born into a world that has placed women in, and socialized women to assume, a role that is much less than equal to our male counterparts. Our inequality covers all spheres: political, economic, social, civil and cultural.

This century in particular, Canadians have seen a number of social changes that have advanced women's equality, but many unresolved struggles remain. Women have succeeded in forcing society to acknowledge male violence against women as a crime, yet it is not clearly understood as an equality rights issue. We have entered the paid workforce in greater numbers and changed employment ads advertising key positions asking for males only. We have the right to file for divorce and have custody of our children. We have the right to post-secondary education and to run for office. We are named in the Charter of Rights and Freedoms. The question remains, though, as to how these rights are respected, facilitated, protected and enjoyed.

It has been during the last decade that a clear, organized and orchestrated backlash against the feminist movement and feminists has emerged and made itself present. Mixed in with the aggressiveness of the global capitalist economy, it has made a deadly cocktail of anti-feminist forces. Our government, political parties, the mainstream media, certain educational institutions and even elements within the "social justice movement" have proven to be feminism's opponents in different ways. The backlash architects never tire of claiming that "feminism is dead!" or making the more misguided comment that "we are living in a post-feminist era." Among feminists themselves, the weary refrains "feminism does not speak for me" or "our national women's organization (NAC) does not speak for me" echo from time to time. Different media focus on the notion that feminism has gone too far and it is men who now are going through an identity crisis and who need to catch up.

For many women in Canada and globally, the backlash has the force of a Mack truck mowing them down. Feminists have been forced to stave off the erosion of the gains made and to fend off attacks instead of advancing the next steps of our agenda. Feminism has always been about the full and equal participation in all spheres of life by women, children and men. Yet, in Canada, we are still struggling for such everyday issues as pay and employment equity; daycare; freedom from all forms of violence and racism; elimination of poverty; and access to education and training programs, credit and loans, and political power. Women still perform two-thirds of the household work and are still the primary caregivers. One can gather from this fact, that the notion of full co-parenting and sharing of household chores has not taken root in the majority of male-female relationships. Seventy percent of the over 5.3 million people who live in poverty in Canada are single mothers. Seventy percent of young, unattached females (many students), 80 percent of Aboriginal women, depending on whether they live on or off reserves, 70 percent of single mothers and 60 percent of older women over 85 live in poverty.

Economically, Canadian women still experience a wage gap. Women earn, on average, 73 cents to the male dollar. For "self-employed" women, it is 67.3 cents. For women with disabilities, young women, Aboriginal women and new immigrant women, it is 50 cents on the average. The differences within the economy do not end there. Within the global capitalist economy and the era of neo-liberalism, women have been increasingly streamlined into non-standard work — part-time, homework, outsourced work, contingent and seasonal employment. We make up 70 percent of the part-time work force, even though more than 50 percent of us say we want full-time jobs. Canada has the second highest rate (next to Japan) of low-paid female jobs of all the countries that belong to the

> ## My Definition of Feminism
>
> Feminism is the full participation of women in the political, economic, social, civil, cultural, intellectual, spiritual and sexual spheres of life. Feminism works with race equality, sexual rights, disability rights, economic, social and education equality, age rights and gender equality at its centre.

Organization for Economic Co-operation and Development. Male violence against women is still a scourge in women's lives. Although there is more awareness in society, the solutions are still largely not based within an equality seeking perspective. As a result, government continues to treat this as a law and order issue versus one of women's human rights. The equality-seeking women's organizations — shelters, rape-crisis centres — that have taken the lead on this issue and advanced Canada's work in these areas are the same ones that have come under attack politically and financially.

Feminism cannot claim victory, nor can critics declare it over and done with, when whole communities of women are treated as expendable and disposable. Nor can we claim victory when racism and oppression continue to hinder our work. We saw the full force of racism and white supremacy when NAC elected Sunera Thobani, a woman of colour, in 1993 and myself, an African-Canadian woman in 1996 — two out of the then thirteen presidents in its twenty-seven-year history. These reactions clearly tell us that feminism has much work to do.

It is within this framework that NAC became increasingly aware that there are many roads left to travel within the women's equality struggle and that this is a multigenerational struggle. The cutbacks, the losses, the oppressions affect women of all ages, races and abilities. To ensure that multiple generations are participating in the leadership, organizing, co-ordination and mobilization strategies, the involvement of young women is essential, integral, instructive and non-debatable. During the 1996 NAC-CLC March Against Poverty, the Young Feminists/Women Caucus was born. NAC followed up in 1997 with a Young Women's Forum, in Hamilton, Ontario, and a town-hall style Young Feminist Forum was held at the NAC National Conference and Annual General Meeting in 1998. At this meeting, young feminists were successful in getting the membership to agree to create a new vice-president position to promote the leadership of and inclusion of feminists under thirty within the NAC organization.

NAC is under siege financially and politically. Yet NAC is not without hope or aim. The involvement of feminists under thirty lends a strong sense of continuity and ownership by women of all ages to the organization and the movement. The leadership of NAC and the membership recognize that it is in these crucial times that it is essential to keep the struggle alive and well by using the resources within our reach. Feminists under thirty are present in the anti-racism movement and the labour rights movement; they are in the struggle for gay and lesbian rights and disability rights; they are fighting for environmental protection and social justice; they are participating in electoral politics both as candidates and campaign managers. Feminists under thirty are policy-makers, organizers and activists. In countless ways, they debunk the mythology of aimless and apathetic "young people."

We do not all have the same understanding of feminism. Feminism is based in our life experiences and who we are. For Aboriginal women, the legacy of genocide, colonialism, racism and white supremacy are part and parcel of their feminist struggle, in addition to sexism. For women with disabilities, disability rights must be an integral part of feminism. For women under thirty, the notion that they must "follow and learn" and that they are being "groomed" to take over is being replaced. Women under thirty of all abilities, races and social statuses are leaders too in this movement and are bringing new and vital analysis to the issues we continue to face.

We live in a country founded on patriarchy, colonialism, genocide, racism, sexism, homophobia and ableism. These are the major oppressions and forms of discrimination. Add to these the economic system of capitalism, which thrives on exploitation of the oppressed, and you have a clear overview of how our society is structured. It is this structure that feminists must fundamentally change.

Feminists under thirty were born in times that have seen new and radical ways of working. Their experiences equip them with a tenacity and fortitude that differentiates them from long-time feminists. Their understanding of entitlement versus giving is one that informs their strategic thinking and organizing. If the last three decades of feminism indeed constituted the "second wave," then feminists under thirty constitute the power and energy of the third wave. From natty dreads to grey ponytails, feminism is alive and kicking, and multigenerational contributions and inspirations will make sure the revolution roars on!

My Top 10 Feminist Influences
(or almost)

1. Adina Graham, my grandmother
2. Idell Grant, my mother
3. Sojourner Truth, abolitionist and Black feminist

4. Nanny, strategist and leader of the Maroons (Africans who refused to be slaves when taken to the Caribbean and who won battles against the British)

5. Mary Pitawanakat, Aboriginal woman activist, leader, environmentalist
6. bell hooks (Gloria Watkins), author, educator, black feminist
7. Eva Smith, founder of Eva's Place for young people in Toronto and pioneer of programs geared for black youth in the Toronto school system
8. Carolyn Egan, feminist, women's health activist, anti-racist, workers' rights activist
9. Angela Y. Davis, African-American author, activist, scholar

My Bio

JOAN GRANT CUMMINGS is an African-Canadian feminist who works within an anti-racist, anti-discriminatory feminist framework. She has worked at and participated in the development of many feminist grassroots organizations, including the Immigrant Women's Health Centre, Women's Health in Women's Hands, Working Skills Centre For Women, New Experiences For Refugee Women and Intercede: An Organization for Domestic Workers, Migrant Workers and Live-In Caregivers Rights. She recently completed her term as the thirteenth president of the National Action Committee on the Status of Women, Canada's largest feminist lobby group, and now lives in Jamaica.

SCREAMING AS LOUD AS THE BOYS:
Women in Punktopia

H e a t h e r   D a v i s

The punk/hardcore scene offers a unique space in which women can express themselves through writing and music, as well as through organizing distros and shows. However, women, as traditionally marginalized subjects, are still extremely underrepresented at shows and in the musical aspect of punk. Punk music offers a way to express oneself through aggression. Women have been socialized to be passive, so many do not participate. But the women who are participating and making their voices heard through punk music are beginning to challenge patriarchy in very significant ways. Many women in the punk scene use the aggressive music as a way to express the rage that they feel at always being "second-class citizens" in a male-dominated world. Through the range of vocal spaces, women are challenging dominant concepts of gender as well, often opening up doors to a space where "third" genders fit.

The punk scene purports to be an anti-sexist, anti-racist space. In a lot of ways, the punk movement sees itself as operating in a utopian space outside of dominant culture; it sees itself as free of the stereotypes that are a part of the dominant sphere. The punk scene attempts to open up a space for self-reflection and for dialogue where all voices will be heard. In many ways, it does accomplish this. You often hear a performer say during the show, "If you have anything to say, any objections, please talk to us after the show." This scene is a place where people can talk about politics. As well, the extremely prevalent Do It Yourself (DIY) ethic in punk allows for participation by many more people, including women. This ethic says that it is okay if you do not know how to play your guitar "properly." This ethic helps to deconstruct notions of expertise and opens up space for multiple voices. Many women cite this as one of the main reasons that they turned to punk. Kathleen Hanna, member of Bikini Kill and a leader of Riot Grrrls, says, "[We realized] how important the whole punk you-can-do-anything idea was for women. It didn't matter if what the girls said was politically correct, or if they were good at their instruments; the point was simply to make some noise." [1]

However, the punk scene remains dominated by white male punks. Despite its good ideals, punk needs to look at itself critically and see how it reproduces the values of the dominant ideologies without intending to. For example, there is a fairly large backlash within the punk movement against the idea of all-women spaces. This includes distros, bands or zines. One zine writer wrote:

> I do not believe that anyone has the right to be sexist, racist or homophobic. I do not believe, therefore, that women

have the right to hate men … I have much less chance of getting a decent job in the future than my sister because I am male … Thanks to Affirmative Action, being a white male anglophone has basic-ally sealed my doom.[2]

Sometimes women run up against blatant sexism, something that they expect in their everyday lives but are not prepared to deal with in a punk scene. For example, one woman in the early DC punk movement recalls:

We played Wilson Centre and I really made a mistake cause it was the new generation of skinheads. We were playing and they were throwing lit cigarettes at me and saying things like, "take off your shirt." I'd written an anti-rape song and I said, "The next song is about rape, which I've been through." These stupid boys, who just discovered their penises, all said, "fuck you!" Man, I was so angry. That made me never want to play or go to a hardcore show again.[3]

My Definition of Feminism

Feminism involves challenging patriarchal systems of power and knowledge. This includes challenging gendered binaries, categories of "male" and "female," both in terms of critiquing them at a "theoretical" level and confronting them as they manifest in material oppressions. Furthermore, feminism has to include a recognition of the ways in which racism and sexism work together to marginalize women of colour.

Sexism shapes the everyday lives of women in punk and not only marginalizes them but also influences whether they will join a band or not. Gender socialization also influences women's participation. Women are told that it is "unladylike" to yell and scream and make noise. Yet, punk offers women a wider range of musical styles. Although most women in punk stick to the standard guitar plus screaming, many are branching out to create new experimental sounds.

However, some critics have argued that there is more going on than women simply being discouraged from playing music. As Susan McClary puts it, "there are additional factors that still make female participation in music riskier than either literature or the visual arts ... [T]he composer-performer often relies heavily on manipulating audience response through his [sic] enactments of social power and desire."[4] A man enacting his sexuality is very different from a woman enacting hers. Women on stage are perceived as sexual commodities, regardless of their appearance; and frequently women are expected to pay sexual favours in order to have a career in music. McClary goes on to say that yet another reason women have been denied access to music is because "music is always in danger of being perceived as a feminine or effeminate enterprise altogether. And one of the means of asserting masculine control over the medium is by denying the very possibility of participation by women."[5]

The punk scene is extremely masculine in terms of the music and the appearance that it projects. Anger is a significant part of the scene; anger is also one of the few emotions deemed "appropriate" for men to display. As well, the concept of the mosh pit is inscribed with the rituals of male bonding (being able to touch each others' bodies) as well as with elements of fighting. James Messerschmidt argues that "there is a dominant ideal of masculinity in the United States. This model transcends boundaries of class and race and involves characteristics of dominance, control, and independence."[6] The norms of male subcultures merely reflect the valorization of masculinity: the cool pose, the sexual objectification of women, the disdain of the feminine world of learning and the valorization of violence.

This masculinization helps to position punk in opposition to mainstream culture through its aggressive rejection of that culture, but it also takes with it many forms of the mainstream. Lauraine Leblanc argues that these subcultures are indeed specifically constructed to be hypermasculine in order to compensate for perceived challenges to working-class boys' masculinity in mainstream culture.[7] Theorists have argued that when adolescent males encounter constraints of class they turn to a celebration of masculinity in their creation of an acceptable "subcultural solution."

These standards of masculinity put women in a peculiar position. On the one hand, they are expected to enact this masculinity, to be tough in order to fit in, yet on the other hand they are supposed to maintain their heterosexual desirability, which means that they still must conform to some areas of femininity, specifically, those governing appearance and grooming. This strange space that is opened up for women somewhere between masculinity and femininity can be extremely liberatory and useful in challenging the binary notions of gender.

The Riot Grrrl movement, in particular, offers a way for women to enter into the hardcore scene without erasing their gender. The Riot Grrrl movement emerged at the beginning of the '90s with such bands as Bikini Kill, Babes in Toyland, L7 and Hole. Musicians in the Riot Grrrl movement appropriate masculine punk music to express anger and outrage at the sexist culture that surrounds them, both within and outside punk circles. The performance of these bands enacts an impersonation of the toughness, independence and irreverence found in male punk. Riot Grrrl musicians bring an extra feminist element to this demystification of music-making in that it rejects "boy" notions of excellence and expertise. It is ironic that much of Riot Grrrl music sounds like English punk and US garage, some of the most masculinist (and mysogynist) rock ever.

Through appropriation of this musical style and sound women have found legitimacy when enacting a parody of the "original" music. However, they do not stick with simply parodying masculinity; instead much of what they parody is femininity. Many Riot Grrrls dress in ripped baby-doll dresses, with clownish or whorish makeup. Through this dress they enact the contradictory elements of feminine sexuality, namely, that of the whore and the innocent virgin. However, through the symbol of the torn dress, these women allude to the sexual violence that many women go through as children, referring to the grim and horrific elements of girl sexuality. The performance of Riot Grrrl bands, such as Bikini Kill, has been described as "though one of Charcot's female patients has taken charge of her own theater of hysteria and transformed the humiliation of being an exhibit into an empowering exhibitionism."[8]

Many question whether the Riot Grrrls have been effective. Joy Press and Simon Reynolds pose an interesting question: How can Riot Grrrls significantly challenge patriarchy while still sounding (with the exception of the vocals) exactly like a male punk band? There have been many times when I have mistakenly thought that a band was all-male, because the music was extremely fast, heavy and aggressive. If women are appropriating this masculine style of music, are they actually being heard? In the case of Bikini Kill, they compensate for the aggressive punk sound by the use of extremely female-oriented, feminist lyrics. Also, their use of dress and the association with Riot Grrrls helps to define themselves as women. Thus, they do avoid being co-opted into the male subculture.

The appropriation of punk by women and the emergence of women into extremely heavy hardcore bands have allowed women entrance into spaces that were previously reserved for men only. It is, indeed, extremely empowering to be able to use a typically exclusionary genre as a means of liberating traditionally marginalized groups. As well, this appropriation has allowed women to challenge ideas surrounding masculinity and femininity. What does it mean if a woman is able to enact an extremely masculine role? This sort of question begins to break down the assumptions that these roles are "natural" and highlights the performative aspects of gender. As well, they enable women to express some of their rage at living in a patriarchal, capitalist society.

Many women in experimental music, within the punk/hardcore scene and outside of it, have been involved with dislocating gender roles. One woman describes this process as one of the most empowering and "interesting way[s] that people are challenging patriarchy, by completely taking apart gender roles and revealing the whole thing as a construct."[9] The possibility of playing out the masculinity role, either through music or through dress, is also one of the major factors that draws women to punk: "having rejected the femininity game, a number of punk girls turned to male models of punk style as alternatives. Carnie, who said that one of the main factors that attracted her to punk was the pleasure of seeing 'a girl look like a guy' is one such girl."[10] Thus punk is a way to express certain attributes that are repressed within mainstream culture. "The point of 'female machisma' is not simply to emulate and assimilate but to invade men's exclusive realms of privilege and freedom …"[11]

Anger is one of the ways that punk and feminism have merged and continue to compliment one another. Feminist critics have realized the importance of this emotion in reclaiming the "personal as political." As anger is the one emotion that has been deemed masculine, women's reclamation of this emotion to critique patriarchal society is an extremely effective political tool. Anger plays a large role in liberating women in the punk scene, allowing for a critique of mainstream culture, as well as punk itself. In fact, for some women, this anger has become central to their identity: "The next time you see me at a show, don't think about what a bitch I am … The isolation, separation and neglect I have felt is not only mine but it belongs to every [straightedge] girl … If I am not angry, I am not alive."[12]

As this woman notes, anger can be a mechanism to group women together, to recognize a common oppression and act against it, without erasing the boundaries that separate women. Recognizing the anger that women feel at being surrounded by a sexist culture can be extremely liberatory, and punk provides a unique format for that anger. Punk itself is an expression of anger, in the styles of dress and through the aggressive music. It is an outrage at the injustices and banalities of mainstream culture. Emily White describes how "Riot Grrrl was organized in the wake of the 'angry girl mood' … After a while, this anger didn't feel like a fad, it felt like hope — compelling certain girls to organize meetings every week, start calling themselves soldiers and messengers."[13] Anger then becomes the organizing tool for punk feminists.

Riot Grrrls manifest anger in punk music through screaming. Screaming is seen as a liberatory device in the sense that it allows for the expression of the otherwise inexpressible and also has very specific female connotations. Screaming is vastly associated with orgasm and childbirth, both very charged emotional events. Thus the scream is a shocking juxtaposition of sex and rage, yet retains an association of femininity that can effectively challenge dominant ideologies. Screaming is used "not as ... therapy, either, for the point isn't letting it out and feeling better ... but enlisting other screamers — and they're doing it in the public eye, which the authorities hate. 'Screaming,' says Kim Gordon 'is a kind of vehicle for expressing yourself in ways society doesn't let you.'"[14] Screaming also has a twofold resistance: it is a resistance to the injustices of mainstream society and a culture of apathy, as well as resistance to the confining role of femininity. Anger is also an embracing of masculinity and is another example of gender-bending.

Throughout the punk scene there are many women challenging both patriarchy and the consumerism inherent in mainstream society. Riot Grrrls have given voice to women in punk and have pushed open the dialogue that allows them to be heard. Although progress has been made, there are fewer women than men performers. But the women who are present are screaming just as loud as the boys.

Notes

1. Emily White, "Revolution Girl Style Now," in Evelyn McDonnell and Ann Powers, eds., *Rock She Wrote* (New York: Dell Publishing, 1995), 399.

2. Packetman, *Void* (Ottawa, circa 1996–99).

3. Sharon Cheslow, Leslie Clague, and Cynthia Conolly, in Lydia Ely et al., eds., *Banned in DC: Photos and Anecdotes from the DC Punk Underground* (Washington: Sun Dog Propaganda, 1988), 79–85.

4. Susan McClary, *Feminine Endings: Music, Gender and Sexuality* (Minnesota: University of Minnesota Press, 1991), 151.

5. Ibid., 151-152.

6. Lauraine Leblanc, *Pretty in Punk: Girls Gender Resistance in a Boys Subculture* (New Brunswick, NJ: Rutgers University Press, 1999), 108.

7. Ibid., 109.

8. Simon Reynolds and Joy Press, *The Sex Revolts: Gender, Rebellion and Rock 'n Roll* (Cambridge, MA: Harvard University Press, 1995), 262.

9. Vinita Ramani, interview with author, November 1999.

10. Leblanc, *Pretty in Punk*, 150.

11. Neil Nehring, *Popular Music, Gender, and Postmodernism: Anger is an Energy* (Thousand Oaks, CA: Sage Publications, 1997), 164.

12. Daisy, *Not Even Zine* (Ottawa, circa 1996–99).

13. White, "Revolution Girl Style Now," 397.

14. Nehring, *Popular Music*, 154.

My Top 10 Feminist Influences

1. bell hooks
2. Toni Morrison
3. Jeanette Winterson
4. Emmy Pantin
5. Kim Gordon
6. Tori Amos
7. Natasha Jategaonkar
8. Judith Halberstam
9. Emma Goldman
10. Trinh T. Minh-ha

My Bio

HEATHER DAVIS is a student at Trent University in her fourth year of a Cultural Studies degree. She thinks that it is important to get her writing outside the walls of the university, so she writes zines. She is currently working on a Super 8 film, and she enjoys working with video and photography too.

AGEING RADICALLY

Lisa Mesbur

This reflection began in May 1999, when, on a rare afternoon off work, I attended Toronto's Reclaim the Streets parade. Reclaim the Streets, an international festival now in its fourth year, bills itself as an anti-car, anti-corporate, anarchic street party that celebrates spontaneity, non-conformity, tribalism and creative spirit; a political event, essentially, but not of the placard-carrying/"Hey hey, ho ho" chanting variety. Since I've become a decided crank when it comes to rallies and protests, this event sounded right up my alley.

I bicycled east along Bloor Street, hit the march at Church Street, and wove myself into the crowd along its edge. Down the middle of Bloor, floats draped with bodies wheeled along to the pounding of drums, and flyers proclaiming secret parties and conspiracy theories slipped from hand to hand. Nervous onlookers, perched above the street in safe restaurants and office towers, peered down as the mass of freaks and renegades hooted, hollered and gyrated their way by. I kept pace, pedalling slowly along the parade's margins, ringing my bike bell as the horde rolled forward, taking up space and generally disturbing the status quo. But something was nagging at me, and by the time the parade wound up at Brunswick Street, culminating in a massive dance party, a tiny voice in my head had grown audible above the crowd's din. "Face it, Lisa," it whispered as I straddled my bike at the curb, watching the young activist types laughing and moving their lithe bodies to the funky beats, "you're too old to be here."

Spotting a friend, I rode up to her and we surveyed the scene together. "I feel old," I told her.

"The average age here is probably twenty," she confirmed, looking a little crestfallen.

It was a strange and humbling revelation. I rode home soon afterwards, perplexed and a bit depressed, reflecting upon my new status: somehow, inexplicably, I was no longer a central insti- gator or participant in the event itself, but a casual witness, a voyeur, even an alien. An image of myself from the perspective of a parade organizer emerged in my head — a tolerant, gently smiling, ageing hipster, appreciative and yet also fundamentally out of touch. I suddenly saw that a group of youngsters was filling the space I used to occupy, and it worried me.

> *My Definition of Feminism*
>
> The understanding that local, nation- al and international oppression of women and girls is a fact and a reality. The belief that oppression of women and girls is inseparable from myriad other oppressions that arise from imbalances of power and privi- lege. The conviction to fight these intertwined oppressions in any form we see fit.

That night, I saw an advertisement for Coach leather goods in *Vogue Magazine*. The ad featured Gloria Steinem, smiling gen- tly, a creamy 500-buck Coach bag swinging nonchalantly over one slim, smooth shoulder. The caption read: "Gloria Steinem, writer." Oh my God, Gloria too, I thought miserably. What is it about ageing that makes us lose our edge? How can we continue to think like radicals in a culture that allows youth the license to participate in political radicalism but excludes adults as some kind of punishment for our early need to shake things up?

***

I became politically aware and politically active when I was in my late teens and early twenties. For me, the transition from mildly irritated adolescent to completely enraged activist flowed from my move to Vancouver to attend university and continued on past my degree and into my young adult life. Anger swept me into political activism. As I educated myself about the complex web of local and global injustices, I developed the language to articulate my feelings and opinions. I learned to carry my anger like a knife, and I learned how to attack, unhesitating, fast and certain.

As a young woman newly activated, I wore many labels proudly, but none more proudly than radical and feminist (though never "radical feminist"; not even in past misanthropic phases did I hope to eliminate males entirely from my life). As a self-identified feminist radical, I wrote articles about queer bashing and about women's carpentry in a community garden. I attended anti-fascist rallies, pro-choice rallies, Pride Day rallies, prison justice rallies. I built trails through endangered rainforest and blocked logging roads. I refused to shave or wear makeup.

My friends and peers felt similarly about most issues; we knew who the "good guys" were, knew the enemy by his face, his vocation, his clothes, his car, his language. Through my political involvement, I grew to understand more about hierarchies, power and control, economics and the many varied faces of oppression. As a radical and a feminist, I marched and yelled, chanted and wrote, argued righteously and defended confidently.

I can find traces of my former self in photographs. One particularly fine example is the one of me holding a placard at a rally in front of the Vancouver police station. I pull it out of the box in my closet and examine it closely. In this photo, I stand looking at something to the right of the camera lens — at a heckler on his way out of the methadone clinic across the street, if I remember — and my face speaks the language of activism. In this photograph, my eyes are narrowed into focus, my mouth shouts a series of retaliations, my stance is solid, confrontational. One of my arms points back to the steps of the police station, where a woman had just emerged from trial, while the other points forward, accusing and enraged.

Underneath this photo I find a more recent one, from this past winter. In it, I stand with my partner and my parents at a wedding, their arms enclosing me on both sides. There is no defi-ant grin here, no fury. Just some well-applied makeup, clean smooth calves visible through sheer stockings, fitted red dress, groomed hair, a quiet smile into the camera's eye, sharing some-thing, falsely intimate. This photograph does not reveal the sub-tler reality, my new full-time job, my reasonably peaceful rela-tionship with my parents or my partial assimilation into a society I once disdained, but I know they are there all the same. I stare at these photos for a few minutes, getting used to the contrast. I can't help wonder what a younger me would see in this contrast between then and now. Would I see Yuppie Before and After shots? Would I see a sell-out and a conservative, jaded and bound by convention? Would I scribble on the back of the more recent photo: Politics? What politics?

Over the course of six or seven years, between these pho-tographed moments, I made a slow and almost imperceptible per-sonal shift out of activist mode. I started noticing my own and others' hypocrisy, how many collectives functioned badly, how the world seemed to carry on whether or not I was at that weekend's event or not. I grew tired of being righteous and tired of fighting. Gradually, my overtly political work slowed to a trickle, though I never consciously chose to abandon it.

Like many young radicals and activists, I sometimes feel that I've slid into conservative patterns and out of radicalism as I've gotten older. "She'll get over it," some relatives of mine used to laugh when I launched into yet another tirade or decided to boy-cott yet another company that oppressed women. Although I don't feel particularly different about most issues, in their eyes, I did "get over it." After all, they are witnesses to the person I have become — aesthetically manageable, delightfully accepting of the behaviour of others, proud holder of a "proper" job.

Why is it that in our culture, youth is so powerfully linked to radical thought and activism, while getting older suggests mellowing out, giving up, growing apathetic, conservative, cal-lous, even cruel? Is it truly possible to stay radical as we age, to continue to fight in the face of the strange and strangely seductive condition called adulthood? Haunted by the eerie image of myself staring prettily and uncritically out of that wedding photograph, I propel myself into the world one afternoon to seek wise words from my women friends on the topic.

One friend suggests a genetic explanation to the problem: "As we get older we want babies, we want stability. Young people are breaking away from the tribe, all those hormones surging ..."

Another sighs, "I'm definitely more conservative. I'm more accepting of the way things are now. The world is so messed up — what can you do?"

Others are more reflective, "I feel like I'm doing my bit through working in the arts."

"Yeah, it's a problem, for sure."

"I just think I'm more realistic now."

Frustrated, I finally give up and head home, turning their responses to my question over in my mind. My women friends, all politically minded, all smart enough to assess their own choices and values, can't provide me with the secret to staying radical. While none of us have completely abandoned our political ideals, we seem to share a sense of guilt, a sense of having given something up as we moved from youth into adulthood. (I have a brief, alarming vision of a future in which all the formerly political people support nuclear energy, shop at fashion designer clothing stores, eat "Stay-Slim-Nutbars" to "feel good," watch the six o'clock news religiously every night, believing it truth.)

When I arrive home, I pull the photos out of my closet one more time. Looking back is painful. Sometimes, I think that my younger, former political self is a mere apparition, an unidentified floating object I can (and often do) pin qualities onto. "Oh, yeah," I can say, if necessary. "I was such a little politico then." It's a badge of honour, this former identity, and I don't want to let go of it. In a way, it's how I justify my current choices, my adult life.

It is in the unexpected form of my favourite aunt that a new vision of radicalism finally emerges. Perhaps it is no surprise that my aunt is twenty-three years older than me, a former hippie, a 1970s-educated feminist and mother of two incredibly well-adjusted, unsexist teenaged boys. One gift of age is insight and perspective, and at this point, I feel I have neither.

When I tell her that I'm working on a piece about why people seem to get more politically conservative as we age, she smiles. "I don't think I'm getting more conservative as I get older," she tells me in her matter-of-fact way. "In fact, in some ways I'm getting more radical."

Astonishment. "Really?" I ask.

"I'm more confident now," she says calmly. "As an adult, I have more power in the world; I speak my mind more. I don't care what people think, and I have the ability to effect change in a way I never did as a younger person."

I think of my own increased abilities to speak out as she tells me this, considering the potential benefits of being an adult in a society where adults hold a great deal of the power.

"Remember, Lisa, teenagers are the worst conformists. They're trying as hard as possible to be different, they don't realize they conform completely to fit into their peer groups."

I think back to my experiences as a younger person and the various pressures to speak, dress and interact in specific ways. This pressure, too, was a part of my "radical" life.

After speaking to my aunt, I begin to notice politics in action in many unlikely places. I see the friend who claims that she's "accepting of the way things are" learning about alternative medicine and volunteering at a women's crisis hotline. I see the friend who says she gave up on collective process making zines and short films. I start to notice powerful words scribbled in women's bathroom stalls, ads for women-only boxing classes, co-workers speaking out against workplace racism and homophobia. I notice teachers teaching conflict resolution to kids in schools, nurses and civil servants performing in queer cabarets. I look critically at my own life and notice my own "political" work with a shock: I work for a feminist literary magazine, eat organic food, teach special needs kids, write smutty poetry ...

I begin to reframe radicalism.

Maybe the secret to staying radical as we age is not, as I thought, segregating ourselves into small social worlds where we are unlikely to encounter those with contentious opinions, organizing only with those with whom we share a great deal. It may not only be going to rallies, working for particular organizations or walking and talking particular walks and talks, although these actions are an enormously significant part of social change movements. It is probably not about trying to cover all the "right" political bases every day, all the time, either. It is certainly not about aesthetics.

Rather, truly radical is the notion that the world is a complicated place and that to live in it is not a straightforward business where we can always know "the good" from "the bad." As we get older, perhaps we can see our own battles better, thus improving our abilities in areas where we can do the most. Truly radical, perhaps, is the notion that radical politics can be a form of subterfuge. We can acknowledge that not all is visible, that radical action cannot always be identified or categorized. We can trust that that which is truly radical is passing around and through us every day, sight unseen, potent and undeniably subversive.

My Top 10 Feminist Influences

1. My women friends: smart, opinionated, inspiring, dazzling
2. My great-grandmothers, grandmothers, and mother (of course!)
3. Bessie Smith, blues singer
4. Emma Goldman, kick-ass Jewish feminist anarchist and rabble-rouser
5. bell hooks, *Teaching to Transgress*
6. All poetry and fiction by Grace Paley
7. Zora Neale Hurston, *Their Eyes Were Watching God*
8. The spoken words and deep grooves of Vancouver's Kinnie Starr
9. *Bust, Bitch, Ms.,* and the many other voices of feminist publishing
10. My female students, the life-blood of feminism's future tense

My Bio

LISA MESBUR is a writer and teacher living in Toronto. Her current fixations include learning how to box, writing for young adults, playing guitar and acting radical.

A DAY IN THE LIFE OF DEBBIE STOLLER & BUST MAGAZINE

Jennifer O'Connor

Debbie Stoller has what may be the world's only anatomically correct Barbie doll. Barbie lives on a shelf in Stoller's New York City apartment. Stoller pulls down the brunette vixen's leopard-print pants to show me a tiny round groove between her legs. "She has this little thing there," Stoller says, pointing at the spot. "I don't know if it's supposed to be her clit or her vulva." Does she want input on this? I shrug; Stoller returns Exhibitionist Barbie to the shelf. "I don't know if she's the only one like that, with a clit."[1]

She is one of a kind — Stoller, I mean. She's the ever-sexy rebel girl (yes, she calls herself a girl even though she's thirty-six), and looks the part in a side-slit skirt, platform boots and a breast-shaped ring. For the past six years, she's been co-editing *Bust* (under the pen-name Celina Hex), along with co-editor Marcelle "Betty Boob" Karp and art director Laurie "Areola" Henzel. It's a low-budget, sassy, feminist magazine for women who are a little too brazen for *Ms.* and way too smart for *Cosmo.* Bust has grown into a magazine with a circulation of 37,000, has won an Utne Reader Alternative Press Award, and published a book, *The Bust Guide to the New Girl Order,* which has sold 23,000 copies and is now in its fifth printing. And Stoller's been everywhere in the press. Among other things, she's made guest appearances on MTV and National Public Radio, and played pundit on MuchMusic's

"Girl Power" special. She's contributed to *Ms., George* and *The Village Voice,* and writes a column for *Shift Online,* where she's a contributing editor. Not that she wants to be a writer. Really. "I'm into feminism and trying to make a difference in the world. There's no way to get those ideas out without writing. I love being on TV. I love being 'Pundit Spice,' but I hate writing more than anything."

But write she must. Stoller is the voice of *Bust,* and *Bust* is the "voice of the new girl order." The third wave of feminism is here, and like Stoller it's all about sex and brains and rock and roll. If second-wave feminism was based on breaking down barriers that excluded women, then third-wave feminism is about embracing a separate subculture, reclaiming language and images. The emphasis on the third wave is on pop culture, sexuality and the bratty girl. Born out of the punk rock, Riot Grrrl, Do It Yourself aesthetic of zines from the '80s and early '90s, *Bust* is Stoller and company's take on third-wave feminism. Flipping through the magazine, you learn the basic lessons of Bustology:

Lesson #1: "If we fuck on the first date, it doesn't mean I am waiting for an engagement ring to appear on the second date."[2]

Lesson #2: "Bad girls are 'femmenistes'; we like our dark Nars lipstick and LaPerla panties, but we hate sexism, even if we do fuck your husbands/boyfriends. We understand men, we love them, us hetero/bi bad girls."[3]

Lesson #3: "C**t is taboo, and taboo things are scary and powerful. Somebody else isn't going to own that word. I figure it's so fucking dangerous, and it's so intimately about my anatomy, that it's going to be mine, too. Yes way."[4]

Lesson #4: "If you really want to do something for yourself, go get a vibrator. If as many women bought themselves vibrators as they do implants, the world would be a better place."[5]

Lesson #5: "Even those of us who were absent on that day in school when they taught you how to do romantic relationships know we can ace the friendship exam. Marilyn, you see, had it all wrong. A girlfriend is a girl's best friend."[6]

The illustrations that accompany these articles are a curious mix of clip art, pin-up photos and collages, like Martha Stewart's head on a dominatrix's body, but the best has to be their subscription form. It's a copy of Jane Fonda's mug shot where she has her fist in the air, holding a copy of *Bust* in her grip. The caption reads "Get Busted." *Bust* also has a Web site (www.bust.com) featuring The Lounge (a chatroom), The Girl Wide Web (links to hundreds of Web sites), and Let's Go Girl (a travel guide).

What else would you expect from a "bad, smart girl" from Brooklyn? She was the one who would sneak into the woods with the other "bad" girl scouts to smoke. The one who cut school to go to Manhattan with friends and "pretend we were beatniks." SUNY Binghamton gave her a $250 scholarship to help pay for her degree in psychobiology, but she still had to take on odd jobs because her father wouldn't sign the financial aid forms. She hated the school and finished a four-year program in two-and-a-half years, sufficiently impressing "Mr. Yale," as she calls whoever it was at the university who offered her a full scholarship. She spent the next six years there, getting her MA and PhD so she could get into the typing pool at Nickelodeon, the children's television station.

In 1992, she met Marcelle Karp in the cubicles there. One day, Stoller mentioned starting a magazine, even though neither she nor Karp had any publishing experience. They put together the first issue a year later, in April 1993. The theme was "A Day In The Life" and would cover stories about anything, with one condition: it had to be something that wasn't being covered in the mainstream media. One woman wrote about her feelings and blow jobs: "I have a very complex, uneasy relationship to blow jobs, as do many of my women friends. Something about being silenced, about dick in your face as if it would obliterate your identity with its demand."[7] Karp, who by then had left Nickelodeon, met Stoller at the Nickelodeon office around seven. The office was an odd mix of a "Nine to Five" corporate culture motif with a funky look. They had typed up the articles: the first step was copying them. They were going to use Nickelodeon's copier, but it's best not to get caught using company property, at least not in your own office, so they went upstairs to the Xerox room at VH1 to run off 500 copies of the first issue of *Bust*. On their way back downstairs they ran into the VH1 President. They said that the photocopiers at Nickelodeon were broken; lying was the easy part. They went back to Stoller's desk to put it together. The text ran really close to the edge of the page, so they had to be careful not to cut off any of the words as they stapled each booklet. "Our wrists would be, like, urrggghhhh," Stoller says. This was the unfun part.

That was the only issue they ever put together like that. Laurie Henzel joined the co-editrixes to put

> **My Definition of Feminism**
>
> If I had to define feminism, I would say that it's not only about achieving equality rights for women in the social, economic and political spheres, but also about embracing and taking pride in girl culture and challenging attitudes about femininity and sexuality.

out the second issue, the "Fun" issue. And they didn't sneak around copying 3,000 issues, which was now the circulation. *Bust* went to a printer. Five thousand people subscribe to the magazine today, and they receive about 140 submissions for each issue (none of the writers are paid).

Speaking of being paid, Stoller has gone to Laurie Henzel's apartment to work on the layouts for the "Money" issue of *Bust* (Karp is in Australia). Henzel has a huge studio space, complete with hardwood floors, an autographed photo of Yoko Ono and, in one corner, a computer where Stoller finishes putting the pages in order. Stoller then takes some dummy pages to a table at the other end of the room and begins piecing together performance artist Ann Magnuson's guide to getting rich and staying poor. Stoller gives Henzel the layout. Now all she has to do is write the decks for the columns and get the product shots done for "The Shit," a beauty column reviewing stuff like Polish Mood Shades (PMS) nail polish. "I'm gonna lay down and close my eyes for two seconds and see if I can get my personality back," Stoller says. "Sorry, this is what it's like working on *Bust*."

Not that everyone appreciates Stoller's work. In a now infamous *Time* article, Ginia Bellafante slams not only *Bust* but also third-wave feminism as part of "the culture of celebrity and self-obsession, a flighty, silly movement deployed by lesser minds."[8] "Feminism at the very end of the century seems to be an intellectual undertaking in which the complicated, often mundane issues of modern life get little attention and the narcissistic ramblings of a few new media-anointed spokeswomen get far too much," she writes. Bellafante counts *Bust* among the frivolous. Why, she asks, can't *Bust* be about "women's roles, status, and pay" (like *Ms.*), instead of "wacky sexual exploits?" While she says that *Bust* has good intentions with its sexual openness, she doesn't appreciate the tone, young lady. "The message is often lost in the magazine's adolescent tone; read about an adult woman's first-time vibrator discoveries," she writes. "*Bust* offers a peek-a-boo view of the world of sex that leaves one feeling not like an empowered adult, but more like a 12-year-old sneaking in some sexy reading behind her parent's back."

"Has Madonna taught us nothing?" Stoller asks, responding to the criticisms. "It's not worth fighting for all these rights if you still feel that you're ignored by the culture. It's very empowering to make your voice heard." And women are listening. "It really speaks to me," says Allyson Mitchell, a PhD student at York University (and an editor of this collection). "I'm really concerned with making feminism accessible and sexy and fun, and *Bust* is the epitome of that for me."[9] "We talk about how shitty women's magazines are. This is what we want," says Lisa Jervis, editor of *Bitch* magazine. "*Bust* is what we'd like in its place. *Bust* takes the grassroots thing and takes it to a wide audience, which is really powerful."[10] Yeah, *Bust* might not make women pick up placards, but it's not supposed to. "*Bust* is not about educating people about feminism," Stoller says. "The women who read *Bust* are too smart to be anything but feminist."

"*Bust* struck a chord with young women, and there's going to be a lot of people doing the same thing to cash in," says John Turner, who hired Stoller to do her column for *Shift Online*. Magazines like *Jane* and *Nylon*, monthlies with full-time staff and cheques for freelancers, are aimed at the same audience — and the same advertisers. The thing is that they have two things *Bust* doesn't: money and a business plan. "There's a lot they could do. Otherwise they run the risk of losing the magazine," Turner says.[11] What they need is enough money to publish more than twice a year, pay the writers and hire a copy editor.

And there's a big problem: *Bust* has to make money without selling out. The magazine has entertained offers from parent companies, but what Stoller would prefer is subscribers — her goal is 500,000. All she has to do is figure out how to get them. There is the "boob-tique," part of the *Bust* Web site, a marketplace of girlie delights (like tank tops that say "toughtitties" across the chest), but that hasn't brought in the bucks yet. And Stoller knows that *Bust* will never get any big-name ad campaigns: "Then we'd have to quit running articles on butt sex. I like it. Maybelline may not."

We're lounging at Stoller's apartment. Her boyfriend, Michael, is watching the nightly news. Booty the cat has crawled out of a drawer to play with his toy Sex Bunny. "Doing the magazine has totally changed my life," Stoller says. "I get the feeling I'm doing something that matters. It's an incredible thing." No doubt she's made Exhibitionist Barbie proud.

Notes

1. All quotes by Stoller come from an interview with her in New York City, January 1999. This essay first appeared as an article in *The National Post*, "Weekend," 4 December 1999, 6. Reprinted here with permission of the author.

2. Betty Boob, Miss Mara, John-Boy and Jimmie C-A-Go-Go, "Don't For Boys," in Debbie Stoller and Marcelle Karp, eds., *The Bust Guide to the New Girl Order* (New York: Penguin Books, 1999), 151.

2. Courtney Love, "Bad Like Me," in Stoller and Karp, eds., *The Bust Guide to the New Girl Order*, 313.

3. Jayne Air, "A Vindication of the Rights of C**t," in Stoller and Karp, eds., *The Bust Guide to the New Girl Order*, 298.

4. Debbie Stoller, Editorial, in Stoller and Karp, eds., *The Bust Guide to the New Girl Order*, 95.

5. Debbie Stoller, "Really Rosie," *Bust* (Summer/Fall 1998), 4.

6. *Bust* (April 1993), 5.

7. Ginia Bellafante, "Feminism: It's All About Me!" *Time* (June 29, 1998), 48-54.

8. Allyson Mitchell, interview with author, Toronto, Ontario, January 1999.

9. Lisa Jervis, interview with author, Toronto, Ontario, January 1999.

10. John Turner, interview with author, Toronto, Ontario, January 1999.

My Top 10 Feminist Influences

1. *Bust* (surprise). This magazine tells it like it is. It's got everything a grrrl mag should have: honesty, a sense of fun, sexiness and brains.

2. *The Awakening* by Kate Chopin: I read this for an English class. I cried at the end.

3. *A Vindication of the Rights of Woman* by Mary Wollstonecraft. It was after reading this that I said "I am a feminist."

4. Liz Phair. Listen to her albums. I mean it.

5. Gloria Steinem, "I Was A Playboy Bunny." I read it to remind myself of why I went into journalism.

6. *The New Our Bodies Ourselves.* Everything I wanted to know about sex but was afraid to ask.

7. Madonna. My girlfriend and I would bond over singalongs to "Material Girl."

8. *Trifles* by Susan Glaspell. I read this in drama. It was incredibly simple (and short) but spoke volumes about how women are treated in society.

9. *The Bell Jar* by Sylvia Plath. Required reading for any confused adolescent.

10. *Absolutely Fabulous.* I said to a guy friend that my best girlfriend and I are like Patsy and Edina. He didn't get it. I told another girl the same thing. She nodded in approval. Girls understand. No matter how fucked up your life gets, as long as you have a girlfriend it's gonna be okay.

My Bio

JENNIFER O'CONNOR is a Toronto-based freelance writer. She also edits the ezine *Cherry* (www.cherrymag.com).

OUT OF THE MOUTHS OF BABES

Chris Mitchell and Madelyne Beckles

4 … 3 … 2 … 1 … OKAY!!!!

Hello. My name is Chris Mitchell and I'm here interviewing Madelyne Beckles, my daughter. And how old are you Madelyne?

Seven years old.

And what year is this?

The year 2000.

And what's the date today? February the fifth.

Yes (hee hee).

And we just came from … what did we do today?

We went and saw *Mella Mella*.

What was *Mella Mella*?

A play.

Right, and who was Mella Mella.

A girl.

What about her? What was the story about?

She saved Zimbabwe.

How did she do that?

She, um, didn't care if she died, she just wanted her dad to get better.

Do you think that she had Girl Power?

Yah.

What is Girl Power?

It's, um, stuff in every girl that makes you a girl.

Like what?

Do you want me to give you an example?

Yes please.

Well, um, hummm, it's something that makes a girl a girl and sometimes inside you feel scared but outside you just do what you need to do and it doesn't make you afraid to be a girl cause you're just a girl and it makes you one. But a girl who does not have Girl Power would be a girl without anything ... she ...

Do you think there's girls that don't have Girl Power?

Nope.

Do you think that all girls have Girl Power?

Um hummm, a girl that didn't have Girl Power would be a boy, or a boy with Girl Power.

What do you think boys think about Girl Power?

Umm, I think that they think it's silly.

Why do you think that?

Because they don't believe in it.

Why do you think they don't believe in it?

Because they're boys.

Just because they're boys they don't believe in Girl Power?

They don't believe in Girl Power.

Why not? It seems like you feel very strongly about that, why?

Because, um, I think that boys think that boy power is better than Girl Power.

Really? Why would they feel that way?

Because they're boys, Mother.

What do you think is better? Is one better than the other?

No I think they're both good cuz if they didn't have boy power they wouldn't be a boy they'd be a girl and if a girl didn't have Girl Power they would be a boy, it makes them what they are.

Good answer.

Good answer?

I think that's a good answer.

What else did I want to ask you? Umm, do you know what the word feminist means?

Yes.

What does it mean?

It means you think that girls and boys should have equal fairness.

Have you ever heard that word before?

Yes.

Where have you heard it?

From you.

From me? You never heard anyone else say that word?

No.

No? Are you a feminist?

Yes.

Why are you a feminist?

Because I think that everybody should go fair and square and have equal things.

Doesn't matter whether they're a boy or a girl?

No.

Do you think there are people who think differently than that?

Yes.

Yeah? Who? Do you know anybody who thinks differently than that.

No, but I think there is some people.

The other day you were telling me an interesting story about heroes and heroines. Can you tell me about that again?

I was talking to Patrick.

He's a boy in your class?

Yes, and um, I told him that heroes are as good as heroines and Patrick said. "You're joking." I said, "No." He said, "Name one." I said "Joan of Arc." He said, "What did she do?" I said, "She saved a city in France." And he said, "That's it?" And I said, "That city would not be alive if she wasn't alive." And Patrick said, "Don't you like heroes?" And I said, "Yes, and I like heroines too."

Then what did Patrick say?

Patrick said I was a goof ball.

He did?

Yes.

So do you think boys and girls can be feminists?

Yes.

Can you name some other girls or women who are feminists that you know?

You, my auntie Ally, Lex, Daddy, Grace, Grandma, Nana and Grampy, Freddy and Frankie [her grandparents' cats ... Mom laughs], Michael and Amy and Chris.

Yeah, so everybody that you know that's close to you is a feminist?

And Auntie and Granny and it goes on and on.

Yeah? Do you know anybody outside of your family who is a feminist?

Yes.

Who?

Molly and Alexandra and Sarah and Hilary and Caitlin and it can go on and on and on and on and on on on.

Do you know any grown ups outside of your family who are feminists?

Yes. My mommy's friends.

Yeah? What makes you think they're feminists.

Because they treat girls and boys fair.

What do you mean by fair? What means fair to you?

Um, if there was an apple and everybody wanted it, they would give everybody a piece. They wouldn't just give a certain person a small piece like all the girls a big piece and all the boys a small piece. They would give them the same amount.

Can you give me another example of what equal fairness for boys and girls means. Besides sharing things equally, can you think of something else?

No.

No?

343

No.

Um, ok. What else do you know about feminists, anything?

No.

What else do you know about Girl Power?

Nothing else.

That's it? Would you like the interview to end now?

Yes.

Do you have anything else to say, final wisdom about feminism?

Good night. Au revoir. See you later.

Thank you, Madelyne.

— Lisa Mesbur

MADELYNE BECKLES is seven years old, goes to school, loves ice cream, wants to learn how to snowboard and enjoys hanging out with her friends.

CHRIS MITCHELL likes art, running, cooking and being with her family. When she grows up she wants to be a photographer, right now she is the vice-president of an import/export company.

R is for Revolution

GLOSSARY

Accessibility: A term used to highlight the way mainstream society has yet to remove innumerable physical, legal and political barriers to groups of people because of (dis)ability, race, class and gender.

Ageism: Discrimination based on age.

Agoraphobia: The fear of open spaces and public places.

Alienation: A sense of exclusion based on class, race or gender, among other things.

Alternative school: A school outside the regular school system established to meet the needs of a target group of students (such as queer youth or single sex).

Anarchism: A movement against the organized government and laws currently in place.

Androcentric: Male-centred.

Binary: Describes "either/or" thinking or concepts that offer two opposing sides to the exclusion of others.

Biphobia: The fear or hatred of bisexual people.

Bisexuality: To be sexually attracted to either or any sex.

Bitch: While potentially an insult, some parts of the feminist movement have reclaimed it as a term that allows women to break free from the stereotypes that they must always be nice, accommodating, self-sacrificing. As a reclamation term, it allows women to feel empowered in finding their voice, even if that voice says something that is counter to perceptions of what is "gender appropriate."

Bollywood: The Indian movie-making industry.

Butch-Femme: Forms of gendered self-stylization among queers whereby butch performs, imitates, parodies and undermines the clichés of heterosexual masculinity in an erotic difference to femme, which is a form of feminine self-stylization that imitates, parodies, negotiates, appropriates and plays with heterosexual forms of femininity.

Camp: Performance of gender and sexuality that is affected and often exaggerated for ironic and critical effect.

Class: Social divisions along economic lines, as defined by Karl Marx. Class is a key factor in maintaining capitalism as the lifestyle of the upper-class (bourgeoisie) depends on the labour exploitation of the working class (proletariat). Without a class system where "workers" provide cheap labour for "owners," capitalism (and the current economic structures of the world) would collapse. In feminist theory, class is considered to be an important difference among women as well as an identity and a culture.

Collective agreement: A labour movement term for a contract determined through the bargaining process and collectively agreed upon through membership voting.

Colonized: Literally means to settle and establish communities in another's country/territory. The term is also used to refer to women's bodies being claimed and defined by racist or sexist others.

Community: While community is often determined by geography, it can also be defined by culture or affiliation. For example, you can belong to a lesbian community and a Jewish community, as well as the community in which your home is located. One can belong to more than one community at a time.

Critical race theory: The body of mainly legal scholarship that looks at the social construction of "race" through government policies and laws.

Culture jam: This term is said to have been formulated by the audio-plunder group Negativeland and has been greatly popularized by *Adbusters Magazine,* however it extends beyond the realms of audio-collage and adbusting. A good "jam" involves creative revitilization of some cultural product, message, script or environment that comments, critiques or satirizes. It is a playful activity that involves creativity and often improvisation. The word "jam" alludes to jamming musicians, jamming the system (i.e., putting a wrench in the machinery) or even to make jam (the preservation of something sweet).

Cunt: It has been used in derogatory or insulting ways to refer to both women's genitalia and women in general. The word has now been reclaimed by some feminists as a celebration of women's sexuality and women's wisdom.

Deconstruct: To take apart. Used in post-structuralist theory as a method of critical analysis that exposes unquestioned metaphysical assumptions and internal inconsistencies in language and texts.

Degradation: Reduction to a lower rank or status.

Diaspora: The geographically dispersed members of an ethnic or cultural group across the world (Jewish Diaspora, African Diaspora).

Dichotomy: A division into two opposites. For example, concepts of women that categorize women as either "virgins" or "sluts."

Dildo: A sex toy that is generally in the shape of a penis and is used for penetration.

Discriminate: An act of power that has the effect of, intentionally or unintentionally, denying an individual or group treatment or opportunities "equal" to others. Discrimination occurs on a personal, structural or institutional level. Discrimination may be practised on the basis of race, ethnicity, colour, nationality, creed, gender, age, sexual orientation and ability.

Distros: A slang term for the distribution of zines and independent music informally rather than through the commercial system.

Do It Yourself (DIY): An anti-establishment politic and aesthetic that commands and conveys an urgency for people to create their own culture and not rely on the mainstream to do it for them.

Drag: A subversive kind of gender performance or play often, but not always, in opposition to what is considered biological sex. A deliberate presentation of gender, frequently based on pardodying gender stereotypes.

Dyke: Slang for lesbian. While this word has had a negative connotation, it is now reclaimed by queer women as an empowering way to refer to themselves.

Embodiments: How ideas and concepts are made concrete though our bodies.

Ethnography: A branch of anthropology which is dedicated to studying cultures. Feminist ethnography, in particular, has attempted to recognize the cultural imperialism that has often occurred and so has taken up and critiqued these practices to give voice to marginalized communities.

False consciousness: The notion that the set of beliefs that one holds may be at odds with their interests. This does not necessarily imply that the beliefs are untrue, just that there is an element of self-deception. In Marxist thinking it is the consciousness raising of the proletariat, becoming aware of their shared experience of exploitation, that will lead to revolution. There is much debate on and around this concept between different streams of feminism.

FAT activism: Organizing to expand public awareness and acceptance about FAT issues.

Femininity: A historically and culturally constructed set of gendered traits linked to the subordination and undervaluing of women in society.

Gender transition: The process of moving from to, between or among a range of biological, anatomical or performed genders.

Genocide: The systematic killing of a group of people based on race, culture or ethnicity.

Girl Power: A third-wave term originating from Riot Grrrls describing the strength and empowerment of girls and women when they unite. The term has been appropriated by pop culture to commodify feminism.

Hegemonic: A set of dominant discourses and ideologies that create common sense understandings of the world and have material effects and implications on peoples lives, making us complicit in our own oppression.

Heterophobia: The fear or hatred of heterosexual people. People of marginalized sexualities may experience this because of a loss of power.

Heterosexism: The assumption that heterosexuality is both normal and natural and the way that society is organized around this.

Ho: Slang for whore.

348

Homophobia: The fear or hatred of gay, lesbian, bisexual, transgendered and transexual people.

Identity politics: A set of politics that emerged in the 1980s and is formed around identity.

Ideology: Some of the definitions currently in circulation, as suggested by Terry Eagleton in *An Introduction to Ideology,* include the process of production of meanings, signs and values in social life; a body of ideas characteristic of a particular social group or class; ideas that help to legitimate a dominant political power.

Imperialism: The rule of one country or culture over another. Often used to describe white or western domination over people of colour. To overpower and dominate another country's socio-cultural economic and political structures.

Individualism: The belief that the rights of the individual are of primary importance over those of the collective.

Indoctrination: The act of being taught the fundamental rules, ideas and beliefs of an ideology (generally seen as a negative process).

Internalized racism: Adopting oppressive ideas about one's race into one's own system of beliefs.

"Isms": Slang referring to sexism, racism, classism, sizism, ableism and other forms of oppression ending in "ism."

Leftist: Refers to people who are aligned with the political "left," those who espouse a left-wing political perspective on such issues as social justice, equality and workers' rights.

Marginalization: To be located on the margins, to be excluded from or to be on the outside of a group or culture or society at large.

Masculinity: A historically and culturally constructed set of gendered traits linked to the dominance and prestige that are assigned to males in this society.

Matricide: To kill one's mother.

Media literacy: The ability to critically assess and engage with mass media messages. To be media literate is to understand the who, what and why of the industry, and to identify the agenda behind advertising, writing and programming.

Misogynist: A hatred of women.

Multi-layered oppressions: Muliple experiences of oppression occurring simultaneously. This can include race, sexuality, ability and class.

Neocon: Short for neo-conservative, the contemporary expression of right-wing conservative politics.

Oedipal: The "Oedipal complex," identified by psychoanalyst Sigmund Freud, is characterized by a boy's unconscious desire for his mother, which leads to his being jealous of his father.

Oppression: The use of political, social, economic, ideological, psychological or physical forms of power to deny particular groups justice and equity. The conditions and experiences that result from subordination and injustice.

Other: One who does not belong to the dominant group (social, racial, etc.) and who, as a result, is treated differently, usually experiencing stigma and second-class status.

Paki: A derogatory term for people of Pakistani descent, often used against anyone with brown skin.

Panic disorder: A mental illness that is characterized by sudden and unexpected attacks of fear or terror, often appearing without obvious reason. Symptoms are not only psychological, but are often physical as well (dizziness, sweating, choking sensation).

Patriarchy: A belief system that supports the sexist ways in which society is organized; by maintaining female dependence and subservience, male power, control and domination is upheld.

Pedagogies: Theory of teaching methods. Feminist pedagogies attempt to explore and critique relations of power and the exclusion of women, race, ability, class and sexuality in learning.

Personal narrative: Everyone has a personal narrative that helps them make sense of the world. This narrative is constantly evolving and is made up of personal experiences, perceptions and interpretations. These narratives reflect our sense of self.

Phallus: Symbolizes a penis and the power that it represents.

Post-colonial: Technically "after colonialism." Post-colonial also refers to a body of anti-imperialist writing and theory.

Postmodern feminism: The term captures streams of feminisms that share an understanding of power relations as decentred, that seek to deconstruct universal truths about the world, and that recognize the multiplicity or differences of experiences and perspectives in the world.

Post-structuralism: An area of criticism that departs from the claims of objectivity and comprehensiveness made by structuralism. Instead it emphasizes plurality, recognizes that meaning comes from the reader and rejects the fixed binary oppositions of structuralism and the validity of authority.

Pre-Menstrual Syndrome (PMS): A series of physical and emotional changes — from bloating, to cramping, to heightened emotional sensitivity — that can be related to the nearing or onset of one's period.

Puritan: An individual who practices or advocates strictness in religion, ideology or morals and attempts to impose those notions on others.

Queer: An inclusive term for a variety of sexualities counter to the norm.

Queer theory: Calls into question seemingly obvious categories (such as man, woman), oppositions (such hetero/homosexuality) and equations (gender = sex), all of which are the basis for notions of sexuality and identity as we know them in the western world today. Queer theory critically examines the structures of their intelligibility.

Reclaim: The process of reclaiming involves shedding negative associations and attributing new and positive perceptions to a word or term. For example, queer has been evolved from an insult to an inclusive and positive political term by those in the community.

"R"eligion: Capital "R" signals a questioning of the traditions and prescriptions of institutionalized religion.

Revolution: The overthrow of one political system or government and putting another in its place. Revolutions are organized from "below" or from the grassroots.

Riot Grrrl: A movement that began in North America in the 1990s, through which girls could organize and empower one another to make inroads into musical and cultural scenes from which they had previously been excluded.

Sanctioned violence: Violence that is approved of or tacitly allowed.

Second-wave feminism: The feminist movement that began in the late 1960s and early 1970s. This "second wave" provided most of the underlying feminist principles and theories that inform current feminist thought. The first wave refers to the early 1900s and the suffragette's fight for the right for women to vote.

Sex-positive: A stream of feminism that celebrates and reclaims the many forms and expressions of women's sexuality.

Sexist: Attitudes and practices that discriminate against women.

Sexual harassment: Unwanted sexual advances involving behaviours ranging from derogatory remarks to physical contact. It often (but not always) happens in a situation where the harasser is in a position of power, such as in the workplace, at school or in housing.

Sexuality: A term to describe various aspects of an individual's sexual self. It includes their sexual interests and desires, as well as their sexual orientation (heterosexual, bisexual or lesbian). A technicolour spectrum of biology, experiences, psychology, behaviour and society. It includes gender roles, sexual activity, sensuality, sexual orientation, choice of partners, sexual ideology and politics, gender identity, reproduction.

Silenced: A sense of being unable to speak, either as the result of fear or persecution or of being misunderstood.

Sisterhood: A term meant to imply a connection among women. Using this word within a feminist context is controversial, as the women's movement has not proven to be an inclusive movement. Women of colour, queer women, disabled women, Aboriginal women and poor women have all been excluded (at different times and in different ways) from the feminist agenda and have therefore challenged the use of the term "sisterhood" within feminism and its implication of equality and connection among all women.

Sizism: Discrimination based on size.

Social construction: Belief systems created by society rather than a result of an innate quality or meaning.

Stigmatized: To be negatively labelled and then be treated according to the assumptions that are attached to that label.

Subculture: A group of people or an activity that falls outside of mainstream culture. A subculture often has its own styles, politics and ideals.

Subordination: Working under the control or authority of another person.

Take Back the Night: An annual night-time march/protest in which women both fight for and reclaim the streets. The event is organized to rally around women's right for safety from all forms of violence, both outside and inside the home.

Third wave: The third wave of feminism both builds on and differentiates itself from the second wave through its sustained homage to 1970s mentors and its sustained critique of the same. Third wavers — emerging and beginning to define themselves only since the mid-1990s in North America — are a diverse group of primarily young women, born into a world changed by feminism and other social justice movements and trying to put their diverse feminisms into practice in this world, acknowledged to be complex, contextual and ever shifting. For this generation, feminism should prioritize not just gender but all of the intertwining axes of identity and experience including race, class, ability and sexuality. The third-wave movement and aesthetic is associated with cultural activism (zines, riot grrrl bands, guerilla subvertising), the challenging of identity boundaries and a revelling in female power whether through our bodies, sexuality, work, art or activism.

Toxic Shock Syndrome (TSS): A potentially fatal bacterial infection accompanied by symptoms such as fever, rash, vomiting, diarrhea and a drop in blood pressure, associated with the use of tampons.

Trade union movement: The organization of workers into unions in order to collectively protect and promote fair working conditions and wages.

Transgendered: Someone who transgresses societal gender norms, either open-endedly or with a specific goal in mind, and who chooses to describe part of their identity as derived from or related to that transgression.

Wicca: The practice of witchcraft from a female-centred spiritual perspective.

Women's Studies: A field of academic studies, and more recently, a degree-granting university program, that emerged in North America out of the social and political context of the women's movement and other social movements of the 1960s and 1970s (e.g., the civil rights movement, lesbian and gay liberation, the peace movement). Women's Studies is concerned with how gender operates at the subjective, symbolic and social level in the making of self, knowledge, culture and society. Gender is understood to be formed through overlapping forms of power such as race, sexuality, class, dis/abiltity and so on.

Women's symbol: An icon used to signify women. It has been taken up as a political symbol by feminists. ♀

Zine: Sounds like the "zine" in magazine. Any form of independently produced media, which are usually photocopied for distribution or posted on the Internet. Zines provide an arena for personal expression and networking. Producers of zines experience a level of freedom of expression because they do not need to satisfy advertisers, editors or audiences of mainstream culture.

READ THIS!

Books

Baumgardner, Jennifer, and Amy Richards. *MANIFESTA: Young Women, Feminism, and the Future.* NY: Farrar, Straus, and Giroux, 2000.

Black Girls Editorial Collective. *Black Girl Talk.* Toronto: Sister Vision Press, 1995.

Bondoc, Anna, and Meg Daly, eds. *Letters of Intent: Women Cross the Generations to Talk About Family, Work, Sex, Love and the Future of Feminism.* New York: The Free Press, 1999.

Bordo, Susan. *Unbearable Weight: Feminism, Western Culture, and the Body.* Berkeley: University of California Press, 1993.

Bowen, Jan. *Generational Feminism.* Toronto: HarperCollins Canada Ltd., 1997.

Brant, Beth. *Writing as Witness: Essay and Talk.* Toronto: Women's Press, 1994.

Brooks, Ann. *Postfeminisms: Feminism, Cultural Theory and Cultural Forms.* NY: Routledge, 1997.

Carter, Sarah. *Capturing Women: The Manipulation of Cultural Imagery in Canada's Prairie West.* Montreal, McGill-Queen's University Press, 1997.

Chancer, Lynn S. *Reconcilable Differences: Confronting Beauty, Pornography and the Future of Feminism.* California: University of California Press, 1998.

Chesler, Phyllis. *Letters to a Young Feminist.* New York: Four Walls Eight Windows, 2000.

Coppock, Vicki, Deena Haydon, and Ingrid Richter. *The Illusions of "Post-Feminism": New Women, Old Myths.* London: Taylor and Francis Ltd., 1995.

Crosbie, Lynn. *The Girl Wants To: Women's Representations of Sex and the Body.* Toronto: Macfarlane, Walter and Ross, 1993.

——, ed. *Click! Becoming Feminists.* Toronto: Macfarlane, Walter and Ross, 1997.

Currie, Dawn H. *Girl Talk: Adolescent Magazines and Their Readers.* Toronto: University of Toronto Press, 1999.

Dean, Jodi. *Solidarity Among Strangers: Feminism after Identity Politics.* Berkeley: University of California Press, 1996.

Decter, Ann, ed. *She's Gonna Be: Stories, Poems, Life.* Toronto: McGilligan Books, 1998.

Douglas, Susan. *Where the Girls Are: Growing Up Female with the Mass Media.* New York: Random House, 1994.

Edut, Opheria. *Body Outlaws: Young Women Write about Body Image and Identity.* Seattel: Seal Press, 2000.

Else-Mitchell, Rosamund, and Naomi Flutter, eds. *Talking Up: Young Women's Take on Feminism.* North Melbourne, AUS: Spinifex Press, 1998.

Faludi, Susan. *Backlash: The Undeclared War against American Women.* New York: Doubleday, 1991.

Farrell, Amy Erdman. *Yours in Sisterhood: Ms. Magazine and the Promise of Popular Feminism.* Chapel Hill: The University of North Carolina Press, 1998.

Findlen, Barbara. *Listen Up: Voices From the Next Feminist Generation.* Seattle: Seal Press, 1995.

Gaskell, Jane et. al., eds. *Claiming an Education: Feminism and Canadian Schools.* Toronto: Our Schools/Our Selves, 1989.

Glickman, Rose L. *Daughters of Feminists: Young Women With Feminist Mothers Talk about Their Lives.* New York: St. Martin's Press, 1993.

Gold, Jodi, and Susan Villari, eds. *Just Sex: Students Rewrite the Rules on Sex, Violence, Activism, and Equality.* Maryland: Rowman and Littlefield Publishers, Inc., 2000.

Heywood, Leslie, and Jennifer Drake, eds. *Third Wave Agendas: Being Feminist, Doing Feminism.* Minneapolis: University of Minnesota Press, 1997.

hooks, bell. *Where We Stand: Class Matters.* New York: Routledge, 2000.

____. *Feminist Theory: From Margin to Center.* Boston: South End Press, 1984.

Hughes, Kate. *Everygirl's Guide to Feminism.* Toronto: Pearson Education Canada, 1999.

Inness, Sherrie A. *Running for Their Lives: Girls, Cultural Identity, and Stories of Survival.* Lanham, MD: Rowman and Littlefield, 2000.

Karp, Marcelle, and Debbie Stollar. *The Bust Guide to the New Girl Order.* NY: Penguin, 1999.

Klein, Naomi. *No Logo: Taking Aim at the Brand Bullies.* Toronto: Knopf Canada, 1999.

Kostash, Myrna. *The Next Canada: In Search of our Future Nation.* Toronto: McClelland and Stewart, 2000.

Kramarae, Cheris, and Paula A. Treichler. *Amazons, Bluestockings and Crones: A Feminist Dictionary.* London: Pandora, 1992.

Larkin, June. *Sexual Harassment: High School Girls Speak Out.* Toronto: Second Story Press, 1994.

LeBlanc, Lauraine. *Pretty in Punk: Girls' Resistance in a Boys' Subculture.* New Brunswick, NJ: Rutgers University Press, 1999.

Lorde, Audre. *Sister Outsider.* Trumansburg, NY: The Crossing Press, 1984.

Manji, Irshad. *Risking Utopia: On the Edge of a New Democracy.* Vancouver: Douglas and McIntyre, 1997.

McRobbie, Angela. *Feminism and Youth Culture.* Second Edition. New York: Routledge, 2000.

Nagle, Jill. *Whores and Other Feminists.* New York: Routledge, 1997.

Proweller, Amira. *Constructing Female Identities: Meaning Making in an Upper Middle Class Youth Culture.* New York: State University of New York Press, 1998.

Rebick, Judy. *Imagine Democracy.* Toronto: Stoddart Publishing, 2000.

Rebick, Judy, and Kiké Roach. *Politically Speaking.* Vancouver: Douglas and McIntyre, 1996.

Robbins, Trina, and Carla Sinclair. *From Girls to Grrlz: A History of Women's Comics From Teens to Zines.* San Francisco: Chronicle Books, 1999.

Taormino, Tristan, and Karen Green. *The Girls Guide to Taking Over the World: Writings from the Girl Zine Revolution.* New York: St. Martin's Press, 1997.

Walker, Rebecca. *Black, White, and Jewish: Autobiography of a Shifting Self.* New York: Riverhead Books, 2000.

——, *To Be Real: Telling the Truth and Changing the Face of Feminism.* NewYork: Doubleday, 1995.

Walter, Natasha. *On the Move: Feminism for a New Generation.* London, UK: Virago Press, 2000.

Whelehan, Imelda. *Modern Feminist Thought: From the Second Wave to "Post-Feminism."* New York: New York University Press, 1995.

Wolf, Naomi. *The Beauty Myth.* Toronto: Vintage, 1991.

Magazines, Journals and Articles

Bell, Lee Anne. "In Danger of Winning: Consciousness Raising Strategies for Empowering Girls in the United States." *Women's Studies International Forum* 19, no. 4. (1996), 419-427.

BITCH: Feminist Response to Pop Culture.

BUST: For Women With Something to Get off Their Chests.

Campbell, Denise, and Bindu Dhaliwal, "Challenge the Assumptions!" *TG Magazine* (1998).

Canadian Woman Studies/Les cahiers de la femme. "Young Women: Feminist, Activists, Grrrls" 21, no. 1 (Spring 2001).

Fireweed. Especially these issues: *FAT* Issue 67 (Fall 1999); *Revolution Girl-Style* Issue 59/60 (Fall/Winter 1997); *Sex Work* Issue 65 (Spring 1999); *Trans/scribes* Issue 69 (Summer 2000).

Herizons. See Lisa Bryn Rundle, "Make Room, Sister: The Next Generation is Here" (Fall 1998).

Hypatia. Special Issue, *Third-Wave Feminism* 12, no. 3 (Summer 1997).

Reluctant Hero: By girls, For girls.

Rundle, Lisa Bryn, Goli Rezai-Rashti, and Angela Miles. "Third Wave Feminism: Antiracists, Transnationalists, and Young Feminists Speak Out." In Nancy Mandell, ed., *Feminist Issues: Race, Class and Sexuality.* Third Edition. Toronto: Pearson Education Canada, 2001, pp. 1-22.

This Magazine. Check out Lisa Bryn Rundle, "Who Needs NAC?" (March/April 1999).

Web Sites

(commentary by Krista Scott-Dixon)

* http://www.houseoffun.com/action/zines/ **Action Girl Online** isn't an on-line zine, but it's a cool girl site that tells you how to make your own print zines.
* http://www.chickclick.com/ **Chick click** is a dynamic, fun portal site with a variety of departments. The "society and politics" link rewards you with a series of interesting and readable articles on everything from body image of women of colour, to media critique, to human rights abuses.
* http://www.digitaleve.com **Digital Eve International** is a global women's technology organization which is "committed to providing a supportive, educational community for women."
* http://www.disgruntledhousewife.com/ Nikol Lohr serves up her special smorgasbord of biting wit and acidic pop culture examination with a heaping helping of neurotic anger. Wickedly funny, **Disgruntled Housewife** carves up the dark and tasty secrets that we all keep inside our tasteful bungalows of life. "Secret Confessions" and "The Dick List" are two of the juiciest pieces of voyeuristic gluttony I've ever chewed on which delightfully reveal the social indigestion of the masses.

- http://www.fabulamag.com/ "This ain't your mama's feminism."
- http://www.fatso.com/fatgirl/ Fat dykes and the women who love them. This zine takes it all on — fat, identity, sexuality, body image and politics, with an in-your-face attitude. Includes fat grrrl wallpaper and pics for you to download. FaT GiRL's efforts at reclaiming negative body stereotypes, particularly in the discursive sense, are analyzed briefly in the research paper. The ezine also examines the intersection of fat with class and sexuality. Best reclamation piece title: "A Fat, Vulgar, Angry Slut."
- http://www.feminista.com/ A wonderful port in the storm of on-line drivel.
- http://www.geekgirl.com.au/ The Aussie grrrl zine by Rosie Cross (aka Rosie X), geekgirl extraordinaire, social commentator and frequent contributor to *Wired Magazine*. In the words of Rosie X, as "the world's first cyberfeminist hyperzine," "geekgirl rox."
- http://www.girlcrushzine.com/ A webzine for girls 13-18, **GirlCrush** was created "because 'feminist' and 'girly' are NOT opposites."
- http://www.mmotion.com/girlrights.html One of two zines discussed in detail in the MRP, **Girlrights** is the product of Rachel Mariko Pilitteri's teenage feminist angst. A snapshot of an evolving feminist consciousness, Girlrights contains Pillitteri's poems, drawings, rants and raves about everything from body image to capitalism, plus a couple of articles by feminist theorists, Riot Grrrl band reviews and pithy quotes from other grouchy grrls.
- http://www.gurlpages.com/ Find more work by our cover artist Missy Kulik and other great stuff.
- http://www.heartless-bitches.com/ **Heartless Bitches** asks, "Are you sick of lazy women who use emotional and sexual manipulation to get what they want instead of using their own brains and muscles?"
- http://www.marigoldzine.com/ Audra Estrones lists this site as "60% slumber party, 40% political rally," which I think neatly sums up the entire modus operandi of third-wave feminism. Fantastic design and layout, featuring everything from politics to arts to chat forums. Plus, it's Canadian.
- http://www.technodyke.com/ Girl geeks and the women who love them.
- http://www.wench.com/ "Wench charts the social and political terrain in which women live, and helps women and men alike understand where we all need to go."
- http://members.aol.com/Critchicks/index2.html Read about **exoticize this!** in Carmela Murdocca's piece.
- WARNING: Something of note for savvy surfers, fake girl zines are everywhere, multiplying like overfed bacteria. It bugs me when a cool girlzine format gets co-opted by a corporate agenda. Be careful out there.

EDITORS' BIOS

Allyson Mitchell is a Toronto artist who just
can't stop. In 1995 she was suddenly overcome with an
urge to stop watching and start making. She started gathering young feminist materials that others had written
and began working on projects of her own. She has completed eight films and videos: *Don't Bug Me, My Very Own
After School Special, Chow Down, Bad Brownies, Cup
Cake, Candy Kisses, Road Side Attraction* and *TV Did This
To Me* (all are available through the Canadian Film-
Makers Distribution Centre; check out their Web site and
Allyson's films at www.cfmdc.org). Mitchell's work is all
about sharing the toys and knowledge so in 1996 she co-
produced *3 Minute Rock Star,* a project that got fifty first-
time filmmakers to make Super 8 films for $50 each in
less than fifty days. Recently she has joined forces with
Alexis Vaughn to create Bucky and Fluff's Craft Factory,
a multi-medium venture that has resulted in products
such as postcards, rabbit's feet, big-eyed girls and band-
aid art. Most recently they have completed two
films: *Itchy Ya Ya* and *Hair Pie;* catch them at a
lezzie/gay film festival near you. Allyson is also a founder
of the FAT activist group "Pretty, Porky and Pissed Off,"
an organization dedicated to eradicating myths like fat
chicks gotta wear moo moos. You can find her writing in
Fireweed: A Feminist Quarterly's special FAT issue and you
may be extra lucky and find her stickers in a bathroom

stall one day. In her spare time Allyson works on her PhD in Women's Studies at York University and teaches first year Women's Studies.

See Allyson's Top 10 Feminist Influences at the end of her piece "The Writing's on the Wall."

Lisa Bryn Rundle is a 26-year-old writer and editor with a master's in Women's Studies from York University who hails originally from Bowmanville, Ontario. She has written about young feminists for T*he Toronto Star, Herizons* and *This Magazine;* contributed a chapter on third-wave feminism to the most recent edition of *Feminist Issues;* and spoken about issues concerning young women on *CBC Newsworld* and the Women's Television Network. She is a former member of the editorial collective of F*ireweed: A Feminist Quarterly,* a current board member of a new Toronto rag, *Trade: Queer Things,* and the assistant to the editor at *Saturday Night Magazine.* She recently showed her first collection of photographs — The Daily Grind: A Day in the Life of One Very Red Vibrator — with co-conspirator kristi-ly green in Toronto. Lisa is a woman-lovin'-woman who also loves men, a vegetarian who enjoys the odd roast beast and a distinct non-athlete (yoga still isn't a sport, right?) who recently ran her first half marathon; she is learning not only to expect complexity but to love it.

Lisa's Top 10 Feminist Influences

1. My mother and her mother.
2. Laura Ingalls and Anne of Green Gables (book and TV versions of both).
3. So many teachers (often found in schools and women's centres).
4. Strong and loving aunts.
5. My fabulous women friends — goddesses every one.
6. bell hooks, Toni Morrison, Adrienne Rich, Audre Lorde and countless other women whose writing blew my mind, opened my eyes, challenged me to grow and made me want to spend my life working with words.
7. Jerky men (throughout life) and great men (who proved not all men were jerky men).
8. ani difranco and Dar Williams.
9. Rebecca Walker and all the brave and thoughtful contributors to *To Be Real.*
10. My sister and her new daughter.

Lara   Karaian is a 27-year-old academic and activist. Currently a PhD candidate in Women's Studies at York University, where she is a teaching assistant for a course on women and the law, she has aspirations to teach feminism and postmodern legal theory. She has participated in the Toronto branch of the Women's Legal Education and Action Fund (LEAF), walked the picket line in York's record-setting seventy-eight day CUPE strike and was tear gassed protesting against the Free Trade Agreement of the Americas in Quebec City. Her most recent projects include helping to organize a conference on the human rights violations of women in Afghanistan and two conferences on the United Nations Convention on the Elimination of All Forms of Discrimination Against Women (CEDAW). Following the CEDAW conferences, Lara went to New York to attend the 43rd Session of the United Nations Commission on the Status of Women, where she worked on the CEDAW Optional Protocol with a non-government organization. Though she's not quite the media darling that her two co-editors are, Lara has spoken about women's legal and gender equality issues on Talk 640 AM Radio (*before* it became "Mojo's talk radio for guys"). She is published in the *Encyclopedia of Feminist Theories* and in the *Pop Culture* Issue of *Fireweed*. In her spare time, she likes to run, pretend that she knows how to knit and, most recently, pretend that she knows how to paint with water colours.

See Lara's Top 10 Feminist Influences at the end of her piece "High School Feminism 101."

7